'This remarkable collection of essays explores the intersecting dynamics of shame and temporality. If our ability to construct the narrative arc of time makes us human, shame makes us social beings—forced to reflect on the norms we have breached, and compelled to repair our damaged person-hood. Shame arrests us in time, delivering us to a double temporality: morbidly reliving past humiliations and rehearsing future disgrace. While intense shame is corrosive to the self, the contributors show that shame is also a teacher, a moral emotion that contributes to civility, integrity, and depth. Readers will be richly rewarded.'

—**Laurence J. Kirmayer**, MD, FRCPC, FCAHS, FRSC,
James McGill Professor & Director, Division of Social &
Transcultural Psychiatry, McGill University, Canada.

'This unusual conjunction of topics, temporality and shame, proves to be quite remarkable through the editorial synthesis of Willemsen and Hinton. Each chapter explores and develops another dimension of the intersection of these aspects of psychological experience through the reflections of diverse, erudite scholars, analysts and authors. Trauma studies serve as a backdrop to many of the discussion, making poignant human suffering a canvas upon which the themes unfold. As the examinations proceed, essay by essay, the emergence of a complex network of association in philo-sophical space appears constructed by the weaving of analytic threads. A unique collection that deserves rereading to fully savor its subtle richness.'

—**Joseph Cambray**, PhD,
Provost, Pacifica Graduate Institute, USA.

'This book's cross-disciplinary content, that includes anthropology, psycho-analysis, technology, culture, the law, [and] philosophy, yields authoritative accounts of emotionally rending and thought-provoking mental and physi-cal depravity and their after-effects in our time. The dynamic structural relations that bind the notions of temporality and shame are at work in both the *synchronic* eternally present time and the *diachronic* passage of histo-rical time. This portentous book is essential reading for its depiction of a world wherein the contemporary pervasiveness of shamelessness is uncon-tained in ethical time and poses an exponential threat to Darwinian *fitness*.'

—**Ann Casement**, Licensed Psychoanalyst/Fellow
of the Royal Anthropological Institute.

'This fine collection of papers is distinguished by a rare integration of psy-choanalytic, philosophical and Jungian perspectives. Its authors include clinicians, scholars and anthropologists and this refreshing combination offers an unusually wide-ranging, thought-provoking and original explora-tion of shame and its relation to various aspects of temporality.'

—**Warren Colman**, Jungian analyst and consultant editor of *The Journal of Analytical Psychology*.

Temporality and Shame

Temporality has always been a central preoccupation of modern philosophy, and shame has been a major theme in contemporary psychoanalysis. To date, however, there has been little examination of the critical connection between these core experiences. Although they deeply implicate each other, no single book has focused upon their profound interrelationship. *Temporality and Shame* highlights the many dimensions of that reality.

A core point of this book is that shame can be a teacher, and a crucial one, in evaluating our ethical and ontological position in the world. Granting the fact that shame can be toxic and terrible, we must remember that it is also what can orient us in the difficult task of reflection and consciousness. Shame enables us to become more fully present in the world and authentically engage in the flow of temporality and the richness of its syncopated dimensionality. Such a deeply honest ethos, embracing the jarring awareness of shame and the always-shifting temporalities of memory, can open us to a fuller presence in life. This is the basic vision of *Temporality and Shame*. The respective contributors discuss temporality and shame in relation to clinical and theoretical aspects of psychoanalysis, philosophy, anthropology, and genocide, as well as the question of evil, myth and archetype, history and critical studies, the 'discipline of interiority', and literary works.

Temporality and Shame provides valuable insights and a rich and engaging variety of ideas. It will appeal to psychotherapists and psychoanalysts, philosophers and those interested in the basic philosophical grounds of experience, and anthropologists and people engaged in cultural studies and critical theory.

Ladson Hinton, MA, MD, is a psychoanalyst who practices and teaches in Seattle, Washington, USA. He is a graduate of the C.G. Jung Institute of San Francisco and a founding member of the New School for Analytical Psychology in Seattle. Recent interests have been shame, temporality, and the deepening crisis of western culture.

Hessel Willemsen, DClinPsych, is a training analyst of the Society of Analytical Psychology, UK. A member of the Editorial Advisory Board of the *Journal of Analytical Psychology*, he practices, consults, and teaches in London, UK. Recent interests include time, temporality, affect and the body, and the authoritarian other.

Philosophy & Psychoanalysis book series
JON MILLS
Series Editor

Philosophy & Psychoanalysis is dedicated to current developments and cutting-edge research in the philosophical sciences, phenomenology, hermeneutics, existentialism, logic, semiotics, cultural studies, social criticism, and the humanities that engage and enrich psychoanalytic thought through philosophical rigor. With the philosophical turn in psychoanalysis comes a new era of theoretical research that revisits past paradigms while invigorating new approaches to theoretical, historical, contemporary, and applied psychoanalysis. No subject or discipline is immune from psychoanalytic reflection within a philosophical context including psychology, sociology, anthropology, politics, the arts, religion, science, culture, physics, and the nature of morality. Philosophical approaches to psychoanalysis may stimulate new areas of knowledge that have conceptual and applied value beyond the consulting room reflective of greater society at large. In the spirit of pluralism, *Philosophy & Psychoanalysis* is open to any theoretical school in philosophy and psychoanalysis that offers novel, scholarly, and important insights in the way we come to understand our world.

Titles in this series:

Jung's Ethics: Moral Psychology and his Cure of Souls
Dan Merkur, edited by Jon Mills

Temporality and Shame: Perspectives from Psychoanalysis and Philosophy
Edited by Ladson Hinton and Hessel Willemsen

Temporality and Shame

Perspectives from Psychoanalysis and Philosophy

Edited by
Ladson Hinton and Hessel Willemsen

To Pat — in
appreciation for the
many fond memories
we share of the past!

love 'Jod..

Routledge
Taylor & Francis Group

LONDON AND NEW YORK

First published 2018
by Routledge
2 Park Square, Milton Park, Abingdon, Oxon OX14 4RN

and by Routledge
711 Third Avenue, New York, NY 10017

Routledge is an imprint of the Taylor & Francis Group, an informa business

British Library Cataloguing in Publication Data
A catalogue record for this book is available from the British Library

Library of Congress Cataloging in Publication Data
Names: Hinton, Ladson, 1958- , editor. | Willemsen, Hessel.
Title: Temporality and shame: perspectives from psychoanalysis and
    philosophy / edited by Ladson Hinton and Hessel Willemsen.
Description: New York: Routledge, [2017] | Includes bibliographical
    references and index.
Identifiers: LCCN 2017021118| ISBN 9781138702332 (hardback: alk. paper) |
    ISBN 9781138702349 (pbk. : alk. paper) | ISBN 9781315203683 (master) |
    ISBN 9781351788762 (web PDF) | ISBN 9781351788755 (epub) |
    ISBN 9781351788748 (mobipocket/kindle)
Subjects: LCSH: Shame. | Time—Philosophy. | Psychoanalysis.
Classification: LCC BF575.S45 T456 2017 | DDC 152.4/4—dc23
LC record available at https://lccn.loc.gov/2017021118

ISBN: 978-1-138-70233-2 (hbk)
ISBN: 978-1-138-70234-9 (pbk)
ISBN: 978-1-315-20368-3 (ebk)

Typeset in Times
by Swales & Willis Ltd, Exeter, Devon, UK

For my wife Darlene, with love and gratitude
                              –L.H.

For James and Logan
          –H.W.

Contents

List of figures   xi
Notes on contributors   xiii
Acknowledgements   xvii

Introduction   1
LADSON HINTON AND HESSEL WILLEMSEN

1 Shame and temporality in the streets: consumerism,
  technology, truth and raw life   14
  LADSON HINTON

2 The unbearable shame of the analyst's idealization:
  reiterating the temporal   33
  JON MILLS

3 A time for shame: Levinas, diachrony and the hope
  of shame   57
  ERIC SEVERSON

4 Lacan: *Nachträglichkeit*, shame and ethical time   74
  SHARON GREEN

5 Abject bodies: trauma, shame, disembodiment and the
  death of time   101
  ANGELA CONNOLLY

6 Existential shame, temporality and cracks in the 'ordinary "filled in" process of things'   119
   SUE AUSTIN

7 Shame and evanescence; the body as driver of temporality   139
   HESSEL WILLEMSEN

8 The pharmacology of shame, *or* Promethean, Epimethean and Antigonian temporality   158
   DANIEL ROSS

9 Justice, temporality and shame at the Khmer Rouge Tribunal   186
   ALEXANDER LABAN HINTON

10 The four modalities of temporality and the problem of shame   214
   MURRAY STEIN

11 Disavowal in Jungian psychology: a case study of disenchantment and the timing of shame   242
   MICHAEL WHAN

   Index   261

Figures

9.1 Vann Nath, aged 32, at S-21 in 1978. Courtesy of the
     Documentation Center of Cambodia (www.dccam.org)   191
9.2 S-21 prisoner in cell (Tuol Sleng Museum of Genocide
     Crimes), painting by Vann Nath. Courtesy of the
     Documentation Center of Cambodia   192
9.3 Vann Nath at Duch Verdict Distribution, August 12, 2010.
     Courtesy of the ECCC (www.eccc.gov.kh/en/gallery/
     photo/duch-verdict-distribution-8)   204
9.4 Duch verdict, painting by Vann Nath. Courtesy of the
     Documentation Center of Cambodia   205
9.5 Vann Nath sketch, 'Self-portrait with a mirror' (1995),
     introduced as evidence at the ECCC in 2009. Image
     courtesy of the ECCC   207
10.1 Four modes of temporality   215
10.2 Times four   233
10.3 The Ring *i*   234
10.4 Times four and the Ring *i*   235
10.5 Levels of temporality   236

Notes on contributors

Sue Austin, PhD (Australia), trained with the Australian and New Zealand Society of Jungian Analysts. She is a training analyst with ANZSJA and specializes in working with adults with eating disorders and supervising clinicians who work in the field. Sue is an assistant editor of the *Journal of Analytical Psychology*. She has given numerous clinical workshops and seminars in Australia, New Zealand, Europe, the USA and Canada, Singapore, South Africa, and Russia, and has published a book *Women's Aggressive Fantasies: A Post-Jungian Exploration of Self-Hatred, Love and Agency* (Routledge, 2005) and several clinical and theoretical papers.

Angela Connolly, MD (Italy), is a psychiatrist and Jungian analyst in private practice in Rome. She is a faculty member, training analyst and supervisor of the *Centro Italiano di Psicologia Analitica* (CIPA). She lived and worked in Russia from 1996–2001 and since then has continued to teach, lecture, and supervise internationally. She was deputy editor of the *Journal of Analytical Psychology* for five years and is currently on the advisory board. She was the honourary secretary of the International Association of Analytical Psychology from 2010–2013 and vice-president from 2013–2016. She has published widely in English and Italian and has had articles translated into Russian and German. Her latest publication is 'Broken Time: Disturbances of Temporality in Analysis' in *Time and the Psyche: Jungian Perspectives*, edited by Angeliki Yiassemides (Routledge, 2017).

Sharon Green, MSSW (US), has a private practice of psychoanalysis and clinical consultation in Seattle, Washington. Sharon's analytic work and teaching reflect her commitment to analysis as a dialogic process that transcends any particular theory or dogma. She is a member of the International Association of Analytical Psychology and a founding member of both the New School for Analytical Psychology and the Lacanian Study Group of Seattle. Her reviews and articles have appeared in the *Journal of Analytical Psychology* and she has presented at numerous international conferences. Current interests include the intersection of ethics and psychoanalysis and the impact of globalization and neo-liberalism on these contemporary subjects.

Alexander Laban Hinton, PhD (US), is director of the Center for the Study of Genocide and Human Rights, Professor of Anthropology, and UNESCO Chair in Genocide Prevention at Rutgers University. He is the author of the award-winning *Why Did They Kill? Cambodia in the Shadow of Genocide* (University of California Press, 2005) and nine edited and co-edited collections. His most recent publications are *Man or Monster? The Trial of a Khmer Rouge Torturer* (Duke University Press, 2016) and *The Justice Facade: Trials of Transition in Cambodia* (Oxford University Press, 2018). In recognition of his work on genocide, the American Anthropological Association selected Hinton as the recipient of the 2009 Robert B. Textor and Family Prize for Excellence in Anticipatory Anthropology. Professor Hinton is also a past president of the International Association of Genocide Scholars (2011–2013) and was a member/ visitor at the Institute for Advanced Study at Princeton (2011–2013). In 2016, he served as an expert witness at the Khmer Rouge Tribunal.

Ladson Hinton, MA, MD (US), trained in psychiatry at Stanford and served on the Stanford Clinical Faculty for twenty years. He is a graduate of the C.G. Jung Institute of San Francisco; he is a member of the Society of Jungian Analysts of Northern California, the International Association for Analytical Psychology, the Institute for Contemporary Psychoanalysis in Los Angeles, and a founder of the New School for Analytical Psychology in Seattle. He serves on the editorial board of the *Journal of Analytical Psychology*, and practises, consults, and teaches in Seattle. In 2009, he received the Award for Distinguished

Contributions to Psychoanalytic Education from the International Forum for Psychoanalytic Education and was nominated for the 2016 Gradiva Award for his article, 'Temporality and the torments of time' in the *Journal of Analytical Psychology*. Recent interests and publications are in the areas of French psychoanalysis, truth and shame, temporality, and the historical and philosophical grounds of psychoanalysis.

Jon Mills, PsyD, PhD (Canada), is a philosopher, psychoanalyst, and psychologist. He is Professor of Psychology and Psychoanalysis at the Adler Graduate Professional School in Toronto and is the author of many works in philosophy, psychoanalysis, and psychology, including 18 books. The recipient of many awards for his scholarship, he was given the Otto Weininger Memorial Award for lifetime achievement in 2015 by the Section on Psychoanalytic and Psychodynamic Psychology of the Canadian Psychological Association. He runs a mental health corporation in Ontario, Canada.

Daniel Ross, PhD (Australia), is a philosopher and filmmaker, the author of the book, *Violent Democracy* (Cambridge University Press, 2005), as well as many papers on the work of Bernard Stiegler, and co-director of the film *The Ister*. He is the translator (from the French) of eight books by Stiegler, including *States of Shock* and *Automatic Society, Volume 1* (published by Cambridge University Press, 2004), as well as of Stiegler's articles, lectures, and chapters. From 2015–2016, he was a Prometeo researcher at Yachay Tech, Ecuador.

Eric Severson, PhD (US), is a philosopher specializing in the work of Emmanuel Levinas. He is the author of the books *Levinas's Philosophy of Time* (Duquesne University Press, 2013) and *Scandalous Obligation* (Beacon Hill Press, 2011), as well as editor of several other works. He lives in Kenmore, Washington, with his wife Misha and their three children, and currently teaches philosophy at Seattle University.

Murray Stein, PhD (Switzerland), is a graduate of the C.G. Jung Institute of Zürich and of Yale University, Yale Divinity School and the University of Chicago. He is a founding member of the Inter-Regional Society of Jungian Analysts and the Chicago Society of Jungian Analysts. He was president of the International Association for Analytical Psychology from 2001–2004 and president of the International School of Analytical Psychology (ISAP) Zürich from 2008 to 2012. He has lectured internationally and is the author of *In MidLife, Jung's Map of the Soul, Minding the Self, Soul – Retrieval and Treatment* (Chiron Press, 2014) and *Outside, Inside and All Around* (Chiron Press, 2017). He lives in Switzerland and is a training and supervising analyst with ISAP Zürich. He has a private practice in Zürich.

Michael Whan, MA (UK), is an analytical psychologist with the Independent Group of Analytical Psychologists, an emeritus member of the Association of Independent Psychotherapists, the College of Psychoanalysts, an international member of the C.G. Jung Clinic in Zürich, the International Association for Analytical Psychology, a registered Jungian analyst with the United Kingdom Council for Psychotherapy, the International Society for Psychology as a Discipline of Interiority (ISPDI), and a senior associate of the Royal Society of Medicine. He has published in various journals, notably in *Spring Journal* and *Harvest*, contributed chapters to four books on analytical psychology and the paranormal, psychotherapy regulation, psychoanalytic schemas, and analytical psychology and alchemy.

Hessel Willemsen, DClinPsych (UK), studied chemistry at Delft University, the Netherlands, clinical psychology at Leiden University and completed his analytic training at the Society of Analytical Psychology (SAP), London, where he is a Training Analyst. He is on the editorial advisory board of the *Journal of Analytical Psychology*. A member of the International Association of Analytical Psychology he practises, teaches and consults in London. Recent interests include affect, the body, time, temporality and philosophy and the work of Primo Levi. He has published and taught on affect and the body.

Acknowledgements

Hessel Willemsen and Ladson Hinton

Both of us would like to thank Linda Carter for her support in initiating our project, Jon Mills for his warm welcome to the series and his unflagging kindness, Charles Bath for his patient guidance through the publication process, and Pramila Bennett for her wise and helpful editorial contributions. We are grateful to our colleagues from the *Journal of Analytical Psychology* whose friendship and professionality led to much creativity. We are indebted to all contributing authors of this book; without their commitment, enthusiasm, time, and hard work the project would not have developed and come to fruition.

Ladson Hinton

Many people come to mind when I think of the conception and creation of this volume. First, I want to express my gratitude to my early philosophical mentors, F. G. Friedmann at the University of Arkansas and the University of Munich, and Kurt Reinhardt at Stanford University, who inspired and facilitated my passion for philosophy. I am also very grateful to my wise teachers at the C.G. Jung Institute of San Francisco who gave me a deep appreciation of psychoanalysis as an ever-evolving exploration rather than a mere technique. In addition, my posthumous thanks to my close friend and colleague Michael Horne whose stimulating and generous presence rekindled old interests in philosophy and psychology. My colleagues at the New School for Analytical Psychology have provided valuable intellectual stimulation, as we built a new forum for teaching and learning in Seattle. I thank my sons, Ladson, Devon, and Alex, for their support and valuable advice, and Alex for his important contribution.

Finally, my deepest appreciation to my London colleague and co-editor, Hessel Willemsen, whose dedicated efforts have been essential to our project, and whose personal warmth and spirit have made the process a pleasure.

Hessel Willemsen

I am grateful for the editorial support I received from Barbara Wharton who, apart from being my supervisor when I trained, taught me how to cast a critical eye on both text and content of my own and others' written work. Her firmness, kindness, sincerity, and warmth have characterized our conversations and my work with her. Richard Carvalho has been most instrumental in helping me discover the excitement I now have for analytic thinking and analytic work but, importantly, for his deep understanding of the role of the body and affect in analysis which has complemented my thinking and allowed me to be so much more comfortable with my patients. I owe a debt of gratitude to my US colleague, friend and co-editor, Ladson Hinton, whose wide academic interests are infectious, whose gentleness made the work flow and whose warmth and generosity are unstinting.

Introduction

Ladson Hinton and Hessel Willemsen

As is familiar from the Book of Genesis, Eve picked the fruit of knowledge from the Garden of Eden, but nothing escaped God's omnipotent gaze. He spied the truth of the transgression and forthwith expelled Adam and Eve from the Garden, thereby banishing them from an eternal, blissful, timeless, one might say profoundly unconscious, state. Ejected from Paradise, naked and ashamed, they became vulnerable to all the vicissitudes of temporality and death. The Christian tradition is based on such a tale.

It is interesting to reflect on an alternate version of the story. What if God had gazed upon Adam and Eve and acted differently; what if He, in His wisdom, commanded them to 'Enjoy!'? Happiness and pleasure would be the imperatives and there would be no shame, no temporality, and no truth or consciousness (Žižek, 2007). How different would human life and history have been if there had been no entry into time, no gaze to challenge one to shame and consciousness? Would failing to actualize an imperative to 'smile and be happy' then result in shame?

This often seems to describe the world we live in, a world of promised pleasures and unrelenting trivialities. Capitalistic consumption promises an endless cycle of pleasures, but the products do not fulfil their advertised promises and only have a limited duration. To continue to enjoy the same level of 'pleasure', we always need more.

With globalization, the automation of work and all the complex technologies that have emerged, there has been a decline in a sense of community and in the general quality of discourse. The editors strongly believe that reflections upon temporality and shame, and their interfaces, can help re-ground us in these times of extreme change. The respective authors will discuss temporality and shame in relation to clinical and theoretical aspects of psychoanalysis, philosophy, anthropology, genocide and the question of evil, myth and archetype, history and critical studies, the 'discipline of interiority', and literary works. So far as we know, no other volume has previously explored the interface of temporality and shame in depth.

A preliminary view might be that the flow of temporality, an awareness of time passing, is what is most basically human, but we can become frozen in time or caught in mere, defensive going-on-being; shame is a signal of the new and the strange, the uncanny and even the monstrous. The disruptions of temporal flow may deeply disturb us, but they are crucial for any process of freedom and individuation. In this view, trauma and individuation are inseparable and it is our task to learn from such experiences to adapt to the changing world around us. Hyldgaard defines trauma and the need for adaptation:

> A trauma is understood as an event without necessity; a cause for the subject as an accidental, contingent event; an event without immediate purpose; an event that does not make sense, or rather a senseless event that has to be made sense of, an event that hereafter will be made the foundation of sense.
>
> (2000, p. 235)

During the twentieth century, the horrors of wars, genocides and the after-effects of imperialism and colonialism often exceeded the capacity of our minds to assimilate them (Caruth, 1996; LaCapra, 2014). We endlessly redact and over-simplify events and experiences to survive psychologically (Hinton, 2016). The realities of our history have gradually eroded our confidence in steady progress into a reliable future. Faith in reason itself has been undermined. Increasingly, people are fearful that their jobs will be automated out of existence. Work is not satisfying to many because the 'system' requires less and less contribution of human *savoir faire*. There is a large supply of 'Symbolic Misery', a bypassed shame that is mainly unconscious (Stiegler, 2014). No longer do we have *trust* that life will turn out well for ourselves and our children: the shame that could slow us down and enhance reflection is largely unconscious.

As an escape, we begin to consider that the 'establishment' has failed to protect the world from disasters, or to enable us to have satisfying lives. There is a general loss of confidence in ordinary political processes, not least because our children can expect a less affluent life compared to our life now, and because people are aware of increasing socio-economic disparities in their communities, nationally and globally. Everyday life feels increasingly uncanny. There is a loss of civility, a breakdown of international structures, and anxiety about minorities and unfamiliar religions, epitomized by fanatics of all religions. Amidst the turmoil, there is a surge toward authoritarian solutions which deny historical events and offer simple answers to complex questions: we become vulnerable to the seductions of shameless tyrants (Glad, 2002).

Despite these worrying trends of our era, temporality and shame are what lie at the core of the human condition, although we may note them more frequently by their absence or distortions in everyday life. There seems to be a growth of narcissism and a decline of civility and regard for the other. This has dimmed the lenses that magnify and give stature to who we are, that can highlight the truth of what we can and can't know in the face of a vast and puzzling universe. Although clinging to the false safety of a temporal sameness, a mere going-on-being, unexpected disruptions evoke threads of shame, disquiet, reflection, and hope.

The fundamental link of shame and temporality is seldom noted in the literature, and that link will be a core emphasis in this volume. The chapter authors have diverse backgrounds, and all their perspectives borrow heavily from other disciplines to convey an expanded awareness and understanding. The abundance of singular viewpoints stimulates deep reflection about theory and practice and many dimensions of contemporary life. More knowledge and awareness of these topics are crucial at this transition point in history.

A core point of this volume is that shame can be a teacher, and a crucial one, in evaluating our ethical and ontological position in the world. Granting the fact that shame can be toxic and terrible, we need to remember that it is also what can orient us in the difficult task of reflection and consciousness. Without shame, we would become amoral psychopaths. Without temporal awareness, we could not anticipate the shameful harm we might do (Baskin-Sommers, Stuppy-Sullivan & Buckholtz, 2016).

Much has been written about shame as psychopathology and the need to get rid of its troubling presence. Indeed, addictions are often desperate evasions of shame, but shame is more an alarm, a signal that things are out of joint. It has an essential connection to the pursuit of virtue and slows us down in time so that we can wonder and reflect. A shameless person or culture is dangerous, as are those who are pervaded by unconscious or unacknowledged shame. Without the perspective that shame contributes to our awareness, life is often lived out of a grim stoicism that feels frozen and lifeless, or a rampant narcissism that runs roughshod over the needs of others.

Writings about time and temporality seem to emphasize either those, like Plato and Augustine, who describe a dimension of 'timelessness' like the regularity of the heavens performing their circuits in the sky, and tend to regard everyday material reality as a derivative of sorts that is in some sense 'lesser' (Augustine, 2009, pp. 220–45); or others, like Kant and Heidegger, who hold that the motions and change of things are the primal experience of time, and that the 'unchanging' aspect of time is an abstract derivative (Khamenei, 2007). In simple terms, the first picture implies that 'essence precedes existence', whereas in the second case 'existence precedes essence' (Flynn, 2013, pp. 17–18). In this volume, we will emphasize the second view: 'temporality' as referring to lived time, the time of our lives, rather than the 'time' of science and mechanical measures of periodicity and motion (Hoy, 2012). Some chapter authors emphasize the more essentialistic view of time, while still valuing the experience of everyday temporality.

During the eras of the Renaissance and the Enlightenment, the authority of the Church weakened, as well as the belief in its monopoly of knowledge of things Eternal. Kant brought a kind of freer-thinking pietistic, Lutheran humility to the conception of how we come to know anything, seeing space and time as conditions of knowledge but not accessible, eternal entities. This undermined belief in direct knowledge of the noumenal, or to Eternal essences, and in turn opened the way to philosophers such as Husserl and Heidegger, who wrote about temporality as the basis for human life, as well as Derrida who described a 'syncopated time' (Pirovolakis, 2010, pp. 43–82). Such ideas have heavily influenced contemporary theology (Caputo, 2006; Taylor, 2007) as well as the editors of this book.

Every person and every culture has an implicit theory or theories of time, and this affects many perspectives, including truth and justice. Western culture tends to deny death and constantly privilege youth and novelty. This has been exaggerated to the extreme by technologies which are hollowing our ordinary relationships. One can tell a great deal about conflicts between and within cultures by examining the temporal contexts, and this became apparent in events such as the Buddhist and Western perspectives on justice at the Cambodian Tribunal (Hinton, 2016).

Temporal awareness is uniquely human. According to Tulving, animals have no more than a rudimentary sense of time (2005). They do not create complex languages or cultures. Our concern for the future and our memories of a past are the basis of cultural creation. We worry about what might happen, or what did happen, and we prepare for what may come. We try to overcome the errors of the past, especially memories that invoke shame.

Ancient man must have begun to anticipate mentally how his rudimentary tools and weapons could improve his future effectiveness in hunting and self-protection, and eventually the appurtenances of settled agricultural life. To starve due to a failure in hunting or to be devastated by inter-group violence could evoke a sense of shame and vulnerability. The attempt to change the future in light of past experience is the basic human project. The lore of tool-making, a set of memories about rudimentary technologies, was the ancestral basis of the complex technics of our present, and is based on anticipation of the future (Stiegler, 1998). We question how effective cultures are in fostering a meaningful way of life for their citizens, so that they don't fear for the future and feel pride in their daily work rather than shame.

Attitudes about shame evolve in tandem with attitudes regarding temporality. The experience of shame, conscious or unconscious, usually slows down the temporal flow. At the extreme, intense shame can freeze the process of our lives, our capacity to be in the flow of temporality. We all have pockets of shame that can stop us short, startle and terrify us, make us want to disappear from the gaze of others and from our own gaze. Tomkins felt that stranger fear was the origin of shame (1995, pp. 5, 140). When we are ashamed, we look to exclude the gaze of the 'dangerous other' from our midst. The Evil Eye is the most pervasive of all human symbols (Seidler, 2000, pp. 68–71). The nearly universal use of scapegoating is a pathological manifestation of getting rid of shame and fear and has been used by tyrants throughout human history (Girard, 1989).

It is all too common to resist the slowing effect of shame, its interruption of flow, out of fear of what might erupt when we stop and look. This reticence seems mostly due to anxiety about a loss of control and the psychic pain that is involved. What might bubble up within us if we 'gave it time'?

Would we be further shamed by what emerges? Speed and spectacle are often conjoined in the present times, illustrating a massive collective avoidance of the shame of the truth of the present.

Speeded-up time is itself a kind of addiction, strongly reinforced by our desire to emulate the speed of our inorganic technologies (Fong, 2013). Their light speed and their apparent intuition make us organic creatures feel shamefully inferior. We become more and more dependent on the superior memory and artificial intelligence of our technologies. This dependence results in a sense of unease, or even a 'shame of being human' (Stiegler, 2014). We question the worth of our all-too-human *savoir faire* in the face of such automated efficiency.

Reflections on shame and temporality can enable us to become more conscious of all times, as well as our own times. To reflect on oneself is to augment our awareness of the other.

Memory lies at the heart of our sense of temporality. Speculations about the eccentricities of memory have become more common in the literature, and it seems to have become an accepted fact that memory is never foundational, never final, never complete. The psychoanalytic process itself elicits an endless re-examination of memory and of shifts and levels of temporality. Shame is often connected with memories, and that may stop us short. When we look back at the past from every developmental level over time, we invariably see subtle or drastically different perspectives. Gerald Edelman has described how this accords with the findings of neuroscience, using the analogy of an iceberg that melts seasonally, but how each season the streams and rivulets take a somewhat different form (Edelman, 2004, pp. 52–3). We, however, cannot invent a wholly other reality, and change always appears in a context. There is no such thing as a 'blank slate'. When I dream of my parents, they are and are not the same parents I remembered when I first went through analysis decades ago, but the fact of their historical presence remains. As the old saying goes, 'My parents get smarter every day.'

These shifts in memory and temporality can make all knowledge more suspect and uncertain and can lead to shame and disillusionment at our limitation (Hinton, 2015). On the other hand, this is the process of our freedom. If memory was final, time would come to a halt, and life would become endless repetition. As movingly described by Borges in his short story 'Funes the Memorius', such total memory would be a torturous horror (1994, pp. 107ff.).

Transitional objects carry an enigmatic aura that enables human creativity. Without this gap of uncertainty or undecidability, there would be no movement in time. Movement in time also involves a movement in our experience of truth, if we describe truth as *aletheia*, an ongoing process of disclosedness that is never final (Mills, 2014). It seems today that many or most workers have lost the sense of a meaningful future (Stiegler, 2014). This escalates both a sense of lack and shame.

An incident in the life of C.G. Jung illustrates how his attitude toward shame and temporality evolved. In 1910, at the peak of his inflated ambition as the chosen favourite of Freud, he had written to him describing his expansive ambitions for psychoanalysis:

> I think we must give it time to infiltrate among people from many centres ... ever so gently to transform Christ back into the soothsaying god of the vine ... for the *one* purpose of making the cult and the sacred myth what they once were – a drunken feast where man regained the ethos and holiness of an animal.
>
> (Jung, 1973, pp. 17–19)

This was the thought of the younger man, excited and inflated about their 'discovery of the unconscious' (Ellenberger, 1970, pp. 657–748). It was also before World War I and the other deflating events of the twentieth century. It manifested a budding messianic inflation.

Fifty years later, at the age of 83, after a lifetime of immersion in the storms of shame and temporality, a young student wrote him to question his earlier point of view. Jung replied by acknowledging his shame regarding the inflated ambition of his youth:

> Best thanks for the quotation from that accursed correspondence. For me it is an unfortunately inexpungable reminder of the incredible folly that filled the days of my youth. The journey from cloud-cuckoo-land back to reality lasted a long time. In my case Pilgrim's Progress consisted in my having to climb down a thousand ladders until I could reach out my hand to the little clod of earth that I am.
>
> (1973, p. 19, footnote 8)

This is the powerful statement of a man in old age looking back at a fully lived life. He had continually immersed himself in the turbulent flow of time, living courageously and intensely on the personal, scholarly, and professional levels. His shame over his youthful inflation is marked, and he openly acknowledges his follies. From that basis of deep honesty, he had been able to lead a many-sided and creative life.

To become that little clod of earth that we are allows the world to come closer to us in all its sometimes shaming and alarming truth, in all its possibility and ambiguity. Embracing shame and temporality opens the way toward becoming that clod of earth, that vulnerable, singular entity that we are. Shame enables us to become more fully present in the world and authentically engage in the flow of temporality and the richness of its syncopated dimensionality. Such a deeply honest ethos, embracing the jarring awareness of shame and the always-shifting temporalities of memory, can open us to a fuller presence in life. This is the basic vision of our book.

Ladson Hinton's chapter introduces the concepts of temporality and shame in a touching and dramatic encounter with raw life on the streets of Seattle. He discusses a growing feeling of disorientation, due to a lack of capacity to assimilate the traumas of history, globalization, and the ever-pacing technology development. He discusses how the increased spectacles of violence and injustice, along with the general deterioration of civility, damages the sense of a meaningful life for our children. He considers that facing shame and truth of our current situation may provide the ground for rebirth of aliveness and a sense of future.

In the second chapter, Jon Mills discusses past, present, and future in the relationship between the analyst's shame and the phenomena of temporality which casts a particular light on the quality of the lived experience that occurs in treatment. The *archaic primacy* of the past, the *immediational presence* of the current moment, and the *projective teleology* informs the qualitative experiences of lived time. He warns of enactments that may take place when shame, evoked in the analyst, cannot be held in the countertransference. He discusses the horrid mobilization of shame when idealized by two patients, which was negated leading to two different forms of intervention through which Mills was able to transform historical shame by adopting the intentional stance of the other's idealization.

Levinas, diachrony, and shame are central in Eric Severson's chapter. Using Levinas's unique philosophy of shame, he explores the psychological and ethical dynamics of shame, leading to the introduction of two manifestations of shame, calling them *synchronic shame* and *diachronic shame*. Severson considers that improving an understanding, particularly of the intersubjectivity of time will improve the treatment of shame. Shame, he says, points to the unsettling of time, an unsettling of the synchronization of the time of the self by the time of the other.

In her chapter, Sharon Green addresses ethical time which she defines as the temporal dilemma of the subject who must act without knowing or having a guarantee of the outcome of the act, while acknowledging the control we do not have and the leeway therefore needed for accidents and unexpected circumstances. Ethical time has two dimensions of temporality: assuming responsibility for and bearing our constitutional shame. Green's chapter focuses on Lacan's understanding of *Nachträglichkeit* as it appears throughout his teaching beginning with the essay on 'Logical Time'. She discusses the relationship between *Nachträglichkeit* and various Lacanian concepts and concludes with the consequences of the loss of shame and shared values as these have emerged with the rise of late capitalism and late neo-liberalism.

Angela Connolly proposes that the development of temporality depends on the capacity to use metaphor which itself is an embodied and embedded practice. Intense trauma such as that undergone by inmates of the Nazi camps or the victims of sexual abuse leads to a progressive dissociation between psyche and soma which, in severe cases, leads to a loss of the sense of body agency and body ownership, or an abject body, the extreme example being Primo Levi's *Musselman*. The states of disembodiment lead to profound feelings of shame which in turn provokes a destructuring of temporality such that the individual is left suspended in an eternal present with the loss of any felt connection to the past and the future. A vicious circle is thus set up: trauma leads to shame; shame leads to disembodiment; disembodiment leads to the loss of metaphor; and the loss of metaphor leads to the loss of temporality. Restoration of the metaphoric capacity either through what Laub and Podell call 'the art of trauma' or through analysis is needed to open up the vicious circle.

Sue Austin describes her work with patients whose inner lives are dominated by severe and chronic shame. She points to the use of a 'temporal defence'; understanding her patient's unconscious efforts to 'vanish' shame by living an internal life that is so speeded up that all thoughts, feelings, or images related to shame have no chance of registering in consciousness. The intolerable shame is inseparable from states of helplessness and powerlessness, which also contain an opening towards an unknown and unknowable future, thus forming the basis of the analytic treatment. Drawing on Jung and Laplanche, Austin suggests that shame can offer a window on to a crack in subjectivity and, through that, glimpses of the unconscious enigmatic 'othernesses'.

Hessel Willemsen discusses the inevitability of death as driver of temporality, marking the inescapable presence of time which moves as gradient beginning some time *in utero* and ending with the final breath observable through the body's evanescence. He considers that temporality cannot be thought of without considering shame, so important in its ontological meaning, relating to the chronic incompleteness of the person, and therefore without considering the incompleteness of the body. Willemsen suggests that only through re-addressing past experiences, or the process of *Nachträglichkeit*, is it possible to advance the future and come to terms with the evanescent truth of life. The chronic sense of incompleteness and finitude creates a quality of shame in life, varying with particular circumstances. Temporality, shame and mortality are therefore strongly interconnected.

In his chapter, Daniel Ross suggests that today's spur to the question of shame is the contemporary pervasiveness of shamelessness. This epochal changeability raises the question of the relation of this two-sided phenomenon, the question of shame versus shamelessness to technology. The account of technologically-induced shame, however, seems at odds with our experience of consumerist capitalism, which more often resembles a process of disinhibition as described by Peter Sloterdijk. Reconciling these perspectives is possible only with an approach capable of going back to the root sources of these tendencies, which Bernard Stiegler, like Anders, relates to the Prometheus myth, and to the *aidōs* (shame) given by Hermes as the feeling by which the discord wrought by technics can be resolved. But for Stiegler, this must be complemented by a consideration of shame's generational character, which in pathological social conditions produces what he calls the Antigone complex. Today, a kind of extremity is being reached in this socio-psycho-pathological condition, resulting in that proliferation of phenomena that could be described as expressing hyper-shame, but where this new character results in actions and behaviour that increasingly blur the line between the shameful and the shameless.

Alexander Hinton explores the interrelationship of justice, temporality, and shame at the Extraordinary Chambers in the Courts of Cambodia (ECCC). He follows the trial participation of the late Vann Nath, a survivor of S-21, a torture and detention centre operated by the Khmer Rouge. This Maoist-inspired group of revolutionaries implemented policies resulting in the death of up to two million of Cambodia's eight million inhabitants. Hinton argues that, even as they seek to help post-conflict societies like Cambodia 'move forward through justice' (as the ECCC slogan goes), transitional justice mechanism like the ECCC are premised on a set of temporal assumptions and an accompanying shameful 'lack' that emerge from a larger transitional justice imaginary. Hinton argues that scholars and practitioners need to attend to such assumptions and local vernaculars that mediate the understanding and responses of people involved in such transitional justice initiatives, including Vann Nath.

Four modalities of temporality and the problem of shame are the focus of the chapter written by Murray Stein. He relates shame to each modality and discusses how the problem of shame may be integrated into conscious life through an experience of the self. The four modalities are: achronicity, chronicity, synchronicity, and dyschronicity. Organized in two polarity pairs: achronicity–chronicity and synchronicity–dyschronicity, Stein suggests that all play a part in a complete in-depth autobiography and constitute the wholeness of the experience of time and shame within the life of an individual.

In our final chapter, Michael Whan discusses Jung's formidable perspective, which enabled him to develop a psychology open to the historical present. Jung's insights reflect his impressive knowledge of the mytho-poetic soul and psyche's cultural-historical forms. The Jungian project, according to Whan, sought to preserve what might be termed a 'myth of meaning': a feeling for the 'enchanted' depths of existence, underpinned by mythic and religious 'primordial images'. Disturbed by modernity's *disenchantment*, Jung's central goal was to re-enchant individual and cultural life.

Whan explores two of Jung's profound experiences of disenchantment and the evolution of his thinking. Indeed, faced with these insights into the loss of enchantment, Jung went on to disavow them, turning toward a merely personal search for an individual 'myth of meaning'. From that point of view, shame is personal, or 'semantic'. He abandoned the approach of the 'inner dialogue' that had originally led him to awareness of disenchantment as the truth of the historical present. He thus evaded his own awareness of a 'syntactical' or ontological-structural dimension of soul, and a shame that stems from the rending truth of disenchantment. Jung's abandonment of his own experience aborted a basic transformation in his thinking, namely, the profound need for the psyche's self-emptying and self-overcoming of the previous historical soul-forms with all their mythic, religious, and metaphysical expressions. He evaded the more crucial task of the soul's *kenósis,* the profound 'emptying' that can open one to the deeper movements of the soul.

References

Augustine, St. (2009). *Confessions*. New York: Oxford University Press.

Baskin-Sommers, A., Stuppy-Sullivan, A. M., & Buckholtz, J. W. (2016). Psychopathic individuals exhibit but do not avoid regret during counterfactual decision-making. *Proceedings of the National Academy of Sciences, 113*, 50, pp. 14438–43.

Borges, J. L. (1994). Funes the Memorious. In *Ficciones*, pp. 107–17. New York: Grove Press.

Caputo, J. (2006). *The Weakness of God: A Theology of the Event*. Bloomington, IN: Indiana University Press.

Caruth, C. (1996). *Unclaimed Experience: Trauma, Narrative, and History*. Baltimore, MD: Johns Hopkins University Press.

Edelman, G. (2004). *Wider Than the Sky: The Phenomenal Gift of Consciousness*. New Haven, CT: Yale University Press.

Ellenberger, H. F. (1970). *The Discovery of the Unconscious*. New York: Basic Books.

Flynn, T. (2013). Jean-Paul Sartre. In *Stanford Encyclopedia of Philosophy, Fall 2013 Edition*. Stanford, CA: The Metaphysics Research Lab, Center for the Study of Language and Information, Stanford University.

Fong, B. Y. (2013). Death drive sublimation: A psychoanalytic perspective on technological development. *Psychoanalysis, Culture & Society, 18*, pp. 352–67.

Girard, R. (1989). *The Scapegoat*. Baltimore, MD: Johns Hopkins University Press.

Glad, B. (2002). Why tyrants go too far: Malignant narcissism and absolute power. *Political Psychology, 23*, 1.

Hinton, A. L. (2016). *Man or Monster? The Trial of a Khmer Rouge Torturer.* Durham, NC: Duke University Press.

Hinton, L. (2015). Temporality and the Torments of Time. *Journal of Analytical Psychology, 60*, 3, pp. 353–70.

Hoy, D. C. (2012). *The Time of Our Lives: A Critical History of Temporality*. Cambridge, MA: MIT Press.

Hyldgaard, K. (2000). The cause of the subject as an ill-timed accident: Lacan, Sartre, and Aristotle. *Umbr(a)*, Fall issue.

Jung, C. G. (1973). *Letters, Volume 1: 1906–1950*. Gerhard Adler (ed.), R. F. C. Hull (trans.). Princeton, NJ: Princeton University Press.

Khamenei, S. M. (2007). Time, temporal, and temporality. In A.-T. Tymieniecka (ed.), *Timing and Temporality in Islamic Philosophy and Phenomenology of Life*. New York: Springer.

LaCapra, D. (2014). *Writing History, Writing Trauma*. Baltimore, MD: Johns Hopkins University Press.

Mills, J. (2014). Truth. *Journal of the American Psychoanalytical Association*, *62*, 2, pp. 267–93.

Pirovolakis, E. (2010). *Reading Derrida and Ricoeur*. Albany, NY: SUNY Press.

Seidler, G. H. (2000). *In Others' Eyes: An Analysis of Shame*. New York: International Universities Press.

Stiegler, B. (1998). *Technics and Time, 1*. Stanford, CA: Stanford University Press.

Stiegler, B. (2014). *Symbolic Misery, Volume 1*. B. Norman (trans.). Malden, MA: Polity Press.

Taylor, M. C. (2007). *After God*. Chicago, IL: University of Chicago Press.

Tomkins, S. (1995). *Shame and its Sisters*. Durham, NC: Duke University Press.

Tulving, E. (2005). Episodic memory and autonoesis: Uniquely human? In H. S. Terrace & J. Metcalf (eds), *The Missing Link in Cognition*, pp. 3–56. New York: Oxford University Press.

Žižek, S. (2007). *Enjoy Your Symptom! Jacques Lacan in Hollywood and Out*. New York: Routledge.

Chapter 1

Shame and temporality in the streets

Consumerism, technology, truth and raw life

Ladson Hinton

> The cask of ages past is spent:
> it's final.
> The plight of Anima Mundi's song is
> fatal.
> We want to hear it sing again;
> we try,
> Refusing to believe that voice
> did die.
> We urge it to return;
> we cry!
> But nothing comes and nothing will—
> the end seems nigh.
> And mourning speaks as mourning must,
> we sigh.

The Vanishing of the World Soul,[1] Ladson Hinton, 2015

Introduction

Indeed, we sigh! No longer do we experience a world soul, an Anima Mundi that contains and connects all things. The view that there is an underlying unity between the world and all the entities of the world has tended to dominate western thought since the time of Plato (Plato, 2000, p. 16). The alchemists attempted to revivify this idea with the concept of the *Unus Mundus,* a unified world, with a Self that is a carrier of the unity of the individual (Jung, 1970, pp. 537–9). At this time in history, we have lost confidence in such an 'enchanted,' interconnected world sustained by the regularity of the heavens circulating around us. In the face of this loss, we feel troubled and bewildered (Hinton, Hinton, Hinton & Hinton, 2011).

Freud wrote of the threefold narcissistic wounds suffered by humanity in recent centuries, namely the Copernican, the Darwinian and the psycho-analytic revolutions. In other words, an awareness that the earth revolves around the sun, and not vice versa; an awareness that humankind is descended from apelike creatures; and an awareness that reason itself is dubiously based and often blindly irrational (Freud, 1917/1955). Today, we would certainly add the terrible events of the Holocaust, the Khmer Rouge and Rwanda genocides, slavery, apartheid and colonialism. Such histories of profound evil further shook our faith in human progress. Following upon these shattering blows, potent technologies, evolving at the speed of light in the twenty-first century, have far surpassed ordinary human capacities. This crescendo of happenings has created a state of shame and disorientation (Ross, 2006; Stiegler, 2008, pp. 64–96).

Time is speeded up, and our sense of continuity with the past and with our ancestors is tenuous. The world seems to be in a state of violent transition, and raw life greets us daily on the streets as we hurry about, equipped with our many electronic and smart devices, or technics. We have become addicted to spectacles of wonderment and terror, and each morning we glance at the news to see what disaster has transpired. Indeed, Virilio calls the contemporary world a Museum of Accidents (Virilio, 2003, pp. 40–57). When our containing traditions are stripped away, we search for ways to endure the screams and cries that run through us (Eigen, 2005, p. 51).[2] We wonder whether this is, indeed, the end of the Anthropocene, also known as the time when the human being no longer dominates, the end of the era of *homo sapiens* (Ross, 2016). What cyborg or other technologized creature might replace us?

At such a time in history, we need, above all, a capacity for reflection. However, the relentless promotion of consumption promises access to immediate gratification and an escape from the truth of the present. Tempting spectacles are endlessly offered with all of the sophisticated attractions of advanced technics, 'short-circuiting' the deferral of pleasure that sublimates our desires for individual and communal goods (Stiegler, 2013b, pp. 102–8). As a result, there is an increasing 'proletarianization of the mind,' a deficiency in the capacity for long-term thought due to the automation of memory and a general loss of '*savoir-faire*' (ibid., pp. 37–8, 123–6). We have become addicted to short-term fixes and are left with a psyche that is uncontained and unformed, in fact dangerous, because a surplus of unsublimated energy is the truth of the frighteningly 'raw life' that is emerging post *anima mundi* (Stiegler, 2013a, pp. 80–102; 2014, pp. 1–13).

Sequence of discussion

Shame and temporality, along with truth, provide crucial lenses for reflecting upon our present condition, and I will begin by briefly delineating these basic concepts. Following this, I will describe a provocative encounter on the streets of Seattle that provides insight into undercurrents that are visibly emerging in contemporary life. My hope is that this detailed example, along with a few others, will contribute to a deepened understanding of the contemporary scene, enhance the reader's knowledge of shame and temporality, and offer space to reflect upon these basic experiences. In the concluding part of the chapter, I amplify those reflections from the perspectives of several philosophers and psychoanalysts who share a deep concern about the future of the human being.

Shame, truth and temporality

The experiences of shame, truth and temporality are interrelated. In psychoanalytic work, it is difficult to discuss one without the others. The many levels of memory are deeply interconnected with temporality and lie at the core of the analytic process. Individual versions of the ghost of Hamlet's father appear in their several voices, emerging from the past, making their claim to truth, and shaming those who survive into deep reflection about the future. In psychoanalysis, the analyst's interpretations are intended to enhance awareness of unconscious truths, past and present, opening frozen dimensions of the patient's world, and allowing fuller participation in the flow of time. Such insights often provoke turbulent evolution and shame, along with potential new openings towards the future; thus, a brief summary of some salient aspects of shame and temporality and their interrelationship with truth is necessary.

First, shame often involves the question, 'What kind of person am I?' It makes us wonder, sometimes with horror, 'How could I have done such and such a thing?' It stops us cold and makes us want to disappear. Its etymology has to do with covering or hiding. At times, shame seems to combine a sense of the immediate and the particular with questions about the very structure of being (Hultberg, 1986). Furthermore, it can open up further dimensions of temporality because it slows us down from the mad pace of our culture, and when we slow down, we can 'see' more.

As shame often has a very social dimension, we flush with shame when we are seen, or see ourselves, violating our concept of an ideal self (Seidler, 2000, pp. 47–97). 'Skin shame' can be superficial and connected with self-conscious conformity, but deeper shame can motivate us to question our deepest core and most primal sense of meaning. This seems to be true across cultures, and there is evidence that it is biologically innate (Sznycer, Tooby, Cosmides, Porat, Shalvi, & Halperin, 2016; Tracy & Matsumoto, 2008). It seems to involve both emotional and metaphysical stirrings, often inciting us not only to acknowledge a factual wrongdoing but to engage with the question of the very nature of our humanity (Heidegger, 1956, p. 27).

The shamelessness of our times is alarming, but shame often goes unacknowledged and ignored (Giegerich, 2001, p. 34; Morrison, 1989, pp. 121–3). Indeed, Stiegler believes that shame is not lacking but rather that it is present in a pervasive although unarticulated form as 'symbolic misery,' that is, 'the shame of being human' (Stiegler, 2013a, pp. 105–6). In his view, the contemporary deficit of selfhood is a dimension of late-stage capitalism, and we are living through a decadence of industrial democracy. These feelings of shame, very often bypassed and unconscious, result in a 'symbolic misery' (Stiegler, 2013a, p. 5) that is expressed by apathy, disaffection and social collapse. It is, in many ways, a product of mass media and the technologies of consumerism to which we have become addicted.[3]

While we can often delineate guilt and obtain a pardon, it is much more difficult to atone for shame. It requires a full, total examination of self. However, throughout the history of psychoanalysis, shame has been perceived as an inferior emotion that is typical of women, cultural and racial minorities, and colonized others (Aron & Starr, 2013, pp. 51–64; Bewes, 2011). Western cultures are often portrayed as guilt cultures, and therefore supposedly superior. However, guilt may actually be an evasion of shame, a focus on something that appears to be specific and 'solvable' in lieu of facing the more intractable and searching questions that shame poses. Indeed, guilt can be a seductive way to explain and dismiss one's deeper sense of responsibility (Stiegler, 2013a, p. 24).

Shame and truth are closely interconnected. I am not speaking of Truth as an absolute or foundational Truth, but truth with a small t. It is truth as a process, which the ancient Greeks called *aletheia*.

Truth is related to temporality, '[and] we should view truth not as an absolute category that discloses itself in its entirety but rather as a contextual process that reveals itself a bit at a time and from many different perspectives' (Stiegler, 2013a, p. 9). That is, it unfolds in time. 'Authentic truth . . . seems to be a matter not of what one knows, but instead of how one lives' (Guignon, 1983, p. 348). As new elements of truth are disclosed, others may fade into hiddenness or obscurity.

Giegerich discussed the importance of remembering that truth often has a violent effect on the psyche (2008, pp. 4–8). He employs the story of Actaion and the Hounds as an illustration. In this story, Prince Actaion was out hunting, and by chance, he found the goddess Artemis naked, bathing in a pool with her acolytes. When she realized that he was spying on them, she turned him into a stag, and he was then dismembered by his own hounds (Giegerich, 2001, pp. 105–11, 203ff.).

The story of Actaion dramatically illustrates how we may unexpectedly come across a naked truth about ourselves, thereby creating a dire sense of psychic disruption and inner crumbling that may provoke deep shame. In the longer run, such experiences can open the space for reflection and profound shifts in awareness. It is also the universal tale of the 'otherness' of time unfolding, impacting a psyche that tends to reflexively maintain continuity and an illusion of safety (ibid., p. 28).

This leads to my last theme, temporality, which is the experience of lived time, the time of our lives (Hoy, 2012, pp. xii–xiii). Temporality is uniquely human and is the basis of culture. Awareness of time drives us, inspiring both the nobility of our future purpose and our destructive paranoias (Johnston, 2005, pp. 300–32). However, time is strangely elusive, appearing to vanish as soon as we attempt to describe it: 'Space contains both living and inert bodies, but *only the living human – hence the living psyche – is subjectively concerned with time*' (Scarfone, 2006, p. 810, emphasis added).

Nothing occurs except in the context of temporality. In a profound sense, temporality *is Homo sapiens*.[4] Our temporal being is also our tormentor, driving us on into an unknown future, evoking both shame and truth, which in turn can radically alter the experience of time.

Memory and our sense of the past disrupt us, and we can endlessly dwell on our memories. However, memory is always subject to revision, and its truth is never final. Our identity has changing levels with no final foundation. Due to the effects of *Nachträglichkeit*, or 'afterwardness,' there is a constant reconfiguration of memory, a factor that comprises much of the work of psychoanalysis. This process not only shifts the meaning of the past but also alters the qualities of the future that we envisage (Civitarese, 2010, pp. 96–108).[5] A fear of the future and the projection of unassimilated traumas may result in a kind of frozenness in time (Hinton, 2015, p. 355). Temporality is uniquely human, and it denies us the peaceful complacency of the other animals on the planet as we anticipate our death and the death of others. Such awareness of the truth of our finitude may create deep shame.

'The Man in the Street'

New perspectives often come from the raw, disowned elements of our world. In that spirit, I will describe an experience that I had last year on a street in Seattle, near our home. This incident highlights shame, truth and temporality in a specific context, and it touches upon many questions about contemporary life and the state of psychoanalysis.

We live in the Capitol Hill area, a large neighbourhood adjacent to the urban core that is filled with old family residences in the north half, and apartment buildings, restaurants, bars, coffee houses and occasional half-way houses in the south half.

One day I stopped for bread at my favourite bakery, which is, more or less, in the centre of the Hill. When I returned to my car, I found a mildly dishevelled man, probably thirty years old, lounging against it with a large cup of coffee sitting on the hood. Vaguely wondering if there would be some sort of messy encounter, I started to unlock my door, saying quietly, 'Sorry to disturb.' The man suddenly sprang up to his full height – he was tall and solidly built – and his face dramatically reddened. His eyes became wide and wild, and he began to shout loudly at the surroundings and at me, 'Do you know about what's happening?! Do you know about what's happening?!' There was a sense of panic, almost terror, in the air, as if he suddenly felt shattered.

With hardly a pause, I looked directly at him in a friendly way and said calmly and succinctly, 'I don't have a clue about what's happening.' Those words had come directly to mind, and was the direct truth of what I felt. The man's visage changed within seconds, lost its red-faced wildness, and he looked almost happy. Nodding slightly to me with the hint of a smile, he took his coffee and strolled off quietly down the street. The flow of life was restored.

Reflections on the encounter

My response to him was truly without conscious thought. Indeed, in that moment, I felt a sort of kinship with him. The change in his demeanour was dramatic and memorable. That I did not 'know' or pretend to 'know about' what was happening was somehow profoundly reassuring to him. It was a special 'moment of meeting,' something unforgettable.

Life is often difficult for individuals whose usual lens of experience is from a 'vertex' that differs from the cultural norm, resulting in a painful sense of being an outsider. This kind of awareness may also evoke a different sense of temporality from that of the average person. Frequently, and very uncomfortably, it seems to them that everyone else knows 'about what is happening' except them. Such experiences are disconcerting, even terrifying, and is also endlessly shame-inducing.

The Man in the Street flushed dramatically when he reacted to my intrusion, but it felt much more like shame than anger. If it had been anger, my own visceral response would have been different. I had violently startled him by my appearance, disrupting his peaceful interlude with his coffee and my car.

My sense is that he had been in a fantasy/reverie state in which he was a 'normal person,' a somebody who, for a moment, 'belonged.' He was in a place where he 'had a place,' and that was what I had disrupted in a way that probably felt violent to him (Giegerich, 2008, pp. 4–8). It is also what was made okay by my response, the message that, on some level, I too did not really have a place. That made our relationship more symmetrical. As a result, his shame dissolved. He was no longer reduced to being a defective object in the eye of the surroundings.

I had suddenly disrupted the Man in the Street during a fantasy of access to the vast power of technics, of cars and coffee and commerce, along with their extensive cultural memories.[6] He had been momentarily entranced by the seductions of the consumer society. I had disrupted his simulation of power and connection, throwing him into a state of psychic disequilibrium. My presence was an existential truth. The car belonged to me. The disruption of his reverie was acutely shaming, thrusting him back into the sense of being an outsider, a social outcast, a crazy piece of trash on the street who existed outside cultural time.

In his panic, the man seemed to be appealing to me and the surrounding surprised people on the sidewalks – appealing, in a sense, to the world as a witness, looking for some kind of justice. Without some hope for justice, cultures cannot hold together, although justice is never final but is always in process, as ethics and law. Shame and justice are deeply interconnected (Stiegler, 2013a, p. 18). They are basic cultural elements that hold people together and make possible a sense of future and hope. A lack of hope lays the foundation for violence, terrorism and shameless acts (Stiegler, 2013a, pp. 8–9, 19).

The question posed by the Man in the Street about what was happening expressed his anguished uncertainty about whether there was any coherent order left in the world, something that included him. Appealing to the collective surround, to 'society,' he beseechingly asked if, indeed, *anyone* knew 'about' what was happening in a way that went beyond merely literal facts. He had immersed himself in the emblems of 'belonging,' which provided a fragile sense of gratification and proof that life was worth living. I had shattered that fantasy. Was there anyone who could affirm a world in which there was any consistent hope of 'belonging,' any possible future?

At some level, he was also posing the 'God is dead' question that seems so overtly and covertly present at this time in history. What do we do when there seems to be no coherent discourse to keep things in place, so that we can think about them and lead meaningful lives beyond our driven consumerism? In that none of us really knows what is happening and we feel lost in the frantic pace of things, we are not unlike the Man in the Street. He is us, and we are him.

When I told him that I did not have a clue, he immediately exhibited a profound sense of relief. This acknowledgement that we shared a common human plight evoked a dramatic shift that seemed dialectical. One could surmise there were several levels involved. First, my sudden appearance had shattered his reverie of ownership and his sense of belonging in the cultural present, and thrown him into shame and panic.[7] Second, I responded to his frantic, screaming questions with a negative assertion, rather than with scorn or irritation. The raw truth was that I did not have a clue![8]

In a dialectical movement, these two negations opened up an expanded sense of space and time.[9] I would call this a dimension of soul, of interiority (Giegerich, 2008, p. 3). Indeed, it was as if we shared a secret, some glimmering of a different truth. This seemed to dissolve the shame he had experienced. As he strolled down the street, back into the everyday flow of time, there was a wink of kinship, almost of complicity, that was fascinating and special, a secret that we shared. We both knew that the world is not as it pretends to be. This contributed an undercurrent of freedom and humour. We had glimpsed another dimension of reality together, and this involved interconnected shifts in the experience of shame, truth and temporality (Civitarese, 2016, pp. 485, 490–3).

This experience has continued to reverberate in my mind. Sociological and psychiatric explanations seem not merely less than adequate but almost unethical in their reductionism. Several theoretical perspectives have helped me understand the dimensions of my experience with the Man in the Street.

Wilfred Bion

I begin with Wilfred Bion. In 1954, he discussed the case of a psychotic man, whom he described as having a severe phobia about wearing socks with holes. At that time, his interpretation was that the man experienced the holes as a symbol of castration, turning the socks into terrifying, attacking objects that could sever his leg. The socks became persecutory objects (Bion, 1954, pp. 113–18; 1967, pp. 27–9).

Twenty years later, Bion returned to the case, saying, 'I suggest that the patient did not have a phobia of socks but could see that what . . . [seemed to be] socks . . . [were actually] a lot of holes knitted together' (Bion, 1973/1990, pp. 21–2; Rhode, 1998, pp. 23–6). That is, the man saw the holes as the primary phenomenon, not the socks as intact and unified objects that were penetrated (Hinton, 2007). Bion called this latter medical-rational point of view the 'medical vertex,' which assumes a primal unity and wholeness of the body along with the assumption that signification proceeds from there in a rational chain.

In contrast, viewed from within another perspective that Bion called the 'religious vertex,' the patient could see the holes as barely contained voids opening into an infinite abyss into which everything might disappear, or as openings into an infinite enigma or an inexpressible truth. This awareness was the source of the patient's terror, not the fear of castration that he had originally postulated (Rhode, 1998, pp. 19–20).

This example has remained with me for many years as a wonderful example of the capacity to see the infinite in the ordinary and a potential dimension of interiority of all things (Giegerich, 2007, p. 3). I personally think of 'interiority' as being like the experience of repeatedly reading a good poem, and experiencing how more and more dimensions manifest themselves. Indeed, one could call this perspective a poetics of everyday life, as opposed to, for example, the view of medical psychopathology, which only sees validity in that which is immediately visible.

There is a depth of experience in the everyday that we tend to miss because of the ego's fear of losing control in the face of enigma, of that which we endlessly attempt to grasp or know, but which defies any final knowing. It challenges and torments us. However, for the person subsumed by a pervasive madness the problem is often being unable to perceive any-thing that does *not* seem enigmatic. The challenge is being able to live at all in such a state of being. Artists and theologians often have the ability to 'see' creatively from that perspective, and Bion felt that psychoanalysts also needed to perceive such dimensions of truth. For that to happen, Bion often repeated that one must come from a place that is without memory or desire, a place that does not privilege goals based on a causal understand-ing from the patient's past or from culturally or personally contrived future goals. That perspective has helped me to understand the Man in the Street, and his shifts vis-à-vis shame, truth and temporality.

Wolfgang Giegerich

Bion's perspective resembles that of Wolfgang Giegerich, although Giegerich's theory is broader because it underlines historical and cultural factors that Bion does not include. Giegerich calls his approach the disci-pline of interiority (Giegerich, 2012b, p. 206; 2008, pp. 3–4). That is, it does not rely on the external material characteristics of a phenomenon any more than one could rely on dictionary definitions of the words of a poem to deeply understand the poem. 'Interiority' is a depth of experience that may be revealed by ongoing reflection. This does not mean the inside of things in a literal sense but a quality of interiority, or soul that is poten-tially present in all experiences.[10] From his perspective, 'If psychology wants to establish itself as a discipline of interiority, it must [also] show that it is capable of accounting for external reality, for the "world," *in terms of its own standpoint of* interiority' (Giegerich, 2012a, p. 1; 2012b, p. 43). Giegerich emphasizes a process of 'the negation of a positive, tan-gible, demonstrable reality, [and] a taking off into the interiority of the phenomenon itself' (Casement, 2011, p. 52). Such a profound shift into the experience at hand is vastly different from viewing or imagining things from the outside as positively given objects. This is similar to Bion's religious vertex, which is very different from the medical vertex of unity, positivity, and linear cause and effect.

According to Giegerich, classical Jungian analysis has become problematic because the time of myth is in the past. We are no longer contained on the inside of such signifying structures. Now, what passes as myth, symbol and archetype are often simulacra of a bygone age (Whan, 2015). Thus, Giegerich asserts that an analytic practice relying on dead concepts can, itself, be a form of neurosis because it privileges an illusory quest. In other words, symbolic realization as Jung conceived it, a dialogue of ego and archetype guided by the Self, is no longer possible because those concepts were dependent on myths such as the *anima mundi* that have lost their meaning, and we cannot replace them (Giegerich, 2001, pp. 84–5).

One can view the singular experiences of people such as the Man in the Street as manifestations of the larger movements of consciousness, of the truths of an age.[11] That is, soul truth 'wants to be embodied . . . as a personal reality in people' (Barreto, 2015, p. 16). To become modern adults, we must arrive at where we already are in a reflective way (ibid., p. 17). That is the purpose of the discussion of the Man in the Street. In some way, he loudly broadcast the truth of where we already are, helping us know more about that, reflectively and consciously. Without such an authentic point of departure, there is no journey.

Tanaka's empirical observations

In his clinical studies, Yasuhiro Tanaka creatively and empirically grounds Giegerich's perspective, revealing our cultural situation in stark relief. Tanaka describes a contemporary phenomenon that he calls 'unborn-ness' (Tanaka, 2014). To move on from mere biological birth and become a psychical entity, an infant needs a frame of reference, a matrix of signification, a 'grammar' for articulating inner and outer experience. Perhaps due to cultural and historical changes and the consequent loss of guiding frameworks, Tanaka observes that psychological birth, the capacity for deeper reflection and soulfulness, has become only a distant possibility (Tanaka, 2014, pp. 6–8).

His studies of the patient population in Kyoto over many years reveal a steady diminishing of dissociation or inner conflict. In his view, this is due to a failure of development rather than repression. As a result, there has been an evident decline in the presence of an internal frame of reference or sense of what is going on inside the person (Tanaka, 2013, pp. 3–4; 2014, pp. 13–17). Shame, an important dimension of insidedness, is often lacking, and he speculates that this shift means that individuals increasingly lack the psychological infrastructure for classic analytic approaches (Tanaka, 2013, pp. 7–11).

One could view this as a consequence of the 'God is dead' phenomenon. Shame, as well as the shock of truth and temporality, is necessary to develop the capacity for psychological reflection. If there is a deficiency of a signifying structure, that is, a lack of containment in family and culture, there can be no subsequent experience of leaving the Garden with all its tension, torment and psychological awakening.

Tanaka sees this state of unborn-ness as related to the autism spectrum disorder and feels that it may be a *Merkmal* of our times – a German word for an indicator that is a harbinger of the future (Tanaka, 2014, pp. 5–6). Psychoanalysis originated from the study of the dissociation of personality, that is, the divided, hysterical selves that Janet and Charcot studied at the Salpêtrière in the nineteenth century. This sense of tormenting self-division motivated the kind of reflection that was at the core of clinical work from its beginnings (Ghazal & Hinton, 2016; Tanaka, 2008). Self-division evokes a sense of self that is other than itself and is therefore motivated to reflect on itself. Psychoanalytic thought and practice are based on this fertile ground of anxious self-doubt and self-reflection. However, in the case of a gross deficiency of self-structures, there is nothing to be divided, thus making the transference and dialogue difficult or impossible. Accordingly, for many patients, the classic psychoanalytic quest for truth may be inconceivable.

Tanaka quotes empirical studies of Japanese students over several decades that show an increasing shift from inner-focused anxieties accompanied by emotions, such as shame, towards complaints regarding the 'out there.' The students became increasingly more concrete in their thinking, with fewer psychological complaints that convey self-consciousness (Tanaka, 2013, p. 6). His work indicates a clear decline of inner structure over decades, along with related deficits in the experiences of shame, truth and temporality.

Similar to Giegerich, Tanaka's startling conclusion is, 'the 20th century, which was called "the century of psychology," both temporally and psychologically, has already ended, and its process of decline . . . [can] easily be observed in the history of psychotherapy' (Tanaka, 2014, p. 3). He reflects on possible approaches to patients who lack psychological infrastructure, contending that the new approach will differ significantly from the more 'classical' forms. Indeed, he questions whether psychoanalysis will survive at all!

Conclusion

We no longer feel contained by a world soul. The thrust of temporality inexorably drives us towards an uncertain future, still haunted by historical traumas that we cannot assimilate. The ghosts of the past and the uncanny dimensions of the future, the strange new world to come, disrupt individuals and societies in multiple ways. This disruption makes us prone to raw emotions that strip us bare, and we feel increasing shame at the truth of our helplessness, or we flee into alarming, shameless acts of violence.

The encounter with the Man in the Street summarizes some of the profound dilemmas we face. Similar to an Old Testament prophet, the Man in the Street provokes anguished speculations about shame, temporality and the raw truth of our times.

The works of Bion, Stiegler and Giegerich usefully amplify the dimensions and questions of our contemporary situation, and Tanaka's research provides an important empirical grounding.

One indeed wonders whether deeper psychological birth is still possible in our time. Who are we? Where are we going? What are we? Is this the end of the human age, the end of the Anthropocene? Feeling naked and vulnerable as we face the unknown future, we mourn the loss of the comforting *anima mundi*.

Notes

1   'We must say that divine providence brought our world into being as a truly living thing, endowed with soul and intelligence . . . let us lay it down that the world resembles more closely than anything else that Living Thing of which all other living things are parts, both individually and by kinds. For that Living Thing comprehends within itself all intelligible living things, just as our world is made up of us and all the other visible creatures. Since the god

wanted nothing more than to make the world like the best of the intelligible things, complete in every way, he made it a single visible living thing, which contains within itself all the living things whose nature it is to share its kind' (Plato, 2000, p. 16).

2   'Variations of a scream run through life. We are that scream and much more. But when the smile comes, the scream does not stop. The smile that grows out of the scream is not the same as the seamless smile, one that makes us believe that no scream is there' (Eigen, 2005, p. 51).

3   Technological memory or 'mnemotechnics,' the exteriorization of memory into technical objects and automation, the 'industrialization of memory,' has radically decreased the value of workers' *savoir faire*. This has contributed to a profound loss of a sense of individuation. They become more and more servants of the machine and subject to the spirit of calculation (Roberts, 2012). This contributes to the shame of being human, with a sense of deep discontent and a propensity for violence.

4   The emergence of endogenous attention, which comprises a rudimentary sense of temporality in infants, may create the scaffolding for more complex language development (de Diego-Balanguer, Martinez-Alvarez & Pons, 2016). One may speculate that this is related to the view of Stiegler and Leroi-Gourhan that the development of bipedal posture, freeing the hands for the use of tools and the mouth for speech, preceded and accelerated brain development in *Homo sapiens*. The discovery of *Homo naledi* in 2014 in South Africa, an ancestor from a million or more years ago with modern feet and evolving hands but a brain the size of an orange, lends credence to this theory (Shreeve, 2015). That is, the emergence of technics, the use of tools and the anticipations of their future use over millennia, stimulated the emergence of a larger brain with a capacity for temporality, and also enabled a richer scaffolding for language (Stiegler, 1998, pp. 134–79).

5   The past is always alive, never completed. In this sense, it is like an ever-changing dance floor on which the dance of everyday life takes place. Perhaps this is most apparent when we view Paleolithic cave art, which clearly reflects the 'dance floors' of ancient peoples, now largely indecipherable to us. Stiegler, in his rich development of Husserl's theory of memory, describes this phenomenon with precision. He calls the intricate compositions of memory, perception and protension (anticipation) a kind of archi-cinema (Stiegler, 2014).

6   For Stiegler, technics refers to the technical domain or to technical practice as a whole. It includes things from primitive tools and weapons to systems of writing. It is the very condition of culture. It is necessary to distinguish this from technology or the technological. Technics indicates the basic human need for prosthetics, the fact that the human is not simply a biological being (Roberts, 2012).

Stiegler elaborates his point of view in a discussion on the fault of Epimetheus, the creator-god who forgot to save a special survival attribute for human beings when they were created. Prometheus, his brother, took pity on them and stole fire and other things from the gods and gave these to humans. In mythic form, this expresses Stiegler's view that humankind, from its beginnings, was defined by the 'prosthetic' devices of technics. That is, technics fills a basic default intrinsic to the human (Stiegler, 1998, pp. 85–203).

The control of fire was certainly a crucial human achievement, and with a bit of imagination, one could create a genealogy of the automobile as a fire chariot stemming from the evolution of the mastery of fire. Of course, technics clearly has a downside as well as an upside, considering its present-day effects on the natural and cultural historical environment. However, to understand technics, Stiegler feels that it is also essential to understand that humans and technics are, in a sense, one. That is, technics is not something encrusted on human beings who had originally been in some paradisiacal 'state of nature' (Stiegler, 1998, pp. 82–133).

7 Reverie refers to a capacity to set aside everyday concerns of the ego and to tune in to the interiority of people and things. Within the psychoanalytic world, it is most frequently associated with the work of Wilfred Bion. It requires the capacity to set aside memory and desire, by which he meant a setting aside of fantasies of goals or affect-laden memories that would prejudice our thoughts or behaviour. It is related to the capacity of a mother to tune in to her infant.

8 I had extensive experience conducting verbal therapy with schizophrenic patients during the 1960s and 1970s. Don Jackson, who was trained by Sullivan, was an early supervisor at Stanford (Jackson, 1964). I heard R. D. Laing speak in 1963 and was impressed by his work with psychotic patients at the Tavistock Institute (Laing, 1960). During the 1960s and 1970s, I had extensive contact with John Weir Perry, a Jungian analyst who was a pioneer in the understanding and treatment of psychotic patients (Perry, 1974). Most of these experiences with psychotic patients involved little or no medication and convinced me that psychotic communications have meanings that may be very profound, both personally and culturally. During this period of my clinical work, we often spoke about 'speaking schizophrenese.' This experience has also made me more aware of the value of the insane parts of sane people over the years (Hinton, 2007; Leader, 2012). Therefore, when I encountered the Man in the Street, I was startled, but his language felt instinctively familiar to me, and I did not have to contrive a reply. The words were there immediately, without thought.

9 I am implying, of course, a dialectical shift in this everyday encounter in the midst of life.

In his essay on sublation, "'Conflict/Resolution,'" "Opposites/Creative Union," versus "Dialectics and The Climb up the Slippery Slope,'" Giegerich beautifully elaborates the process of dialectical movement and sublation. He makes clear the difference between the concept of conflict resolution and a dialectical movement to a different level, a *sublation*. With the former, the perspective is exterior, while the dialectical view opens up the interiority of persons and events (Giegerich, 2005).

10 Soul, for Giegerich, is a negative concept (Giegerich, 2012b, pp. 22–3, 52–6). I take this to indicate a quality in the object that exceeds any positivity. This seems akin to Stiegler's description of Winnicott's transitional object as that '[whose] virtue [is that] it does not exist,' but is also what makes life worth living. When that quality is not preserved by family and culture, the result is symbolic misery (Stiegler, 2013b, pp. 1–5). There is no sense of future.

In a similar vein, Laplanche discusses an enigmatic quality of life that hermeneutics endlessly attempts to translate but cannot reduce to positivity (Laplanche, 1999, pp. 138–65). This quality is also highly temporal in its horizon. To quote Laplanche (1999, p. 224): 'the cultural [itself] is an address to another who is out of reach, to others "scattered in the future" as the poet says,' and he further asks, 'why does the Dichter Dicht – why does the poet poetize – except in response to an enigmatic other?' That is, a crucial temporal element is intrinsic to the experience of the enigmatic signifier or the transitional object. In a similar fashion, Giegerich speaks of 'The Soul's Logical Life' as an historical (i.e., temporal) process (Giegerich, 2001, pp. 76–8).

11 As an example, *The Scream,* as well as other works by Edvard Munch, illustrates the emergence of panic and agoraphobia in the late nineteenth century. In the great cities of Europe during the early 1870s, the terror of raw life emerged in the form of agoraphobia and panic. The main symptoms were dizziness, buzzing in the ears, dyspepsia, palpitations and a wax-like quality in the legs. The malady was viewed as generated by the draining chaos of crowds due to the increasing population of cities and the destruction of intimate containing plazas, along with the creation of vast circular spaces, such as the Place de la Concorde in Paris, which were bustling with traffic and the hubbub of pedestrians. One could easily become disoriented by the cacophony of sound and motion within these large, impersonal spaces.

The sufferer felt as a normal person would when looking down from atop Niagara Falls or when peering into a large abyss. This was an evolution of modernity and was the first time in the history of psychiatry that *anxiety* figured as a primary factor shaping the configuration of symptoms. It is not too far a reach to read this as a movement of the *opus magnum*, as Giegerich and Barreto discuss (Barreto, 2015; Giegerich, 2001; Ghazal & Hinton, 2016; Hinton, 2002).

References

Aron, L. & Starr, K. (2013). *A Psychotherapy for the People: Toward a Progressive Psychoanalysis*. New York: Routledge.

Barreto, M. H. (2015). End of man in the modern form of consciousness. Unpublished Paper. Faculdade Jesuíta de Filosofia e Teologia Belo Horizonte, Brazil.

Bewes, T. (2011). *The Event of Postcolonial Shame*. Princeton, NJ: Princeton University Press.

Bion, W. R. (1954). Notes on a theory of schizophrenia. *International Journal of Psychoanalysis, 35*, 113–118.

Bion, W. R. (1967). *Second Thoughts: Selected Papers on Psycho-analysis*. London: Heinemann.

Bion, W. R. (1973/1990). *Brazilian Lectures*. London: Karnac Books.

Casement, A. (2011). The interiorizing movement of logical life: Reflections on Wolfgang Giegerich. *Journal of Analytical Psychology, 56*, 532–549. doi:10.1111/j.1468-5922.2010.01927.x.

Civitarese, G. (2010). Nachträglichkeit. In *The Intimate Room: Theory and Technique of the Analytic Field*, 96–108. New York: Routledge.

Civitarese, G. (2016). Truth as immediacy and unison: A new common ground in psychoanalysis? Commentary on essays addressing 'is truth relevant?' *The Psychoanalytic Quarterly, LXXXV*, 2, 449–501.

de Diego-Balaguer, R., Martinez-Alvarez, A., & Pons, F. (2016). Temporal attention as a scaffold for language development. *Frontiers in Psychology, 7*, 44. doi:10.3389/fpsyg.2016.00044.

Eigen, M. (2005). *Emotional Storm*. Middletown, CT: Wesleyan University Press.

Freud, S. (1917/1955). A difficulty in the path of psychoanalysis. In *The Complete Psychological Works of Sigmund Freud*. Vol. XVII, 139–144. London: The Hogarth Press.

Ghazal, Y. A. & Hinton, D. E. (2016). Platzschwindel, agoraphobia, and their influence on theories of anxiety at the end of the nineteenth century: Theories of the role of biology and 'representations' (Vorstellungen). *History of Psychiatry, 27*, 4, 425–442.

Giegerich, W. (2001). *The Soul's Logical Life*. Frankfurt: Peter Lang Publishing House.

Giegerich, W. (2005). 'Conflict/resolution,' 'opposites/creative union,' versus dialectics, and the climb up the slippery slope. In *Dialectics and Analytical Psychology: The El Capitan Canyon Seminar*. New Orleans, LA: Spring Journals, 1–24.

Giegerich, W. (2007). *Technology and the Soul*. New Orleans, LA: Spring Publications.

Giegerich, W. (2008). *Soul Violence: Collected English Papers*. New Orleans, LA: Spring Journal Books.

Giegerich, W. (2012a). Soul and world. Paper Presented at the Meeting of the International Society for Psychology as the Discipline of Interiority, Berlin.

Giegerich, W. (2012b). *What is Soul?* New Orleans, LA: Spring Journal Books.

Guignon, C. B. (1983). *Heidegger and the Problem of Knowledge*. Indianapolis, IN: Hackett Publishing.

Heidegger, M. (1956). *What is Philosophy?* Lanham, MD: Rowman & Littlefield.

Hinton, D. (2002). Munch, agoraphobia, and the terrors of the modernizing urban landscape. In L. J. Schmidt & B. Warner (eds), *Panic, Origins and Treatment*, 229–252. Berkeley, CA: North Atlantic Books.

Hinton III, L., Hinton IV, L., Hinton, D. & Hinton, A. (2011). Panel: Unus mundus – transcendent truth or comforting fiction? Overwhelm and the search for meaning in a fragmented world. *Journal of Analytical Psychology, 56*, 375–396.

Hinton, L. (2007). Black holes, uncanny spaces and radical shifts in awareness. *Journal of Analytical Psychology, 52*, 433–447. doi:10.1111/j.1468-5922.2007.00675.x.

Hinton, L. (2015). Temporality and the torments of time. *Journal of Analytical Psychology, 60*, 353–370. doi:10.1111/1468-5922.12155.

Hoy, D. C. (2012). *The Time of Our Lives: A Critical History of Temporality.* Boston, MA: MIT Press.

Hultberg, P. (1986). Shame: An overshadowed emotion. In M. A. Mattoon (ed.), *The Archetype of Shadow in a Split World.* Zurich: Daimon Publications.

Jackson, D. (1964). *Myths of Madness: New Facts for Old Fallacies.* New York: Macmillan Publishing.

Johnston, A. (2005). *Time Driven: Metapsychology and the Splitting of the Drive.* Evanston, IL: Northwestern University Press.

Jung, C. G. (1970). *Mysterium Coniunctionis.* R. F. C. Hull (trans.). Princeton, NJ: Princeton University Press.

Laing, R. D. (1960). *The Divided Self: An Existential Study in Sanity and Madness.* Harmondsworth: Penguin.

Laplanche, J. (1999). *Essays on Otherness.* New York: Routledge.

Leader, D. (2012). *What is Madness?* London: Penguin Books.

Mills, J. (2014). Truth. *Journal of the American Psychoanalytic Association, 62*, 267–293. doi:10.1177/0003065114529458.

Morrison, A. P. (1989). *Shame: The Underside of Narcissism.* Hillsdale: The Analytic Press.

Perry, J. W. (1974). *The Far Side of Madness.* Upper Saddle River, NJ: Prentice Hall.

Plato (2000). *Timaeus.* Donald J. Zeyl (trans.). Indianapolis, IN: Hackett Publishing Company.

Rhode, E. (1998). *On Hallucination, Intuition, and the Becoming of "O."* Binghampton, NY: Esf Publishers.

Roberts, B. (2012). Technics, individuation and tertiary memory: Bernard Stiegler's challenge to Media theory. *New Formations, 77*, 8–20. doi:10.3898/NEWF.77.01.2012.

Ross, D. (2006). Democracy, authority, narcissism: From Agamben to Stiegler. *Contretemps, 6*, 74–85.

Ross, D. (2016). The question concerning the Anthropocene. Yachay Tech www.academia.edu/22810427/The_Question_Concerning_the_Anthropocene.

Scarfone, D. (2006). A matter of time: Actual time and the production of the past. *Psychoanalytic Quarterly*, *75*, 807-834. doi:10.1002/j.2167-4086.2006.tb00058.x.

Seidler, G. H. (2000). *In Others' Eyes: An Analysis of Shame*. Madison, CT: International Universities Press.

Shreeve, J. (2015). This face changes the human story. But how? Photographs by Robert Clark. *National Geographic*, September 10. Retrieved from http://news.nationalgeographic.com/2015/09/150910-human-evolution-change.

Stiegler, B. (1998). *Technics and Time, 1: The Fault of Epimetheus*. Palo Alto, CA: Stanford University Press.

Stiegler, B. (2008). *Technics and Time, 2: Disorientation*. Palo Alto, CA: Stanford University Press.

Stiegler, B. (2013a). *Uncontrollable Societies of Disaffected Individuals: Disbelief and Discredit*. Vol. 2. Malden, MA: Polity Press.

Stiegler, B. (2013b). *What Makes Life Worth Living: On Pharmacology*. D. Ross (trans.). Malden, MA: Polity Press.

Stiegler, B. (2014). Organology of dreams and archi-cinema. *Nordic Journal of Aesthetics*, *47*, 7–37.

Sznycer, D., Tooby, J., Cosmides, L., Porat, R., Shalvi, S., & Halperin, E. (2016). Shame closely tracks the threat of devaluation by others, even across cultures. *Proceedings of the National Academy of Sciences of the United States of America*, *113*, 2625–2630. doi:10.1073/pnas.1514699113.

Tanaka, Y. (2008). On dissociation as a psychological phenomenon. *Psychologia*, *51*, 239–257. doi:10.2117/psysoc.2008.239.

Tanaka, Y. (2013). Anthropophobia: An old and typical Japanese neurosis, its conceptual transition and clinical disappearance. Paper presented at the International Jungian Conference, Taipei.

Tanaka, Y. (2014). What is born in the analytic practice for patients with the problem of 'un-born-ness'? Paper presented at the 2014 Conference of the *Journal of Analytical Psychology*, Berlin.

Tracy, J. L. & Matsumoto, D. (2008). The spontaneous expression of pride and shame: Evidence for biologically innate nonverbal displays. *Proceedings of the National Academy of Sciences of the United States of America*, *105*, 11655–11660. doi:10.1073/pnas.0802686105.

Virilio, P. (2003). *Unknown Quantity*. New York: Thames & Hudson.

Whan, M. (2015, Apr.). The logic of image: Simulating 'mythic image.' In Anselm Kiefer's 'Parsifal II.' *The International Society for Psychology as the Discipline of Interiority Newsletter*. Retrieved from http://ispdi.org/index.php/en/newsletter/ispdi-newsletter-april-2015.

Chapter 2

The unbearable shame of the analyst's idealization

Reiterating the temporal

Jon Mills

Although it is common to discuss the dynamics of patients' shame, what is often not discussed in the literature is the analyst's shame: it remains secret and taboo. To discuss shame openly is to reveal vulnerability and psychological motives, and to risk judgement from others; yet, it is the very thing we encourage in the consulting room.

The relationship between the analyst's shame and the phenomena of temporality casts a particular light on the quality of the lived experience that occurs in treatment. As the relational encounter unfolds in the inter-subjective field, psychic reality traverses the whole gamut and continuum of time that springs from (a) the *archaic primacy* of the past, (b) the *immediational presence* of the current moment, and (c) the *projective teleology* of the future as dialectical mediation. Temporal mediacy informs the qualitative experience of lived time in its simultaneous reiteration of the past within the present and the future trajectory of consciousness, hence *re*-presenting mnemonic linkages to affect states and emotional schemata that are stimulated by the therapeutic environment. When the experience of shame is evoked in the analyst, it is linked to a reiteration of the temporal that stands in relation to the analyst's own developmental history within the current transference-countertransference dynamic. Shame may take on polarities in their manifestation, qualia and vectors, from the realm of pure negativity to that of ideality. Therapeutically, the clinician may be temporally surprised by the mobilization of shame to the point that it affects praxis and the treatment frame, hence altering the course and boundaries of the therapeutic process. What becomes more difficult to shoulder is an almost unbearable intensity of emotion that is usually enacted in the countertransference because the therapist feels it would be inappropriate to share such emotions directly with the patient.

Shame is also structurally instituted by the very nature of the analytic milieu where formal parameters of professional space impose a certain constraint on what the clinician and the patient can do, despite the fact that analysis by definition imposes the ethic of honesty on the subject. Here, disclosure becomes asymmetrical from the beginning as does the seduction of the transference predicated on the therapeutic framework itself; the analysand is led to both idealize and devalue the analyst at different temporal intervals in the treatment. We may say that shame is always in the background as unconscious presence, but also in the foreground as the realization that we can never fulfil the patient's desires or expectations while at the same time holding back revelations that are deeply personal and confessional. These conditional dynamics maintain an artificial or constricted ambiance that at times can appear very unnatural, inauthentic and depriving to both parties involved. Therefore, shame is inscribed in the very onto-structural, socio-symbolic matrix that constitutes the analytic encounter.

In this chapter, I discuss the horrid conscription of shame after being idealized by two clients: one a child who was physically abused, the other an adult who revered me as Jesus. This mutual shame dynamic resonated both within the treatment and each patient's own experiential vulnerabilities due to their developmental traumas, as it did in me due to my own abuse history and professed atheism. My inner negotiation of shame led to two different forms of intervention in the transference, one interactive and paternal, the other containing and role responsive. Each treatment led to a creative transcendent function for all participants when I was able to transform historical shame by adopting the intentional stance of the other's idealization. In other words, by adopting the role each patient needed me to play in the idealized transference, shame was transmuted.

On shame

When psychoanalysts speak of shame, it is usually in the context of critical superego functions (Freud, 1917, 1923); group identifications, idealizations and idealized imagoes (Freud, 1921); mobilization of defence and rage, narcissistic vulnerabilities connected to fragile, grandiose, or incohesive self-states (Kohut, 1971); and hypocrisy, dissociation, inauthenticity, and morally corrupt agency (Naso, 2010). It may also be based on insidious toxic introjects that hinder healthy personality structure, self-regulation, and disfigure attachment capacities due to developmental trauma (Mills, 2005). As the underside of narcissism (Morrison, 1989), shame has traditionally been viewed as a negative, emotional, qualitative form of psychic injury – what more contemporary discourse refers to as microtrauma (Crastnopol, 2015).

In considering shame as painful affect states or introjects that assault the integrity of the self and one's self-representations, there are innumerable forms that shame can manifest with regard to content, form, scope, intensity, duration, and qualia. It is in fact the qualia of shame – those qualitative properties and emotional resonance contours – that often give lived phenomenal experience their harrowing character. One decisive experience of shame is psychological *exposure*, that is, how certain aspects of oneself are disclosed, unconcealed, and viewed, hence judged, by another. Such soul exposure, if we want to call it that, is coloured by a certain degree of vulnerability, fear, lack of safety, embarrassment, hurt pride, humiliation, and so forth, which evokes feelings of inferiority, abnegation, psychic castration, and self-defect that are elicited, unwelcomed, exploited, and foisted upon us and are outside of our control. I would refer to this as *imposed* shame, and there is almost always an element of surprise involved, for events sprung on us without anticipation, preparation, or warning are experienced as encroachments on our psychic integrity. While we also displace, externalize, and project disowned shame experiences on to others, as seen in childhood onward, shame is ultimately an intimate self-relation to one's interior mediated by many competing psychological dynamics, contexts, and contingencies. This makes the experience of shame a highly esoteric enterprise, despite the fact that it is a universal emotion derived from intrapsychic conditions that are interpersonally informed.

As Kohut (1985, p. 109) reminds us, shame arises when we can't live up to our own ideals. But shame is much more than that. Shame is the emotive corollary of self-consciousness as the *recognition* of one's failure to live up to one's own self-imposed ideals that brings about self-condemnation and narcissistic depletion. Despite the fact that ideals and values are based on the internalization of one's identifications with one's parents, community, society, culture, and so on, we develop a very intimate relationship with our values, as they form the qualitative bedrock of our own self-relation to self-valuation vulnerable to judgement and criticism from others. Shame, I suggest, is ultimately based in negation, the compromise or devolution of self-value. When you betray your own self-professed values, you sully the self, and hence shame is a logical consequence of self-abnegation as recognition of lack, and in particular, a lack of courage to live up to ideality.

As an assault on self-consciousness, shame becomes amplified when one lacks cognizance or knowledge of themselves. I would refer to this as *epistemological* shame. One instance of this is bearing witness to the other's acute awareness and observation of some absence, failure, or deficit in oneself. Perhaps that is a more intense form of shame because others see your vulnerabilities or weakness, and you now are *forced* to become aware of the other's knowledge of how they see something in you that you did not notice before. Here shame is a lack of self-knowledge given over to us by the mirror image of the other's epistemology. In other words, when others see things we do not see in ourselves, shame is *a fortiori* inevitable, and, more ironically, the analytic arrangement is set up to be where the analyst is supposed to be the one who knows, hence a master discourse.

But looking at shame as an internal self-relation of failing to live up to ideals is a private inner experience clouded in negative feelings that affects the self-esteem of the subject. It is shrouded in avoidance, annulment, dissociation, and denial. I propose that the qualitative felt-injury of exposure is an important aspect affecting the degree and intensity of experiential shame, whether as self-exposure (i.e., as conscious awareness of one's personal limitations and ignorance), or more sinisterly, when others mock, ridicule, denounce, or reject you, especially when there are perceptual acts of humiliation cast upon the subject. Feeling out of control over the affair only accentuates emotive self-derision. Acts of aspersion that are public and witnessed by others are most poignant and emotionally agonizing to anyone. Yet shame is always an internal relation regardless of what others do or say. It is always *mine*: either you experience it or not. Here the quality of *mine-ness* is always an internal self-relation to one's interior.

Time, or to be more precise, temporality as *living* time, is also indispensable for shame to occur, even when it involves conjuring historical memory or its re-inscribed after-effects (*Nachträglichkeit* or *après-coup*), because it is temporally mediated in the present, hence confronting the residue or resurfacing of dishonour felt as tarnished desire and pride.

Despite the fact that shame is memorialized in the psyche, that is, engraved as a negative mnemonic leaving semiotic traces as reminders or recollections of the subject's vulnerability, which occurred in the past, it further elicits an impending realization that nothing can be done now nor in the future to remedy those adverse conditions or emotions tied to archaic events. It must merely be accepted and subsumed in history.

When we fail to live up to an ideal – what we utmost value and prize – we are forlorn and left in the ashes of disappointment, weakened, crushed, maimed. Here I am reminded of Hegel's (1807) beautiful soul as a divided self: spirit (*Geist*) is aware of what it wants and what is right, but it just can't live up to its own values. Instead, sadly, it is interned in 'unhappy consciousness'. In this sense, shame always remains a condemned relation toward the future, as it can never be overcome or surpassed, hence sublated (*aufgehoben*), only forgotten. Here shame is tied to some element of failed perfection – the notion that we can never be or become that ideal (whether in fantasy or reality), itself an artifice based in a fantasy principle. We remain exposed and exploited by our own limitations and must bear witness to our own imperfections, something that can only be mourned. The ego ideal is therefore an illusion.

The ontological conditions of shame apply to everyone, including the clinical practitioner. What I have in mind is to articulate some parameters of the analyst bearing witness to their own shame in professional space, namely, the consulting room, visited by the unwanted imposition of the alien Other, an unconscious remainder of the real. But before venturing into case material, it is important to say what we mean by the temporal.

On temporality

Time is a succession of phases experienced through our river of consciousness, a patterned fluidity of perishing awareness that contains the coming into being and passing away into nothing of previous series of moments, what we may call phenomenal diachronies of difference and change within a transmuting process of persistence. There are beginnings and endings, openings and closings, both ephemeral yet permanent. Time is pure flow and unrest, at once continuous yet spontaneous and fleeting, for as soon as you try to pin it down, it is already gone. Each moment is merely a transitory conduit to a new movement or mode of experience within an interconnected chain of moments containing past, present, and future (not to mention their gradations of closest to farthest, undiscernible to palpable, in their sequence), all standing in dynamic relation to one another as a pressurized holistic systemic. Yet there is a universality to time that is ontologically invariant as sheer process.

Experience is imbued with diachronies that punctuate the pervasiveness of lived time, the essence of what precipitates shame.[1] The diachronic experience of time is that there is a sensation of interruption with ordinary sequential time: it could be that lived time is experienced as long when it is short, minimal when it is quantitatively enduring, fleeting when it is protracted, or unaccounted for, such as a depersonalized loss of time when one is in a state of psychogenic fugue, meditation, or mystical absorption. Here time is both instituted and constituted in the moment of our living experience as we live it, which may entail a (felt) adjournment of consciousness as withering streams of awareness, or conversely, an attunement and intensity of self-consciousness as heightened self-reflectivity that directs our focus of awareness to a particularized moment of lived experience.[2]

Time is not merely a theoretical abstraction, for we feel its presence, its coming and going, that which is momentarily here then gone, only to be cyclically present as a dialectic of passing-over into a ceasing-to-be only to enter into a new movement of becoming that is retained through enduring experience encountered as transient intervals of length and intensity. At the same time, we may view time as an incorporeal condition, an immateriality of pure event, namely, experience itself. Yet experience is a temporal embodiment. On the one hand, time is not an entity, literally no-thing, and in this sense immaterial; yet on the other, it exists as actuality governed by natural laws of patterned continuity, duration, perishing, and succession as a flux of appearing modes of becoming. Time is always coming, going, and is *here*, hence developing, transitioning, succumbing, and expiring yet never fully ceasing, as it is born anew as an eternal presence and recurrence within an ordered series of temporal modalities and periods.

Paradoxically, we may even say there is no such thing as pure time independent of mind, as it is merely a formal concept; rather time is constituted through embodied space, hence its appearance is always enmattered yet nowhere to be seen. To be more specific, because mind is embodied activity, temporal experience is only possible through cognition. Here the notion of time takes on its own phenomenological encounters. Time is neither static nor fixed, nor is it a tangible thing that can be appropriated, for it is invisible and indivisible yet it transpires in a series of spacings each of us inhabit in our mental and material worlds; this is why it is more appropriate to think of our experiential relation to spacetime as a fused event. Here the essence of time is process.

Our relationship to presence and absence, finitude and eternity, flux and permanence, all presuppose our intimate dynamic relation to what I call *temporal mediacy* (Mills, 2010). Here time draws on (a) the *archaic primacy* of our past as the amalgamation of our historicities, ontological preconditions, and developmental trajectories, (b) the *immediational presence* of the phenomenology of our present (concrete and qualitatively) lived experience as mediated immediacy, and (c) the *projective teleology* of the imagined future as a valued ideal, goal, or purposive aim. These three simultaneous facets of temporal mediacy are operative at any given moment in psychic tandem where the past and future convene on the present, or immediate, subjective experience. The presentational encounters of past, present, and future we confront as immediacy become our metaphysical relation to time, phenomenologically realized in the here-and-now.

Psychic organization has a simultaneous temporal relation to the past, the present, and the future: (1) the past is subsumed and preserved within the psyche; (2) the present is immediate mediated experience; and (3) the future (in contemplation and fantasy) becomes a motivational, teleological impetus. Temporal experience is a mediational realization informed by this threefold relation of the dialectic;[3] however, each domain may have competing and/or opposing pressures that affect the other modalities at any given moment. In other words, each locus may pressurize, extol, invade, usurp, coalesce, and/or symbiotically conjoin with others within their interdependent dynamic system. But each domain also has the potential to have a subjective surge, voice, or lived reality of its own, despite the force and presence of the other two realms. Yet such seemingly autonomous moments of individualized expression are relegated to the broader systemic processes that operate within the dialectical mind. In psychoanalytic language, we may refer to these differentiated experiences as a multiplicity of self-states that are operative on parallel or overdetermined levels of functioning within the ontologically monistic, supraordinate agency we call the self.

The past we may refer to as archaic primacy, thus emphasizing the primordial nature of our historicities, including a priori ontological conditions (e.g., constitutional, social, and cultural forces) as well as that which is subjectively (i.e., qualitatively) and developmentally experienced (both consciously and unconsciously). Here we may say this is archetypal, for history always re-enters psychic structure. The present we may call immediational presence, thus stressing the phenomenology of the concretely lived experience presented as subjectively mediated immediacy. The future we describe in terms of projective teleology, which captures the future trajectory of the dialectic of desire, which stands in relation to a valued ideal, goal, purposeful action, or wish-fulfilment. These three simultaneous facets of temporal mediacy are the dialectic in action in the moment of bringing the past and future to bear upon its present, or immediate, experience.

Archaic primacy holds a privileged position in the psyche since the mind always presupposes and draws on the past in all its mental forms, derivatives, contents, and operations. For instance, cognition necessarily requires memory, which is the *re-presented* past, just as the mind itself requires certain ontic relations and neurobiological processes in order for there to be cognition at all. Similarly, the unconscious is lost presence, namely, that which had formerly presented itself (in its multiple derived forms) but had receded back into the abyss. Archaic primacy has a stipulated degree of causal influence over the driving force behind the dialectical psyche since the archaic is always brought to bear upon pre-sentational encounters that the subject confronts as immediacy, which furthermore stimulates projections of a future. The way the present is incorporated into the past, however, may be highly conditional and idio-syncratic given the unique contingencies that comprise the nature of subjectivity, either individually or intersubjectively actualized. It is in this sense that the preservative aspect of mind may be very *selective* in what it retains. Although we may generally say that the past is preserved in some way as our personal thrownness or developmental historicity (and this is certainly true of world history), there are certain elements that are – or have the potential of becoming – omitted or negated and forgot-ten altogether, hence denied, dissociated, and/or repressed. That is, certain aspects of archaic primacy may not be operative, mobile, or caus-ally expressive and, perhaps, may fizzle out entirely in the psyche, while other aspects are selected, secured, harboured, and sustained (especially as segregated schemata within unconscious life).

Immediational presence is the subject's experience in the here-and-now and how it engages what is presented before it (either as an internal event or stimulus, or as an external imposition), thus affecting thought, feeling states, somatic schemata, and action, and their unconscious resonances. The immediacy of the lived encounter highlights the context and exigencies that influence the phenomenology of the emotional, cognitive, and unconscious aspects of personal experience. Although the present immediacy of the moment is largely a conscious phenomenon, immediate experience is already a mediated dynamic by virtue of the fact that archaic primacy already suffuses every lived encounter, which is superimposed as its facticity. This means that unconscious processes always saturate every conscious experience and become a mediatory screen, or template, in which the world is received and perceived, thus influencing the contingency and construction of experience.

Selective retention is particularly operative within immediational presence, as cognition executes certain determinate choices in its relation to mediated experience. In effect, the psyche seizes upon certain aspects of the environment and internally evoked stimuli from the press of archaic primacy while refuting, denying access to, or limiting the range of others that may exert certain degrees of determinate influence on immediate experience – the range and signification of each mediated choice having resonance in the mind's trajectory and orientation toward the future. In every immediate encounter, the past and future are summoned and converge on the present: the archaic superimposes past form and content; the future superimposes goal-directed intentionality in mediated thought and action.

Projective teleology is the future trajectory of a desired state of affairs (as fantasy, wish, intention, or purpose) that is stimulated by presentational processing or mediatory interventions, thus instigating the teleological projection of a goal-directed aim. Like archaic primacy and immediate experience, the projected future may entertain a certain selective aspect to the retention or locus of experience that takes place within the transformative, progressive dialectical processing governing each mediated dynamic. Mediation stands in relation to which the subjective mind experiences as desire. This is fertile ground for shame to materialize. In all three spheres, however, there exists the primacy of ambiguity, uncertainty, and context, for real and virtual time may be suspended within the mind and experienced as radically dissociative, incongruent, or atemporal, yet nevertheless wed to contingency.

At any given moment of experience, the past and future are ontologically operative on subjective immediacy, bringing to presence the vast configurations and pressures of unconscious affect, wish, and defence, and the corresponding conscious reality that is simultaneously evoked and represented, such as in the experience of trauma and shame. Archaic primacy, immediational presence, and projective teleology are functional aspects of orienting the psyche towards dialectical growth, even if regression and decay are activated consequences of the lived encounter. Here it becomes important to keep in mind that the psyche works radically to compress and transpose its multiple instantiations within its mediatory functions. There are multiple realities and self-states or microagents that coalesce, intermingle, compete, vying for attention and expression, and do battle for supremacy by forcing themselves on the pressure cooker we call mind. The teleological motives of the dialectic are therefore informed by the threefold presence of the past, the present immediate context, and the future trajectory to which it is oriented, each vector exerting its own source and constraint on the inner constitution of the subject.

The phenomena of awareness involves our immediate immersion in what we presently desire, feel, perceive, think, remember, emote, cognize, or otherwise experience as an internal temporal relation to intentional objects in reality or fantasy mediated by unconscious agency. Just as Freud (1933, p. 74) reminds us that the unconscious is 'timeless', the nature of consciousness as such is the outgrowth of an unconscious epigenetic instantiation and dialectical contrary that fractures its primordial cosmic eternity by introducing temporal enactments in and through qualitative experience, namely, that which we live. Like the nature of experience itself, it is vast and variegated, punctuated by instances of particularity and its concomitant qualia. Here enters shame.

A better father

Jimmy was 10 years old when he first came to see me. He had a history of violence, hearing voices, and had multiple suspensions from every school he had attended. He had been to several medical and mental health professionals, including his paediatrician, two psychologists and a child psychiatrist, who had diagnosed him with ADHD and a psychotic disorder, and he was prescribed Risperdal and Concerta. His parents were at their wits' end, reporting a history of paranoia, delusions, and physical aggression against themselves, peers, and adults, including being expelled from public and private schools for hitting other people. The day I met him he had just been kicked out of his fifth elementary school for putting his head through drywall because he was mad at a classmate, which escalated to assaulting a teacher when she attempted to intervene.

When he first entered my office, he plunged himself on to my sofa and started to maul the pillows while he avoided eye contact. Then he leaped across the room and did a cannon-ball on my analytic couch, an early 1900s, reupholstered Edwardian antique with original box-springs, and then bounced off on to the floor, where he promptly took his shoes and socks off, and then farted without excusing himself, oblivious to his social surroundings. After I asked his mother to wait in the sitting room, he spoke honestly, somewhat agitatedly, the whole time. Jimmy reported going into rages, feeling out of control over his 'brain and body', and heard both 'boys' and girls' voices' that would direct him to hurt others, especially when he felt teased or picked on, upon which he would feel 'sad' afterward. He said that 'Mother Mary and Jesus' sometimes speak to him and tell him good things, such as he is 'loved,' and that 'they are there to help.' When I asked him what some of his favourite things to do were, he got very excited talking about fishing and wanting to catch a big fish. As an avid bass angler myself, I told him of some of my fishing stories and the best strategies that work for me, and he started beaming, now making full eye contact.

Jimmy had a rather woeful look to him and was somewhat chubby, but his face lit up when talking about what interested him. We had a propitious connection in our initial session, and he enjoyed being listened to. Upon inviting his mother back into my office at the end of the hour, she commented on my authored books I have displayed in my waiting area. Jimmy wanted to see them and know what they were about. He was very much eager to see me again, which I arranged with his mother.

During our second session, he entered my office and immediately verbalized that he wanted to be an author like me. After encouraging him to tell me more about his newfound interest, I asked him to tell me a story he may wish to write about. Without being told to do so, he sat on the edge of my analytic couch and looked at me rather perplexedly, saying 'I don't know what to say.' 'Well, what comes to mind? Say anything that pops into your thoughts; that's a good place to start', I replied. Jimmy went on to talk about a boy who is sad because he is picked on and teased, but also angry for being hit. After encouraging him to expand his narrative and talk about the feelings of the protagonist, I asked him if he could relate to his character in the story and if anything like that ever happened to him. Upon this query, he disclosed that his father sometimes hits him as a form of discipline, such as being slapped in the mouth or in the face when he talks back. He also reported being angry at his mother for not stopping it, but also expressed ambivalent feelings about his father because now he was getting 'special time' with him, unlike in the past. He was perspicacious enough to connect his anger at his parents for why he took his aggression out on other children and teachers at school as a form of displacement. Given that he had a history of violence since the age of 5, including beating up his older sister, initiating fury toward his parents, and needing to be restrained at home and school due to uncontrollable rages, I felt it was prudent for me to acquire more facts before making any decision regarding child protection matters under the law. Instead I empathized with Jimmy and asked him how I could help. I suggested that I meet with his mother to make sure that any physical discipline at home promptly stopped without making the matter worse with his father, and he was happy with that plan of action.

My concern about Jimmy having an underlying psychotic process was due to him reportedly hearing voices since kindergarten and unprecedented acts of violence in childhood, such as throwing chairs at students, beating up classmates, and attacking family members, but all of this would make sense due to his father's abuse as well as attachment pathology based in accruing developmental trauma. I decided the best course of action was to work with the family rather than involve the child protection agency governing my jurisdiction. This was because the physical discipline was not current or ongoing, there was no immediate or imminent threats to Jimmy's safety, and the so-called abuse took place during times when he was out of control and assaulting others, thereby necessitating restraint. Instead I coached the parents on the parameters of the law, my legal responsibility, and the need to stop any form of physical discipline, persuasively educating them on how to be sensitive to his emotional disruptions and on how not to exacerbate the situation when he appeared out of control. This seemed to work, and was also welcome news to Jimmy, who felt I had restored a balance in the family dynamic while protecting him at the same time.

The seeds for an idealized transference had already been incubating, but it had intensified after he told me about the sundry incidents of being bullied at school and in various settings away from his family without their awareness, many of which he did not disclose either because he did not trust them to protect him or remedy the situation, feared being blamed or ridiculed for causing the conflict, and felt they were impotent to do anything about the incidents. He had recounted many emotionally painful and shameful experiences he'd had, perpetrated by boys at school during team sports and while away at summer camp, but when he recalled being assaulted in the bathroom at school by older boys who ganged up on him at the urinal, this is when I was reacquainted with my own traumatized childhood under similar circumstances. Jimmy had his pants pulled down to his ankles while being choked around his neck from behind as he was urinating and then thrown on to the ground helplessly as the boys laughed and sadistically mocked him. He started weeping when recounting the event, reliving the humiliation he felt after 'pissing' on himself, and I felt my eyes starting to well up witnessing his vulnerability.

Like many victims of child abuse, he internalized his secrets while acting out as a form of defence and displaced emotional expression. I am no exception. I was bullied from my early elementary school years until early high school, living in a perpetual state of anxiety and helplessness with no faith whatsoever that my parents could do anything about it. I could neither confide in nor trust them, but when it got so bad I had nowhere to turn but to tell them the truth. To this day I still recall the feeling of being reproached and blamed by my parents, as if it was my fault that I was being physically abused and taunted by school-mates, often older kids, sometimes several years older than me, and sometimes in swarms at a time. As I sat next to Jimmy as he was crying, I was specifically reminded of a similar incident I experienced in the locker room while feeling powerless and naked in the shower after gym class. Here the archaic primacy of my past revisited me in the imme-diational presence of relived shame, while simultaneously invoking the projective teleology for how I had wished things to be. Even now, after putting these words to paper, there persists the lingering aftermath of shame, both in what had happened to me as a child, as well as the con-tempt I experienced for my parents, including writing about it openly in professionally public space.

The identificatory mortification of such exposure to my little patient's helplessness, shame, and derision led to the reverberation of my own countertransference, yet one that led to a turn in the therapy. When appealing to my father's help or advice during times of desperation, he was often insipid and incompetent. Moreover, he was inept at dealing with my feelings and had a way of making me feel it was my fault for not fixing the matter on my own. My mother was equally invalidating and useless. Neither seemed adept at understanding my emotional vulnerability nor doing anything to protect me. I understood Jimmy's pain very intimately. The only thing my parents did of any value was to enrol me in karate classes at my insistence, hoping I would learn how to defend myself. When Jimmy was expressing his sense of anxiety, hopelessness, and fear of future abuse, I could not help but ask myself, *What did I wish my father would have done to help me?*

It was Lacan (1936) who introduced the notion of the mirror stage in the development of the ego, which he derived from Hegel's (1807) theory of recognition as the reappropriation of the other's desire. When I saw the desperation in Jimmy's eyes, I recognized my own as a mirror reflection, but rather than maintain a passive holding environment marked by empathic listening and validation, I decided he needed much more, and I was going to do something about it. I told him I understood how hard it was because I had also been bullied for years at school, and what really helped me was when I learned karate. So I offered to teach him some martial arts moves and self-defence strategies so he could protect himself if kids ever started to threaten him again, and he jumped at the chance.

I have a large playroom that is adjacent to my consulting room and waiting area, so I took Jimmy there to show him where we would begin our lessons next time I saw him. That room also contains a small storeroom, which I had opened to show him where I store all my trophies I had won in martial arts tournaments when I was a national competitor as a younger man, having earned my black belt in Taekwondo. Amidst his excitement, as his mother was returning to pick him up at the end of the session, he said to me, 'I wish you were my father.'

This comment not only brought on an almost unbearable shame, it also conjured up my own conflicted dynamics in relation to my traumatic past as well as profound disappointments with my parents' failures as parents. But over the course of treatment, I had become more comfortable in adopting the role of being a better father to Jimmy, despite being uncomfortable with my heightened idealization.

It was Winnicott (1971, p. 47) who referred to therapy as play, which involves a certain degree of precariousness between two psychic realities that can at times appear quite magical in the development of mutual intimacy within a secure relationship. The playroom became a transformative space of becoming as Jimmy learned the basic stances, blocks, punches, and kicks, and, as he progressed, more advanced techniques at self-defence and in disabling one's opponent or foe. This process had a modifying effect on his self-esteem as he felt more capable of sticking up for himself and not feeling so intimidated. I encouraged his mother to enrol him in a formal club where he could build his confidence even further, learn self-discipline and restraint, and have a controlled (sublimated) outlet for his aggression. And she did just that.

As Jimmy became more involved in the sport formally, our karate lessons slowly began to dissipate; instead we focused on other matters, pursuing other interests. Convincing his parents to stop dispensing his anti-psychotic medication led to a complete remission of voices, which were likely more ego-syntonic in nature and connected to his fantasy life in reaction to internal conflict commensurate with his developmental age. He was getting along better with classmates, had less problems at school and home, and his grades were improving. He was also spending more quality time with his father, and they even went fishing together at my suggestion. I started to teach him the guitar, and he practised throughout the week eager to show me his progress. He also developed an interest in conducting magic tricks, would demonstrate his acts for me, and eventually started performing at his school's talent show and the local public library. As he gained new friends and excelled in his endeavours, after two years of therapy, it was inevitably time to end. And with a big hug. This process was also transformative for me, as I felt I could allow myself to indulge my own fantasy by being a better father with diminished shame, as well as welcome forgiveness for inadequacies any parent is condemned to make by virtue of our ontological imperfections. In the end, I believe we both benefited without shame.

Becoming Jesus

Rachel came to see me after a referral from her family doctor. She was 47 years old, married with no children, unable to have a baby after her hysterectomy, with a 20-year history of depression and anxiety primarily treated with Effexor, Wellbutrin, and Xanax for panic. She grew up in a strictly observing Irish-Catholic home and suffered gross developmental traumas. Her father was described as a 'cruel man' who would 'terrorize' her and her siblings with threats of physical aggression, pound his fists on the table during dinner, and would punish her if she showed any display of emotion or anger. He was totalitarian, demanded unwavering conformity, and would discipline upon the slightest provocation or if his children did not do exactly what they were told. She recalls as a small child crying out at night from her room, only to be beaten for waking up the house. She never cried out again. She used to rub her ankles together until they bled because she could not express her feelings openly and had to internalize everything. Rachel characterized her childhood as constantly living in fear and feeling unsafe, and made to feel responsible and guilty if her parents were upset. When she was 6, she received a doll she wanted for her birthday and started to cry, not out of happiness for receiving the doll but because, she said, 'I didn't deserve it.'

Rachel's mother was described as cold, aloof, unavailable, and invalidating of her feelings and needs, such as when she told her mother she could not have children; her reply was 'You're free.' She 'hated' her mother growing up as she was un-nurturing and never gave her affection or hugs, and 'sicked my father on me' for upsetting her. In short, she never felt loved. Although her father did occasionally show her affection during 'happy times', this stopped after she defied him in her teens, only to be shunned by him ever since.

Rachel mentioned, almost in passing, that she and her husband 'never have sex', but reported that he was 'supportive'. She associated this with how her father would follow her on dates, spy on her, and once assaulted her boyfriend on the street, accusing them of wanting to fornicate. But when she entered the convent at the age of 20, her father wept and begged her to reconsider. She left shortly thereafter.

All three of her siblings were distant and had cut ties with the family, only occasionally speaking to her. She described the onset of her depression and anxiety as the culmination of abuse, relational trauma, and the gradual withdrawal and withholding of acceptance and love, which she feared was becoming 'severe'. At the end of the first session, she disclosed that I had instilled some hope as she found me 'kind'.

Rachel's father was raised in a strict religious home where weekly observance was mandatory for the family. During Rachel's upbringing, her parents always had priests and clergy over for dinner or after church functions, two of whom were arrested for paedophilia, charges the parents dismissed, even though her father's 'best friend' was convicted for molesting boys. As the initial sessions progressed, Rachel described her father acting like a 'jealous lover' who controlled, dominated, and shamed her during her adolescence. She reported that all break-ups with boyfriends were due to her father, and that he would make uncomfortable comments about her body and sex, and even removed the mirror in the bathroom because he accused her of looking at herself naked. Constant references were made about her weight and 'getting fat,' and even her mother once accused her of seducing her father. She felt she was always the object of unjustified blame.

At the beginning of the fourth session, my patient stated that she had felt an almost immediate lifting of her depressive symptoms that had brought her immense relief. Upon my query of what she thought was the reason for her sudden change in mood, she attributed this to me. Although I had sensed the development of an idealized transference, I was not prepared for what I was about to hear. I have a home office separated from the other parts of the house with its own private entrance. As a matter of habit, I always greet my patients standing at my office door after hearing them enter the house and descend the stairs to my waiting area. This is when Rachel said that the first time she saw me she had a vision of me as Jesus waiting for her. She said that she had immediately felt safe and that there would be no judgement of her, only a loving and accepting presence, which I embodied as her 'Saviour'. She even asked if I had a beard when we first met or if I had grown one since our last session. I've worn a beard since high school.

Having been exalted to such a divine position, I immediately felt mortified and defensively wanted to laugh out loud. In fact, I recall blushing, hence feeling the blood rush to my face and having to keep it in, mindful not to appear shaming in any way despite my own feeling of embarrassment. The comical thought of me being deified was about as ludicrous as I could imagine, let alone me allowing the delusion to persist. The immediate sense of shame was particularly intensified because I have been an outspoken atheist most of my adult life, viewing the notion of God as no more than a supercilious idea (Mills, 2017), and to accept the transference projection would be a most profane form of inauthenticity and assault on the truth as well as my sense of personal identity. In fact, as a general rule, I feel it is an ethical duty to challenge such social ideologies when confronted with the topic. But here I felt a curious impulse to remain silent and accept the idealization. Although adopting the posture that I thought the patient required was for technical reasons and was warranted, even now I feel like I betrayed a personal sense of authenticity. When cast in perfectionistic fashions by patients in the course of therapy, I typically defer to the reality principle and suggest it is due to the transference or their need to see me in such romanticized ways, whereas a dis-identification may be a more appropriate stance, or at the very least I would encourage a more holistic appraisal of integrating both good and less worthy aspects of my presence into some meaningful whole where fanciful, fetishized elements are subsumed into more objective dimensions, virtuous as they may appear to be. But here I felt paralysed by Rachel's need to see me otherwise, and indeed felt it would be counterproductive not to adopt the therapeutic role responsiveness she was craving. Was this my countertransference? I am still uncertain, but this question may itself be illegitimate given that we can never entirely separate our personal psyches from the therapeutic encounter. Rather than dissuade such thinking on her part, I merely accepted the protagonist she needed me to be by not challenging her projection. Instead I encouraged her to tell me more about her thoughts and feelings.

After an outpouring of emotions, including feelings of loneliness, emptiness, and loss, Rachel felt she was able to liberate her true inner experiences and talk about them for the first time, released from the childhood prison of her pathological accommodations. I made her feel safe and my office felt like 'home' where she was allowed to have emotions and express them openly. She gradually admitted that she was not so happy in her marriage after all, having come to realize that she picked a man who served as a compromise, resembling both her parents. As she opened herself up to her inner world that previously remained compartmentalized and unformulated, she naturally felt a mourning for living a life that was unconsciously chosen yet consciously denied.

After only ten sessions, her symptoms subsided and she went off all medication. This was also at the point her insurance benefits had been exhausted for the year, but she felt good enough that she did not need to return until the new year when her plan resumed again. The new year came and passed, but she did call to let me know that she was doing fine and did not need to return. Approximately four years later she wrote me a letter to thank me for my help and to let me know that she was estranged from her parents, divorced, and was soon to remarry.

I consider this treatment to be a 'transference cure' where I offered very little in terms of being scarcely more than an idealized selfobject experience providing transitional space via attentive listening, empathic attunement, and validation within a role responsive-holding environment intended to provide a corrective emotional ambiance sensitive to her vulnerabilities and shame. Although there was some interpretive and integrative work that was accomplished, I am left with the humble conclusion that I was neither her saviour nor a successful analyst despite her suggestion otherwise. But I guess we all get lucky sometimes.

Concluding postscript

Psychoanalysts of all persuasions and schools of thought often do not talk about or write openly and honestly about what they truly think and feel, or admit their internal conflicts or complexes, let alone what they actually do and say in the analytic session. This scholarly observation, I suggest, is largely due to shame and fear of exposure, critique, and ridicule by colleagues. When analysts do write freely about what transpired in the session, their experiences become alienated from their personhood and judged by others, whether they like it or not, especially when technical principles, revealed content, and the specifics of interpretation and self-disclosure are ripe for intellectual rape. It is not uncommon to hear analysts from a particular psychoanalytic coterie or camp debasing or belittling analysts from different orientations when it comes to clinical praxis due to group identification, competition, and the narcissism of minor differences. It is largely seen as exhibitionist when therapists discuss their own personal traumas or tragedies in the professional literature, which is often invalidated, condemned, viewed as pathology or a counter-transference enactment, or seen as a narcissistic act of self-expression inappropriate for the profession. But it also takes courage to speak the truth even if we risk verdicts and deprecation from others, whether this be about our own personal lives or what really transpires in the consulting room – not some manufactured narrative, contrived scenario, or massaged vignette that customarily permeates psychoanalytic writings where the sage master demonstrates the perfect interpretation or intervention that all others should aspire toward or emulate. In fact, this conventional practice is somewhat shameful, as it is disingenuous and inauthentic, for it never reveals the whole picture, as is typical of life. We need to be honest with ourselves and with others: if we cannot disclose our personal feelings and conflicts with our fellow colleagues, then how can we advance as a profession? More analysts should be encouraged to be open and genuine when writing or speaking in professional space because we may all learn from what they experience in their practices and struggle with internally. We need to be truthful and real if we are to progress as a discipline, and there is no shame in being human.

We usually do not consider shame to be a philosophical matter, but rather a psychological state of mind we desperately seek to avoid. But shame may very well be one of the most salient emotions that structure subjectivity ontologically and contribute to group identifications and inter-relations politicized within the social fabric of all cultures, hence informing the concrete universals reflective of collective humanity. Here we may say that shame is archetypal, a psychic dominant that is at once interiorized, externalized, and symbolic.

Whether standing in relation to a set of ideals or values, the internalization of one's family, being a member of a group or nation state, or revelling in one's penchant for a particular identification with a cherished object, the problematic of shame yields many philosophical representations. It further carries a modicum of humility amongst a backdrop of anxiety, for it is ubiquitous even when hidden. In fact, the ontic condition of hiddenness or concealment generates free-floating psychic unrest, as this reminds us of our intimate relation to time, which is ticking by-the-way, and freedom, that which is chosen, enacted, or denied. Here we generate time in every act of consciousness as the coming into being of our lived subjectivity, the coming to presence and instantiation of our being. Shame is always lived in time, in living the embodied temporal, whether historical, immediate, or looming. Absurdly, we have no say in the matter whatsoever. Let's simply call this existential inertia – the impotence of freedom, for we just can't will away our emotions, only transform them.

The temporal mediacy of our emotional lives is contingent upon the psychological realities that condition our experience of self, other, and world. As such, the past is unconsciously memorialized and becomes an eternal present from the standpoint of conscious reflection as recollection, while the future is an eternal recurrence of what came before through modified form. Both realms of psychic reality are united when the unconscious artefacts of personal history, as well as history in general tarrying within cultural memory, merge with the 'new now', the presence of the present. Here the presence of the present can retroactively alter the past as re-inscription, which in turn can amend the contemporary, thus revealing the double character of their values, values that are internally divided. As in political economy, values vary over time. Nothing stays the same, although in their purest forms we have memorialization, presencing, and futurity, each supervening on one another as its own self-constituting form of emanationism. When futurity is realized, it becomes the actualization of the archaic, and when the past resurfaces in new patterns or appearances, it is the eternal recurrence of a new presence. There are no unchangeable states, only perspectival shifts when it comes to the temporal, except for the ontological merit that process is invariant and universal, itself an oxymoron but something that can always be counted on. Or perhaps a better word is paradox, the *aporia* of impassable time.

Does shame change or is it re-emblazoned in the 'new now' through temporal alterations and imprints on consciousness? I would surmise that the qualia, intensity, and valence of shame does not qualitatively disappear in memory when revisited, as it is a traumatic (though subdued) reiteration, but it can be mitigated with time. History is never erased. Futurity is uncertain. All we have is now. This ultimately implies that temporality is the emotional instantiation of value.

Notes

1 What I mean by diachrony is how perceived or experiential lived time is marked by constant changes that traverse the domain of the temporal and alter fixed and/or fixated value-relations, what Freud referred to as cathexes, or Jung as psychic energies, based on human development, maturity, and transmogrification of internalized past experiences regardless of their historical accuracy or factual basis. Here temporality makes interiorized values, schemata, and emotional introjects, which change over time.

2 While pondering the infinite, Husserl discovered the double continuity of time-consciousness that apprehends the presence of the past and the future in the immediate present moment of awareness as an intentional act of relating to meant objects (see Mills, 2015; Tougas, 2013, pp. 50–65, for a review). Husserl theorized that the origin of subjective experience sprang from an originating or generative centre in which all appearances arise, and that each moment is

its own centre responsible for engendering time. In *The Phenomenology of Internal Time-Consciousness*, Husserl (1905) referred to this centre as 'a point of actuality, primal source-point' in which time generates itself, 'that from which springs the "now"' (§ 36, p. 100). Each present moment is held together by its simultaneous relation to the past and the future as a doubly continuous instant preserved in dialectical continuity. The double continuity of new presence, of the bipolar reiteration of itself in every fresh moment of experience, ensures that the continuously new presence of the 'now' becomes the ground of all appearances. Our subjectivity of time always corresponds to a 'new now' whether one is reflecting on the past, the present, or an imagined or anticipated future state that has not actually occurred.

Our attunement to presence involves a lived sense of 'passing' and 'enduring' within our moment-to-moment awareness of meant objects, which is both an act of 'transcendence' and 'immanence'. For Husserl, the ego or consciousness is a transcendental structure that generates forms of subjectivity in and through time where there is no formal division of subject from object. Here subject and object, self and world are conjoined as a whole or superordinate totality only separated by moments, hence abnegating the vicious bifurcation between nature and mind. It is in the bracketed act of *epoché* (ἐποχή) or reduction that reveals the world as a correlate of consciousness, which is performed by the pre-reflective transcendental ego. So when Husserl speaks of time as instantaneously transcendent and immanent, he is also speaking of the psyche in general. That which is given to consciousness is as much a transcendent objectivity as it is subjectively constituted. The feeling or thought of something beyond us or in abundance in us that is temporally present to our immediate lived experience is a form of transcendence, as is the notion of anticipating the coming to presence or innateness of that experience arising in us.

3   When I refer to the dialectic, I am specifically referring to Hegel's (1812) *Logic*, which is often misunderstood and inaccurately captured by the pedestrian phrase 'thesis-antithesis-synthesis'. For Hegel, the dialectic is much more complicated and involves a complex movement of mediating opposition while surpassing its immediate shape, which constitutes a simultaneous threefold process as the act of negation or annulment, transcendence, or supersession, while at the same time subsuming or preserving opposition within a higher structural unity of mind (see Mills, 2002, for a review). Hegel's philosophy of mind or spirit rests on a proper understanding of the ontology of the dialectic. Hegel refers to the unrest of *Aufhebung* – customarily translated as 'sublation' – a continuous dialectical process entering into opposition within its own determinations and thus raising this opposition to a higher unity, which remains at once annulled, preserved, and transmuted. Hegel's use of *Aufhebung*, a term he borrowed from Schiller but also an ordinary German word, is to be distinguished from its purely negative function, whereby there is a complete cancelling or drowning of the lower relation in the higher, to also encompass a preservative aspect. Therefore, the term *aufheben* has a

threefold meaning: (1) to suspend or cancel, (2) to surpass or transcend, and (3) to preserve. In the *Encyclopaedia Logic*, Hegel (1817) makes this clear: 'On the one hand, we understand it to mean "clear away" or "cancel", and in that sense we say that a law or regulation is cancelled (*aufgehoben*). But the word also means "to preserve"' (§ 96, *Zusatz*). What this implies is that with each shift of the rotary motions of the dialectic comes various revisitations and enunciations of shame due to mutating occurrences, reincorporations, and changing levels of truth and ignorance mediated by agency.

References

Crastnopol, M. (2015). *Micro-Trauma: A Psychoanalytic Understanding of Cumulative Psychic Injury*. London: Routledge.

Freud, S. (1917 [1915]). Mourning and Melancholia. *The Standard Edition of the Complete Psychological Works of Sigmund Freud*. James Strachey (trans. and gen. ed.), in collaboration with Anna Freud, assisted by Alix Strachey & Alan Tyson. London: Hogarth Press, 1966–95, Vol. 14, 237–60.

Freud, S. (1921). *Group Psychology and the Analysis of the Ego*. In *The Standard Edition*, Vol. 18, 67–144.

Freud, S. (1923). *The Ego and the Id*. In *The Standard Edition*, Vol. 19, 3–66.

Freud, S. (1933). *New Introductory Lectures on Psycho-Analysis*. In *The Standard Edition*, Vol. 22.

Hegel, G.W.F. (1807). *Phenomenology of Spirit*. A.V. Miller (trans.). Oxford: Oxford University Press, 1977.

Hegel, G.W.F. (1812/1831). *Science of Logic*. A.V. Miller (trans.). London: George Allen and Unwin Ltd, 1969.

Hegel, G.W.F. (1817/1827/1830). *The Encyclopaedia Logic*. Vol. 1 of *Encyclopaedia of the Philosophical Sciences*. T.F. Geraets, W.A. Suchting, & H.S. Harris (trans.). Indianapolis, IN: Hackett Publishing Company, Inc, 1991.

Husserl, E. (1905). *The Phenomenology of Internal Time-Consciousness*. J.S. Churchill (trans.). Bloomington, IN: Indiana University Press, 1964.

Kohut, H. (1971). *The Analysis of the Self*. New York: International Universities Press.

Kohut, H. (1985). *Self Psychology and the Humanities*. New York: Norton.

Lacan, J. (1936). The Mirror Stage as Formative of the Function of the I. In *Écrits: A Selection*. Alan Sheridan (trans.). New York: Norton, 1977.

Mills, J. (2002). *The Unconscious Abyss: Hegel's Anticipation of Psychoanalysis*. Albany, NY: SUNY Press.

Mills, J. (2005). *Treating Attachment Pathology*. Lanham, MD: Aronson/ Rowman & Littlefield.

Mills, J. (2010). *Origins: On the Genesis of Psychic Reality*. Montreal: McGill-Queens University Press.

Mills, J. (2015). On Meant Objects, Unconscious Intentionality, and Time. *Jung Journal: Culture & Psyche*, 9, 4, 92–7.

Mills, J. (2017). *Inventing God: Psychology of Belief and the Rise of Secular Spirituality*. London: Routledge.

Morrison, A.P. (1989). *Shame: The Underside of Narcissism*. Hillsdale, NJ: Analytic Press.

Naso, R.C. (2010). *Hypocrisy Unmasked: Dissociation, Shame, and the Ethics of Inauthenticity*. Lanham, MD: Aronson/Rowman & Littlefield.

Tougas, C.T. (2013). *The Phenomena of Awareness: Husserl, Cantor, Jung*. London: Routledge.

Winnicott, D.W. (1971). *Playing and Reality*. London: Routledge.

Chapter 3

A time for shame

Levinas, diachrony and the hope of shame

Eric Severson

Hester Prynne, the heroine of Nathaniel Hawthorne's classic *The Scarlet Letter*, is often strong and defiant, but not impervious to the judgemental and condescending words and glances of her community, nor to the bright red 'A' on her dress. The phenomenon of *shame* plays a central role in Hawthorne's tale. He subtitled the story 'a romance,' but the most powerful emotion at play in the novel might not be love, as one would expect in a romance, but shame. Shame moves in and out of the narrative; it is pushed back and then rushes in mightily. In an unforgettable passage, Prynne is made to stand for three hours, on an elevated platform in front of the town stocks. She is pressured and badgered and humiliated by the townspeople, each trying to make her feel enough shame to reveal the father of her baby. She is sentenced to wear the letter as a permanent 'mark of shame upon her bosom' (Hawthorne, 1982, p. 34). Unlike guilt, which pertains to measurable behaviours and consequences, shame is an internal discomfort, an event in one's relationship to oneself. The goal of the townspeople is not to render her guilty, but to alter permanently her self-understanding. They were, however, unaware of another layer to shame, a kind of shame that opened Hester to a future she could not have anticipated.

Shame plays a fascinating role in both the self and the composition of society. This chapter explores the dynamics of shame as they relate to temporality. Drawing from a wide range of examples, this chapter will first explore the double-edged sword that is 'shame,' then will utilize the unique philosophy of time offered by Emmanuel Levinas to explore the psychological and ethical dynamics of shame. Though shame takes many forms, I will isolate two manifestations in this chapter, calling them *synchronic shame* and *diachronic shame*, which are seen in Hester's relationship to the townspeople and in Hester's relationship to her daughter Pearl, defining the two types as the supposed simultaneity of the experience of time, as most often tracked by clocks and calendars (synchronic) and the non-synchronized experience of time that is unique to the one who experiences it (diachronic). To unlock the differences between these two types of shame, which is crucial for thinking about shame psychologically and philosophically, I will explore the relationship between time and shame. A better understanding of time, particularly the intersubjectivity of time, will improve our psychological understanding and treatment of shame. Ultimately I will argue that shame points to the unsettling of time, an unsettling of the synchronization of my time by the time of the other.

Synchronous shame

Written in 1850, and promptly devoured by eager readers, *The Scarlet Letter* offers insight into the role of shame in the seventeenth-century Puritan colonies. To Hawthorne's credit, he avoids creating an impossibly austere heroine. Hester Prynne vacillates between resisting the pressure to feel shame and denying it with defiance. When her husband, thought to be lost at sea, finds and confronts her in secret, 'he laid his long forefinger on the scarlet letter, which forthwith seemed to scorch into Hester's breast, as if it had been red-hot' (Hawthorne, 1892, p. 52). She is torn between pride and shamefulness, eventually learning that, if she pointed at her letter when she was being mocked by the townspeople, she could maintain her pride and satisfy their need to condemn and condescend (Hawthorne, 1892, p. 224). Her resistance to their attempts to lock her in synchronic shame, in the permanent presence of their condemnation, was not an escape from shame but a shifting of its terms. Synchronic shame attempts to synchronize, to conform, to minimize independence and autonomy in the interest of harmony; it seeks to freeze time.

Contrary to guilt, which principally focuses on what I have done – on actions, behaviours, and infractions – shame aims at *who I am*. Shame stems from wrestling with components of the self that fail to arrange themselves satisfactorily. Hester feels guilt for her wrongdoing, and admits as much to her husband. However, the townspeople sentence Hester to wear a scarlet 'A' for life, and their hope in this sentence is that she will slowly and permanently internalize a jarring truth: she has not merely made a mistake – Hester *is* a mistake. She is to have no hope of salvation, no proper place in society, and no moment when her very appearance in public does not provide a 'living sermon against sin,' at least 'until the ignominious letter be engraved upon her tombstone' (Hawthorne, 1892, p. 34). In this regard, Hester's letter seems like the embodiment of synchrony. Her shamefulness is always to be synchronous with her name and her existence, even in death. The scarlet letter is meant to sink through her clothing and on to her heart, to be permanent, to be unchanging, and to fasten her past sins to her every future moment. Paradoxically, the letter becomes something quite different for Hester, a symbol of her independent and resilient refusal to be synchronized.

This application of synchronic shame freezes time, refusing Prynne any future that is not bound to the eternally present moment of her indiscretion. Shame, as applied oppressively by the masses, is an attempt to rob time of its future dimension, its freedom to renew, to redeem, to resurrect, to overturn, to surprise. When it succeeds, synchronic shame forms a hellish prison around its victims. This appears to be what the townspeople had in mind, with both the letter and the tombstone; they wanted to make sure that Hester began her stay in hell's prison immediately.

This helps explain why shame and guilt are so vividly different in the emotional states of people who experience them. When one has *done* something wrong, something worthy of guilt, there is often the possibility of restitution, of doing differently, of making apology, of righting wrongs. Guilt is fluid. Shame, at least synchronic shame, is without exit. At least that appears to be the intentions of those who seek to apply it. What is refused to the shamed person is *diachronic* time, or the liberation that her unique temporality might provide from the tick-tock of the universal clock. To help someone struggling with this sort of shame is delicate work. The simplest remedy for shame is to rework the pathways that lead to shameful feelings, to minimize the oppressive and synchronizing forces from laying hold on a person. This solution might indeed lead to a loss of shame, but at what cost? As desirable as it might be to minimize shame, might the reduction of shame introduce new psychological and interpersonal problems? Before exploring healthy shame, a shame I am calling *diachronic*, it is important to explore with some depth what is at stake in the concept of shame.

The need for shame

Shame is a deeply complex emotional state. There is a surging interest in the psychological dynamics of shame, as clinicians and scholars demonstrate a growing awareness of the way that shame is both vital and dangerous. The topic of shame is an ancient one, with direct and influential treatments by scores of philosophers and theologians across many centuries. Shame overlaps with religion, culture, morality, and almost every aspect of human nature. For Sigmund Freud (1961), who is both insightful and controversial on the topic, shame is as original to human nature as walking upright (p. 99). In fact, for Freud, the very transition to being bipedal leads to the invention of shame; standing up leaves the genitals exposed and visible. Shame begins, by this interpretation, as an instinctive and self-protective movement. Shame is therefore tied to vulnerability, and to the raw and unprotected exposure of oneself to the radical alterity of the other person.

This raw vulnerability is the root of every manifestation of shame, and certainly both the synchronous and diachronous manifestations explored here. The very idea of a person unable to experience shame is a frightening image. What horrors might flow from the enemy who knows nothing of shame? The surest formula for a Hollywood blockbuster involves the invention of a villain that is truly shameless. We are frightened and fascinated by the alien, the monster, the vicious animal, the zombie, the psychologically deranged. We count on shame to hold back the otherwise dangerous desires and emotions of our fellow human creatures.

Philosopher Robert Metcalf (2006) calls Freud's explanation for the origins of shame a *Promethean* account, noting intriguing similarities between the story of Prometheus, as narrated by Protagoras in Plato's dialogue. In *Protagoras*, during the 'great speech,' Protagoras notes that it was simply not enough for Prometheus to rob the gods of fire and 'practical wisdom.' With fire and basic language, people could find food and achieve basic tasks, but they lacked *political* understanding, a gift that was not available to Prometheus, we are told by Protagoras; it was kept securely by Zeus and his fierce guards. Without politics, the people remained powerless against the wildest animals; they could communicate with one another but knew not how to live together. In search of 'self-preservation,' they found themselves binding together as cities, but they inevitably and repeatedly treated one another in an evil fashion.

Fearing that 'the entire race would be exterminated' (Plato, 2012, p. 178), Zeus intervened and gave humanity the final gifts that allowed for our ascension above the realm of the animals: justice (*dikē*) and shame (*aidōs*, sometimes translated as 'reverence'). These tools provide both 'conciliation' and 'friendship' (ibid., p. 178). They are the tools of coordination, of synchronizing behaviour according to common allegiances, mores, and purposes.

For Protagoras, shame is a crucial gift from the god Zeus, for it is the key to being able to have culture and civil society. Without shame, there is only evil, perpetrated without hesitation. The biblical book of Genesis offers a similar theme: God resolved to destroy the human race because they perpetuated evil without reluctance. The flood is precipitated by the unreserved 'depravity' of humankind, when God saw that 'every inclination of the thoughts of their hearts was only evil continually' (Genesis 6:5, NRSV). Shame breaks the chaotic and unrestrained patterns of desire, which manifests itself as 'evil,' interrupting the animalistic indulgence of the ego. In Plato and in Genesis, to be without shame is to be a monstrosity, to be pre-human or sub-human, or otherwise ill-fit for the communal life.

The first move of shame, of all shame, is its primordial interruption of the self-satisfaction of the ego. The baby that grinds new teeth against the fingers of her caretaker knows only, at first, the soothing of pain in the gums. This soothing, this satisfaction, is interrupted by cries of pain from the caregiver, from outside the immediate experience of the child. Shame is learned, or *awakened*, in the responsiveness for the vulnerability of the skin of the other person. A human with little or no shame moves about the world with a calloused, damaged, muted, or missing vulnerability to the suffering of others.

Freud's understanding of shame echoes the biblical and Hellenistic accounts; without shame, the threads that hold society together are undermined by egoism and self-interest. Freud's fixation on genital exposure is strikingly similar to the echoes of primordial shamelessness that even survived the flood. When Adam and Eve ate the forbidden fruit, their very first reaction was to realize that they were naked: 'the eyes of both were opened, and they knew that they were naked; and they sewed fig leaves together and made loincloths for themselves' (Genesis 3:7). Shame and exposure are interlocked. To know shame is to know exposure. The arrival of shame coincided, for Adam and Eve, with eating from the 'tree of the knowledge of good and evil' (Genesis 2–3). Shame and moral awareness move hand-in-hand. This was a diachronous act, the choice of Adam and Eve to emerge from the synchronous, frozen present of Eden.

We see the dynamics of shame again on display in the story of Ham and Noah in Genesis. When Ham finds his father Noah drunk and exposed, he exploits Noah's vulnerability, though it is unclear exactly what Ham does to Noah (Gagnon, 2001, pp. 63–71). Rather than be embarrassed at the enjoyment he took from his father's exposure, Ham demonstrates no shame and attempts to draw his brothers into the spectacle. The other sons, Shem and Japheth, respond in a way that demonstrates their awareness of shame; they back their way into the tent and cover their father's nakedness. This story demonstrates the necessity of shame to maintain the sanctity of family relations, sexual relations, filial piety, and other mores. Ham is the villain for his lack of responsiveness to the vulnerability of Noah; the plight of his father did not rise above his private enjoyment of the event. Shem and Japheth demonstrate this very virtue; they operate out of shame, out of a shame that turns them toward the vulnerability of the other person.

Even more fascinating is the infamous 'Curse of Canaan,' which Noah utters when he awakes and realizes (or, perhaps, remembers) what has been done to him and feels a 'need for revenge in order to maintain his dignity and self-esteem' (Rashkow, 2004, p. 57). Noah's curse renders Ham's descendants slaves: 'Cursed be Canaan; lowest of slaves shall he be to his brothers' (Genesis 9:25). They are converted from full humanity to human *property*. The lack of shame before genital exposure is indicative that Ham, and, consequently, his descendants, are not worthy of free and full humanity. Noah's response, which some have suspected closely resembles a Freudian defence mechanism, is to *shame the shamer* (Rashkow, 2004, p. 57). The mechanism is a dangerous one, of course, a two-edged sword. Though shame arises to protect Noah, and others, against the unbridled desires of the shame-less, it soon becomes clear that Ham and his ilk will need shame applied where it is missing. Ham and all his descendants must be marked so that nobody ever forgets how shameful such activities are forevermore.

Shame establishes boundaries and protects against vulnerability; it is shame that, supposedly, stands between power and vulnerability. Noah's son is not merely punished, for he is more than just 'guilty' of a transgression.

There can be no path to final atonement for shame; the stain of Noah's curse lasts forever. This movement to apply shame and force it to appear among those who do not demonstrate it, is the move to synchronize. Those who refuse to conform to this synchronization will often find themselves ostracized, treated as scapegoats, imprisoned, or even killed. The synchronic movement of shame may arise from a cultural evolution toward the survival of the community. Friedrich Nietzsche (2001) implies that shame arises from the weak voices of those who are trampled by the powerful (pp. 153–8). Whatever its origins, synchronic shame is a powerful and dangerous force. The challenge of treating people who struggle with shame is surely found in the difficulty of disentangling the synchronic shame from the healthier version of shame that provokes vigilance to the suffering of others. In the case of Hester Prynne, we find the transmutation of synchronic shame into a diachronic form. Instead of attempting to defeat shame, perhaps clinicians should encourage the evolution of synchronic into diachronic shame.

Any phenomenological or psychological evaluation of shame must contend with this double complexity: shame is simultaneously crucial for functional human existence and yet massively dangerous. Shame cuts in many directions and is particularly difficult to treat because clients frequently find the act of seeking help itself *shameful*. Because shame is crucial for the operation of society and fundamental for morality and justice, as Zeus determined, treatment is delicate. Synchronic shame can redouble self-hatred and contribute to dangerous behaviour, including suicide, while the elimination of shame cauterizes the nerves that expose human beings to their very humanity, to their connection to the sufferings (and joys) of the world around them. Even 'good' shame is dangerous, though, sometimes weighing particularly heavily on traumatized and vulnerable persons.

The Showtime television programme *Shameless* (2011–), along with its British counterpart of the same name (2004–13), delves into the dark and comedic realm in which characters experiment with the boundary of shame. *Shameless* depicts the way alcoholism erodes the ability of a person to manage and avoid shame. Freud found shamelessness to be a dangerous state; a person without shame has lost the ability to navigate social relationships without causing immense pain. This can be seen also in bullies who 'are afraid their failures or shortcomings will be exposed' (Lamia, 2010). The bully's sense of shame, or attempts to mask it, lead to the behaviours that classify such a person as a bully.

In *Shameless,* the character Frank, played flawlessly by William H. Macy, appears to be entirely without scruples, and fixates only on appeasing his own alcoholism. The brilliance of the show, however, is manifested in the reappearance of shame even in the midst of this depraved condition: while Frank will risk the lives of his children, rob church collection boxes, steal from blind beggars, and otherwise violate all social moral paradigms, he appears to reach his limits occasionally. Shame seems to restore his humanity, even if momentarily, and restrain him from behaviour that might destroy his relationships permanently. The show actually does not depict *shameless* characters, but deftly plays with the line between inhumanity and humanity. When Hollywood depicts shameless characters, the genre shifts to horror; the truly shameless are zombies, monsters, cannibals, and psychopathic killers.

In *The Republic* (1991), Plato's character Glaucon introduces the ancient Greek myth of Gyges. The shepherd Gyges finds a ring that makes him invisible, and he immediately begins to use it for sinister purposes, manoeuvring for power, pleasure, and wealth. The question pressed to the participants in Plato's dialogue is simple: could anyone remain righteous if they were rendered invisible? The question continues to haunt philosophers and political scientists. The myth of Gyges fascinates because it plays with the possibility of a shame-free existence. If nobody can see me, if no encounter rises up to question my assertion of power on the world, does shame disappear? When my students contemplate Plato's discussion of invisibility, as I often press them to do, the responses are mixed. 'I would be ashamed to take advantage of people, even if nobody ever caught me,' one student told me. Other students insisted that 'God is watching,' even when other humans are not. These may be sophomoric objections (literally), but perhaps they are not entirely misguided.

Does the concept of shame remain even when the anxiety of encountering judgement and accountability are removed? If this is the case, shame may indeed be both gift and curse; it stands between the abuser and the child, between the oppressor and the oppressed. At the very least, shame weakly and quietly summons for justice. Shame protests the abuse and the oppression. For every instance of these injustices, how many have been prevented by the intervention of shame? It is this type of shame, the shame that aims uniquely at the self and heightens awareness of the vulnerability of others, that I am calling diachronic shame.

Diachronic shame

Much is gained from a close examination of what shame tells us about the composition of the human person. Twentieth-century philosopher Emmanuel Levinas devoted considerable attention to this philosophical concept of shame. He contends that shame is not the result of the encounter with judgemental eyes, or even a judgemental culture or historical context. Rather, shame is already present, even before these encounters have begun. The remainder of this chapter wagers that his insights into shame, and the related concept of *time*, prove helpful for our understanding of shame and its manifestations.

The concept of shame plays an intriguing role in the work of Levinas, though it is an evolving role that takes some attention to track. In his 1961 book *Totality and Infinity*, Levinas provides an extended reflection on shame, focusing on the particular way that shame demonstrates a confounding of our typical approach to conscious experience. In his later works, he develops a unique understanding of time, an innovation that sheds new light on the dynamics of shame. In this section, I will first trace Levinas's invocation of shame in *Totality and Infinity*, then I will discuss the way new ideas about time transform his thought in its later stages.

There is a directionality to everyday consciousness that is easy to demonstrate: I direct my attention toward an object and gather its attributes into my thoughts and sensations. Visual phenomena demonstrate this structure of intentionality; I apprehend that toward which I direct my gaze. Though people sometimes see what they do not wish to see, it is more often the case that we choose the object and direction of our gaze. For Levinas (1987), the thinking subject takes a stable and complacent position from which to observe the world, which Levinas, borrowing a phrase from Hegel, calls 'the position of the one who is looking' (pp. 79–80). We are spectators, first and foremost, and the crucial philosophical questions involve the intersection between our spectating minds and the machinations of the world. The spectator chooses to take in the spectacle. But in the phenomenon of shame, consciousness moves in the opposite direction. Simon Critchley (2015) summarizes it by calling shame 'the inversion of intentionality. It's a movement in a direction opposed to that of consciousness' (p. 25). For Critchley, shame comes at me unawares, not as the result of my experiential voyage into the world, but as the arrival of a foreign invader. Shame, as such, is the interruption of the systems with which I make the world present to me, the yelp that the child hears when his teeth first pierce his father's finger. Shame is not as much an event of knowing as it is an event in which one realizes that one is already known, already nominated for responsibility.

Levinas uses 'shame' in a manner that is conversant with discussions of shame by psychologists. Shame is manifest as a loss of naïvety, the death of a delusion. In the wake of the delusion, Levinas points to the awakening of the self to a reality that was before veiled or ignored. This reality, for Levinas, is that we are never alone; even within our most solitary thoughts, we are never free of the other person, of the infinite (1987, p. 58). Levinas points to Descartes, who discovered that even in the midst of radical doubt he could not shake the idea of the infinite, an idea for which he could find no rightful place in the mind of the doubting self. For Levinas, the idea of infinity appears not as a 'blocking force,' but as a way of putting into question the freedom, spontaneity, and independence of a living being. The realization that the infinite is beyond the grasp of the being, beyond the scope of its freedom, is, for Levinas, the original cause for shame (1987, p. 58). The interiority of my finitude is punctured, ruptured, by the infinite; the experience of this rupture is what Søren Kierkegaard (1983) called *despair* (pp. 13–14). Levinas calls this experience *shame*, and it represents for him the rupture of any primordial synchrony.

The presumption of Western philosophy has always been that, at some level, human beings have a sense of identity that is pre-relational, or that can be isolated from the self-hood of others. We could think of this as the kernel of the self, a piece of the 'I' that is not ultimately intertwined with others. For Levinas, shame has everything to do with this presumption. Descartes discovers, in the idea of infinity, that something has appeared within the very solitude of his all-doubting self that cannot find its rightful home there. Other ideas can be doubted and justified despite the doubt that besets them. The idea of the infinite, however, confounds Descartes. How could a finite creature conceive of the infinite? For Descartes (1998), the encounter with the infinite is a momentous encounter; the inexplicability of the infinite is ultimately sufficient, for Descartes, to prove the very existence of God (pp. 69–80).

Levinas famously discovers this infinite in the face of the other person as infinitely other, the face dispossesses the ego of its originary solitude. To look at the face of the other, to see in that face an incomprehensible otherness, is to experience a particular sort of shame. Yet the experience of shame is not that of a bystander; shame is intensely personal. I experience shame when I encounter suffering because the destitution of the other is a summons to respond. This is the shame of a dawning awareness, the realization of a disposition that is not related to anything one has or has not done. Shame as diachronic is not about what I have done but about what I am nonetheless enjoined to do in the future. This shame washes over me – not as an experience that I go looking for in the mode of intentionality, but as a realization that cannot be shaken. The discovery of this responsibility is *diachronic* because the encounter is with something that is utterly outside of the time of the self, beyond the reach of my endeavours to synchronize.

Shame is the realization that I am responsible to the other from time-before-time. Levinas (1998) calls diachrony 'an election without identification, an election that impoverishes and denudes, a goodness that demands' (p. 57). Levinas invokes here the religious concept of 'election,' whereby a people or person might be elected by God without ever being present for the moment of election. Likewise, the person who, through shame, comes to see the suffering of the other is also impossibly late for the appointment. There is no restoration of synchrony, no recovery of the choice to embrace or denounce responsibility. *The election is always in the past.* Diachrony is the break-up of the synchronic march of time that would blind me to this raw responsibility.

The face does not match any a priori idea, or fit into any category. At the same time, the face of the other invokes need, summoning a response from the self. The face of the other renders me responsible without first equipping me for this responsibility. Shame is the discovery that I am without the resources, internally, to meet that which is required of me. To avoid shame or to be shameless is, therefore, to ignore the appearance of the face of the other in its incomprehensible splendour and need. The diachrony of this situation refers to the fact that the election of shame and responsibility is before any preparation, before the establishment of the self, outside of and prior to the time of the self. Levinas (1998) writes: 'In approaching the other I am always late for the meeting' (p. 150). Though Levinas is proposing a complex philosophical idea, the experience of being late is a vivid phenomenological application. The other is hungry, cold, unclothed, in need. This need is presented to me starkly; it arrives before I can prepare for it, before I am aware of the encounter.

The need of the other, however, always precedes this encounter, and the resources at my disposal are never a match for the need that I encounter in the face of the other person.

The act of gathering together my identity, of composing myself, includes the folding in of this primordial responsibility to the other. I find that I have no time that isn't already inhabited by the other person. The experience of shame is, as it was for Freud, Zeus, Adam, and Noah, the experience of exposure. But, for Levinas (1998), this exposure is not an event in the life of the ego, nor an anxiety produced by a particular encounter with the other (p. 90). Rather, exposure is about the unavoidability of responsibility, and the unique way that shame reflects this scandalous obligation. Another person cannot stand in my place, cannot replace me in responsibility. I am uniquely elected by the other to take responsibility for her suffering (Levinas, 1998, p. 15). In the face of this election I am exposed, and ashamed of my inclination to slide away from this obligation.

Diachronic shame can therefore create the opening to one's own humanity, to that which is truest about the ego. To be a human person, according to Levinas, is to be caught in the time before time, in the joy and the need of the other person. Diachronic shame can be ignored and repressed. For Levinas, these moves are done at great peril; they threaten the very heart of what it means to be a human being. In light of this vital function of shame, how might we begin to think about treating people who experience many of the harmful and debilitating aspects of shame?

Some tentative applications

For Freud, the encounter with the other begins in primary narcissism. This is similar to the biblical narratives; humanity emerges from a time in which egoism and narcissism threaten destruction. But Levinas levels a challenge to this pre-original narcissism and violence. For him, the encounter with the other does not begin from the ego, from the self; I do not move, as a human person, into a world and then discover how I will navigate the relationships and complications in which I find myself. The encounter with the other person is diachronous. The first awareness of the encounter includes the discovery of a situation that is already afoot, a responsibility that is older than my time.

Levinas is challenging, here, the fundamental structure of epistemology and ethics in western thought, from Homer to Plato to Freud and beyond.

In the traditional metaphysical configuration of the world, the self is fundamentally separate and challenged with the encounter with others. Shame, by this account, is the result of these encounters, the product of the anxiety produced by the tensions between self and other. Hegel (1902) is perhaps the paradigmatic philosopher of this clash; he is able to explain progress and conflict and hope through the lens of the originary and ongoing encounter between self and world, between self and other (p. 108). Levinas challenges this central and pervasive thesis, and, therefore, the fundamental dynamics of shame and temporality.

What often passes for shame is merely the synchronic mechanism of culture and history, which operates to oppress and humiliate the fictional Hester Prynne and countless non-fictional persons like her. What if shame is not primarily a by-product of the anxiety of the encounter with culture, with the masses, with the world, but rather connects human beings to the pre-original summons of the other person, a summons that does not originate in violence and conflict, but in peace? Levinas (1998) suggests precisely this; he calls it 'the immediacy of peace that is incumbent on me' (p. 139). For him, this 'peace' is the arrival of responsibility for the other person before conflict, in the tranquillity of the time-before-time. Shame has a negative inflection, but for Levinas, shame does not aim at the particular disposition of the ego relative to societal norms; there is no moment when self-meets-world. Instead, shame is the discovery that there is no such thing as a separated 'ego' that can have such original encounters. It is, for Levinas, a sort of anxiety. Diachronic shame is the result of the unsettling of the delusion that consciousness, knowledge, and understanding are products of the self-meets-world epistemological framework. Shame has its positive inflection here; it is the awareness that, despite the trap of self-interest and narcissism, the other person offers a way out. This is the alternative path that Levinas proposes; shame is best understood as a symptom to the dawning awareness that the self is trapped in its self-interest. Responsibility, and substitution for the suffering of the other person, is therefore salvation. This salvation is the transition into diachronic time, into a responsibility for the suffering that never falls to synchrony, for the other person for whom I am responsible for diachronically.

Shame is not the product of conflict, but is the reverberation of a bond older than conflict. Shame is the echo, sometimes barely audible, of a responsibility to others that constitutes the self before the artificial acts of self-constitution are underway. This is why temporality is so crucial for the better understanding of shame. Shame points to this disruption of time, an unsettling of my inclination to stabilize my time with the ticking clock of synchrony; shame points me to the time of the other.

Shame is potentially crippling, but it is the by-product of a pre-original disposition of the self, the for-the-other, which poorly matches the narcissistic, egoistic, self-concerned composition of the self in being. Being is cruel, after all, privileging survival and rewarding narcissism. Diachronic shame is the unsettling sense that there is something more original than the preservation of the ego, something more important than staying alive. Synchronic shame, on the other hand, moves dangerously into our lives and communities and participates full-tilt in the cruelty of being.

If we might follow and extend Levinas's insights on time and shame, a few practical suggestions are in order. Clinicians should, as current practice encourages, help clients identify and acknowledge shame. Clients will often need to dissect valid and invalid sources of shame, and monitor the impact of shame on their responses and behaviours. The danger remains, however, that a client be encouraged toward synchronizing her experiences with cultural and conventional understandings of her behaviour. This turns a client away from diachronic experience of shame and toward the synchronic experience. Attentiveness to diachronic shame may help avoid the perils of indifference and insensitivity to the other person. For Levinas, the turn toward synchrony is a turn away from the humanity of both the self and her neighbour. In particular, I suggest that clinicians encourage clients to unravel one version of shame from the other, treasuring and preserving diachronic shame and identifying and addressing synchronic versions.

Synchronic shame can be used as a weapon, such as when it was wielded against Hester Prynne and in countless historical and present-day instances. Shame as a psychological phenomenon can be crippling and deadly. The experience of shame is potentially the experience of diachrony, of the unsettling of the time of the self. Diachronic shame is indicative of the inability of any person to overcome and satisfy responsibility, which is far from a bad thing. To be unable to achieve 'goodness' or fulfil responsibility is also to be liberated from an egocentric trap. Diachrony positions the self as forever outside the time of the other; though I am never good enough for this election to responsibility, my own goodness is never the point. What lies beneath the dangerous manifestations of unmanaged shame?

For Levinas, the original 'shame' is the anarchic presence of the other person in the midst of the very constitution of the self. Though uncomfortable, this awareness is the hope of liberation from the endless repetition of self-interest. Shame, properly understood, does not point to the failure of the self to measure up to culture, to some ideal, to some potential. Rather, shame refers to the inability of a human being to be her own starting point, to be his own completion.

Hester Prynne is not punished: she is cursed. Yet, the curse of shame laid on her by the judgemental and hypocritical masses carries with it the echo of shame's older and more primitive roots. As Hester's young daughter Pearl grows, Hester is puzzled by the mysterious fascination that the little girl takes with the letter on her mother's chest. The letter, to Pearl, points not toward the synchrony of the town's judgement but toward the diachrony of her mother's independence and defiance in spite of their castigations. The letter continues to play a crucial role as the years pass, and drama mounts with the child's father (Arthur Dimmesdale), and Hester's husband (Roger Chillingworth). Ultimately, Pearl's father stands before the town, confesses his sin openly, and then immediately dies. As he does so, some bystanders think they see a stigma in the form of an A on his chest as well. Here the letter, along with the one that eventually marks the tombstone of both of Pearl's parents, means something quite different than the stitched emblem that was intended to bind Hester to her eternal punishment. The stigma that many saw on Dimmesdale's dying body was his liberation, his refusal to maintain the guise of innocence which had caused Hester and Pearl such suffering. His confession is perhaps the emergence of diachronic shame, the expression of a vulnerability to the suffering of others that demands responsibility over decorum and self-preservation.

Shame, properly understood, points to hope, for it harkens to a past prior to conflict and violence. There is also a sense in which shame points to a way of being human that is liberated from the 'project' of selfhood that produces so many of the negative manifestations of shame. The experience of shame is the opportunity to unravel the various manifestations of synchronic and diachronic shame, and the opportunity to see a new form of life on the other side of the shame that can be so psychologically crippling. Shame is both blessing and curse, for it reminds us that to be human is neither more nor less than being bound irrevocably to the other person.

References

Abbott, P., Faber, G., Pattinson, C., & Threlfall, D. (executive producers) (2004–13). *Shameless* [Television series]. United Kingdom: Company Pictures.

Critchley, S. (2015). *The Problems with Levinas*. A. Dianda (ed.). Oxford: Oxford University Press.

Descartes, R. (1998). *Discourse on Method and Meditations on First Philosophy*, 4th edn. D. Cress (trans.). Indianapolis, IN: Hackett.

Freud, S. (1961). *The Future of an Illusion, Civilization and its Discontents, and Other Works*. James Strachey (trans.). Vol. XXI (1927–31) of *The Standard Edition of the Complete Psychological Works of Sigmund Freud* (1–56). London: The Hogarth Press and the Institute of Psycho-analysis.

Gagnon, R. A. J. (2001). *The Bible and Homosexual Practice: Texts and Hermeneutics*. Nashville, TN: Abingdon.

Hawthorne, N. (1892). *The Scarlet Letter* [Google Play Edition]. H. P. Barnes (Ill.). Boston, MA: Samuel E. Cassino.

Hegel, G. W. F. (1902). *Philosophy of History*. J. Sibree (trans.). New York: American Home Library Company.

Kierkegaard, S. (1983). *The Sickness Unto Death*. H. Hong & E. Hong (trans.). Princeton, NJ: Princeton University Press.

Lamia, M. C. (2010, October 22). Do bullies really have low self-esteem? *Psychology Today*. Retrieved from www.psychologytoday.com/blog/intense-emotions-and-strong-feelings/201010/do-bullies-really-have-low-self-esteem.

Levinas, E. (1987). *Collected Philosophical Papers*. A. Lingis (trans.). Boston, MA: Martinus Nijhoff Publishers.

Levinas, E. (1991). *Totality and Infinity: An Essay on Exteriority*. Pittsburgh, PA: Duquesne University Press.

Levinas, E. (1998). *Otherwise than Being or Beyond Essence*. A. Lingis (trans.). Pittsburgh, PA: Duquesne.

Metcalf, R. (2006). Unrequited narcissism: On the origin of shame. *Studies in the History of Ethics*, 9/2006. Retrieved from www.historyofethics.org/092006/092006Metcalf.shtml.

Nietzsche, F. (2001). *Beyond Good and Evil*. Cambridge, MA: Cambridge University Press.

Plato (1991). *The Republic of Plato*, 2nd edn. Allan Bloom (trans.). New York: Basic Books.

Plato (2012). *Containing Charmides, Lysis, Laches, Protagoras, Euthydemus, Pratylus, Phaedrus, Ion, and Symposium*. Paul E. Boer Sr. (ed.), B. Jowett (trans.), Volume 1 of *The Dialogues of Plato in five volumes*. North Charleston, SC: CreateSpace Independent Publishing Platform.

Rashkow, I. (2004). Sexuality in the Hebrew Bible: Freud's lens. In *From Freud to Kohut*, Volume 1 of *Psychology and the Bible: A New Way to Read the Scriptures*. J. H. Ellens & W. G. Rollins (eds). Westport, CT: Praeger.

Wells, J., Pimental, N., Steam, A., Hissrich, M., Frankel, E., Callaghan, S., & Chulack, C. (executive producers) (2011–). *Shameless* [Television series]. Hollywood, CA: Warner Bros.

Chapter 4

Lacan

Nachträglichkeit, shame and ethical time

Sharon Green

Introduction

There is a basic dilemma to human temporality at the heart of the psycho-analytic endeavour: we make decisions and take actions throughout our lives without the possibility of knowing the results of these actions in advance. We can have good intentions as we anticipate a particular outcome, but with no certainty of that outcome. Additionally, events and circumstances come upon us unexpectedly, sometimes irrevocably shattering our most intimate sense of who we are and how we understand the world. With every failed attempt, unintended consequence, or bungled action, our lack of mastery and control is revealed to both ourselves and to others. When our defences fail, the veil that covers over our vulnerability and our finitude is stripped away. We feel mortified by the shame of our incompleteness, our ontological lack, making shame the constant companion of temporality.

We are so caught up in the flow of time that we rarely contemplate the full significance of our temporal conundrum, and yet how we understand the nature of temporality and shame underlies our assumptions about the goal and end of psychoanalytic treatment. How do we bear the shame that we are not masters of our own fate and yet take responsibility for our actions? Can we resist feeling persecuted and claim some small portion of freedom when we are acted upon by events that are outside of our control? In other words, how do we live as ethical subjects even though we are always already acted upon 'too soon' to understand, or 'too late' to undo the impact of what we have said or done? Imre Kertész (2004), who survived the fate of being sent to Auschwitz, insists, 'if there is such a thing as fate, then freedom is not possible . . . If on the other hand . . . there is such a thing as freedom, then there is no fate; that is to say . . . then we ourselves are fate' (p. 260).[1]

Although we often think of fate in terms of being its victim, 'fate' can also mean the will or *determining cause* by which things come to be as they are. Lacanian psychoanalysis assumes that 'we ourselves are fate' and that through a paradoxical twisting of time, we can become the 'cause' of our own lives. This is possible because of *Nachträglichkeit*,[2] a psychic dynamic in which memories are in constant temporal flux, with meaning always deferred into some indefinite future, with no final ground or presence. *Nachträglichkeit* interweaves past, present and future in a way that allows us to assume responsibility – not only for present and future actions, but also for *past* actions, whether consciously or unconsciously intended. Accepting responsibility – even for those acts we do not intend consciously – is in direct contrast with conventional psychoanalytic goals of 'insight' or 'understanding', which can become defensive ways of refusing responsibility for one's life (Harari, 2002). For Lacan, at the logical end of psychoanalysis, we will have come to accept responsibility for those unconscious processes that have exerted an influence over our lives.

Although Lacan is credited with re-introducing the Freudian concept of *Nachträglichkeit* to the psychoanalytic field, Forrester (1991) and Johnston (2005) both make the claim that he never sufficiently elaborated a theory of time. However, even without an overarching 'theory' of time, temporality resonates throughout Lacan's work, but most explicitly in his reworking of Freud's *Nachträglichkeit*. By the 1950s, Lacan felt that many psychoanalysts had misunderstood Freud's most important ideas about the nature of time and the unconscious. In his break from the traditional psychoanalytic establishment, Lacan rejected the notion that the human subject is primarily a biological being living in the 'natural' time of a linear chronology from birth to old age and death. He also rejected the teleological view that the libidinal being is instinctually driven through genetic stages of psychic development towards a fixed and predetermined goal (Vergote, 1983). For Lacan (2006), the human subject is a 'lack of being' that emerges from the abyss, the groundless void of unconsciousness, as an ephemeral effect of speech in the field of the language and rituals of the big Other.[3] Each so-called 'instinctual stage' is a subjective organization 'grounded in intersubjectivity', i.e., always already constituted by and with the Other (p. 217).[4] Rather than instinctual or developmental 'stages', we are marked by experiences that are purely historical and can only be recalled – and re-translated – through speech:

> What we teach the subject to recognize as his unconscious is his history – in other words, we help him complete the current histori-cization of the facts that have already determined a certain number of the historical 'turning points' in his existence ... Thus every fixation at a supposedly instinctual stage is above all a historical stigma: a page of shame that one forgets or undoes, or a page of glory that obliges.
>
> (Lacan, 2006, p. 217)

For Lacan, temporality is thus intimately related to the repressed and unconscious aspects of our singular history, to the structures of language, and to our lifelong struggle to make meaning from non-meaning, sense from non-sense. One of the goals of Lacanian psychoanalysis is to arrive at the disturbing realization that there is no 'final meaning' to our speech, our memories or our lives, because there is no final authority – be it God or Ultimate Truth or Science – that anchors meaning (Ruti, 2012; Vergote, 1983). Rather, *Nachträglichkeit* reflects time as a vehicle for a perpetual process of transformation wherein we 'come to be who we will have been'. In order for these processes of transformation to occur, we must be able to bear the shame of our constitutional lack – the void of non-meaning around which we are constituted – otherwise we risk becoming frozen in sterile repetitions or we disavow our shame and act immodestly without regard for the impact we have on others. Assuming responsibility for our hidden desires, our unintended actions and most importantly for our own inevitable unconsciousness – while bearing the shame of our constitu-tional lack – are the intertwined dimensions of what I am calling 'ethical time', the time that resonates throughout Lacan's work.

In order to more closely consider these two dimensions of time, this chapter will explore several key Lacanian ideas that link temporality and shame to our capacity to become ethical subjects: trauma and the temporality of *Nachträglichkeit*; time, the other and the act; fate as 'cause'; and subjective destitution. Then, I will consider how the com-panion of time – the affect of shame – can serve as an ethical guide for the historically situated subject.

Trauma and Freud's *Nachträglichkeit*

In his theoretical writings and letters, Freud frequently used the common German terms '*nachträglich*' (afterwards, belatedly) and the substantival form '*Nachträglichkeit*' to refer to his view of psychical temporality (Laplanche & Pontalis, 1974, p. 112). As early as 1896, Freud wrote to Fliess that 'I am working on the assumption that our psychical mechanism has come into being by a process of stratification: the material present in the form of memory-traces being subjected from time to time to a *re-arrangement* in accordance with fresh circumstances – to a *re-transcription*' (Masson, 1985, p. 207). Although this early formulation of temporality seems to apply to the generality of human experience, Freud was specifically concerned with the delayed effect of childhood trauma that appeared in the field of human sexuality due to the delayed onset of puberty (Boothby, 2001, p. 242).[5]

Because the sexual experience arrives 'too early' for understanding in the life of the child, it becomes repressed as a memory trace, since it cannot be psychically represented. When a later event, which is associatively linked to the first, occurs after sexual maturation, the memory of the second event, when recalled even later in time, can activate the first event – not as a *perception* since the experience is over – but now, through a retroactive interpretation – as a *memory*. This unassimilated memory bypasses the attention of the ego and its defences, because the mechanism of the ego is to defend against *perceptions*. The deferred activation of the memory results in a release of 'unpleasure' and the development of a symptom. The unassimilated memory trace is the 'hidden cause' of the second event, which retroactively triggers the effects of the first.

This deception of the ego, which Freud calls the *proton pseudos* ('original lie') is possible because the prematurity of the original experience prepares the way for a release of sexual feeling after puberty that could not have been experienced prior to sexual development. Since all adults have passed through the two phases of sexuality (pre-puberty and puberty), every adult is subject to the effects of traumatic *Nachträglichkeit* (Boothby, 2001, p. 203). Thus, 'trauma' only becomes constituted *as a trauma* later in time when the child has achieved the sexual maturity to understand and thus 'experience' the impact of the memory of the first event. Significance (meaning) can now be conferred upon the earlier event retroactively after the recall of the later event. This process of retroactively ascribing meaning to the memory of an event constitutes much of the work of psychoanalysis.

Temporality, the subject and Lacan's *Nachträglichkeit*

In his famous 1952 *Écrits*, 'The function and field of speech and language in psychoanalysis' (often referred to as the 'Rome Discourse'), Lacan (2006) introduced his rediscovery of the phenomenon of Freudian *Nachträglichkeit* and radically revised it, though retaining the same term. Freud realized that his patients came to him not only with symptoms and memories, but also with hopes, plans and expectations. However, Freud did not theorize 'the future' in his accounts of psychic temporality, because he was reluctant to grant causal authority to future possibilities (Bowie, 1991). It was Lacan who added the Heideggerian emphasis on the *future* and the distinctly human capacity for *anticipation* to the concept of *Nachträglichkeit* (Casey & Woody, 2003).

For Heidegger (1962) – and so for Lacan – the human being does not exist *in* time but exists *as* temporality (Casey & Woody, 2003). Temporality is not an entity, a sequence of self-contained 'nows' moving from future to present to past in linear succession, but is a self-generating and self-transcending process. It is the distinctively human capacity to be at once ahead, behind and alongside oneself (Mulhall, 1996, p. 146). Past, present and future reflect the three dimensions of 'lived time' that relate to each other in a circular movement. Heidegger calls these dimensions the 'three ec-stasies'[6] to emphasize the specific ways in which we stand 'outside of ourselves' as *Dasein*, i.e., as temporal human beings.[7] By being able to distance 'myself from myself' in time – via memories of the past or anticipation of the future – we are freed from a merely biological life of immediacy dominated by continuous bodily need and gratification. In other words, for both Heidegger and Lacan, we are radically alienated (i.e., other than ourselves) in time, allowing us to be different from our present selves by standing outside of ourselves while looking backwards and forwards. This means we can live our lives informed by the context of our unique history while looking towards an undetermined future (Casey & Woody, 2003).

Because we know that we will die, Heidegger says that death *precedes* us, making *Dasein* the originary phenomenon of the future

(Heidegger, 1962). Although 'death' is the limit to human temporality, for *Dasein*, death is not the biological event that marks our demise. For *Dasein*, 'death' is 'being-*for*-the-end' not 'being-*at*-an-end' (Stiegler, 1998). *Dasein* is always *becoming* its 'not yet' – never arriving at a final destination. Being 'futural' means that human life always remains agitated and unsettled, which is reflected in the everyday way we say that the deceased is *finally* 'at peace' or 'at rest'. For Lacan, we never arrive at a final destination, or fixed identity, because we are lacking and our lack sets up the movement of infinite desiring. As he writes:

> The function of desire must remain in a fundamental relationship to death … Shouldn't the true termination of an analysis … confront the one who undergoes it with the reality of the human condition … namely, *Hilflosigkeit*, or distress, the state in which man is in that relationship to himself which is his own death … and can expect help from no one.
>
> (Lacan, 1986, pp. 303–4)

So, paradoxically, the finite human is constituted as a subject-in-process through our relationship to infinite desiring.

The lacking subject is always in relation to *future* possibilities, which 'means that the subject is what it is not yet, in order not to be what it is' (Hyldgaard, 2003, p. 231). Lacan sometimes calls the subject of the unconscious a *manque-à-être,* which means a lack-of-being, or a lack-towards-(a-future)-being (p. 231). Although Lacan formulates different kinds of 'lack' throughout his teaching, this lack-of-being is not lack of some thing or the other. Rather, 'lack-of-being' means we can never satisfy our unconscious desiring, nor achieve our fantasy of originary wholeness, nor gain a sense of completion through relationship with another person. The fantasy of originary wholeness is denied to us due to awareness of our mortality. Shame is the experience of our ontological limitations – our lack-of-being, our finitude (De Kesel, 2009; Stiegler, 1998). This (pre)-ontological lack is a primordial facticity of being human and why 'shame is the definition of being human' (Hyldgaard, 2003, p. 238).

For Lacan, *Nachträglichkeit* as a perpetual process of becoming is constitutive of both speech *and* the human subject. In the 'Rome Discourse', Lacan (2006) presented his original thesis that the proper field of psychoanalytic study is the *speaking* being (a *parlêtre*) that is thrown into an always-already existing system of language (the big Other). He recognized that our ability to create meaning in speech is based on the phenomenon of *Nachträglichkeit*. Following the linguist Saussure, Lacan realized that there is no direct relationship between a word (signifier) and the concept that the words represent (the signified).[8] Language and speech are predicated on the *difference* (or gaps) between signifiers rather than on some foundational ground of pre-existing meaning. In speech, the first words of a sentence are already anticipating the last words, but the meaning of the sentence only comes into being *retroactively* once the last words have been spoken. This sets in motion a process where meaning is in constant flux and always deferred into some indefinite future. Because of this uncanny temporality, in human discourse there is always an element of uncertainty, generating anxiety, as speech always eludes our conscious control and desire for mastery.

For Lacan (1998) the 'subject' of the unconscious is that which fleetingly appears and then disappears in a temporal pulsation from the gaps in the unconscious signifying chains of speech.[9] The 'subject of the unconscious' is not a reified agency – 'the subject' is a non-substantial temporal pulsation, always becoming, that is 'subjected' to the signifiers of the Other.[10] Nor is 'the unconscious' a substantial place or thing; rather it is an always failing *process* that Lacan describes as the 'non-realised', the 'unborn', 'limbo' (Verhaeghe, 1998, p. 170). The unconscious 'is' a void, a pre-ontological abyss with no background of totality or unity – it is a concept pointing to our ontological lack. As soon as the subject emerges from these signifying chains and uses the language of the Other to declare, 'I am *that*' – then through the dynamic of *Nachträglichkeit* – the ephemeral 'subject' has always already disappeared and retroactively become an object ['that']. Having been subjected to the signifiers of the Other and petrified into an object, the non-substantial subject fades back into the chain of signifiers leaving the object in its place. Lacan describes the subject of the unconscious as an *aphanisis* (a fading away) because as soon as it emerges at this 'impossible point' (between pulsation and object) it disappears under the signifier it has assumed. Just as the slip of the tongue, a bungled action or a symptom are the leftover 'evidence' of unconscious processes the subject is also a 'symptom' of unconscious processes and the dynamic of *Nachträglichkeit*.

The subject of the unconscious is a desiring '*want-to-be*' constituted around a lack, a void of *non-meaning*. No matter how many words we subject ourselves to, no matter how many qualities or traits we use to try and define our identity, we can never pin down our most singular self. It is this constitutional lack, the subject as a '*want-to-be*' that sets off the movement of infinite desire that fuels the fantasies that allow us to cover over the void at the centre of our being with an endless series of objects that sustain the illusion of wholeness – 'Everything will be fine once I finish my education . . . get a new job . . . find the right spouse.'[11] As soon as we put something into language, there is always an excess – something 'more' that could not be reduced to the words that are used. This 'something' is the hidden desire for love and recognition silently operating beneath all of our words and efforts to communicate. Our most basic unconscious fantasies are the scenes in which we imagine ourselves to be what we think the Other wants of us in order to gain their love and recognition. When we seek to be the answer to the Other's desire, we fade as subjects and are objectified. Like the living being turned to stone by Medusa, under the gaze of the Other, the subject is mortified. This is the ontological shame of being human and this shame, our finitude and lack, is a dimension of the subject's perpetual process of desiring and becoming. The subject 'is' only as negativity. Lacan, who was influenced by Sartre, recognized that our lack of determinable essence *is* our freedom (Hyldgaard, 2003). We are always 'becoming' and have no substantial essence – like the infinitely deferred meaning in a sentence, the 'meaning' of who we are is also in constant flux and infinitely deferred.

Because we are born into an already existing language, an experience takes on a certain meaning as soon as it occurs. However, certain aspects of the experience are censored, because there is always an *excess* in an experience that escapes the net of language (the 'Real'). Meaning is not fixed or static because when this earlier event is reproduced after the fact in present events, the earlier event undergoes a new historicization. Thus, events are continually transformed through their exchange of meaning. This kind of history is not centred, but discontinuous and reversible. The new experience of the event will depend on whatever meaning is presently active, filtering the effects of the actual experience as it is now occurring (Vergote, 1983). Lacan explains the temporal movement of this transformation of our history via *Nachträglichkeit* through the grammatical future perfect (also called the future anterior) tense:

What is realized in my history is neither the past definite of what was, since it is no more, nor even the perfect as what has been in what I am, but the future anterior of what *I will have been* given what I am in the process of becoming.

(2006, p. 247)

Lacan is describing the conjunction of an absolute past '*what has been*' with a present '*now*' moment that is about to spill into the future of '*what will be*' in a way that creates the future perfect of '*what will have been*'. This future perfect temporality allows the subject to recognize their history from the point of view of their present potentialities but only by virtue of taking into account the possibilities of an undefined future, which allows for the rewriting of who we have been (Hook, 2013, p. 71). Although this may sound like verbal tongue twisting, as we will explore below, Lacan's valorization of the future perfect tense of *Nachträglichkeit* is the key to our freedom and responsibility. The grammar reflects how we can 'become the cause' of our own fate.

Time, the Other and the act

The work of Hegel complicates Lacan's understanding of temporality by bringing into account desire and the Other. Hegel insists that when we fail to recognize our own history and see ourselves as a purely autonomous ego, free of the customs and culture of our world, we are estranged from ourselves (Casey & Woody, 2003, p. 195). Although we are free agents, we cannot know what we are until we act, because we constitute ourselves by acting upon and changing our world in a dialectic tension between self and others (p. 201). It is desire that moves us away from mere contemplation of the world into disquietude and action (p. 196). For Lacan, however, desire is always the desire *of* the Other and *for* the Other. It is the desire *of* the Other because the Other is the field of language and we must use the Other's signifiers. It is desire *for* the Other because beyond mere communication, what we most desire through speech is recognition from the Other.

In an early (1945) essay entitled 'Logical Time and the Assertion of Anticipated Certainty: A New Sophism', Lacan (2006), borrowing from (but revising) Hegel, demonstrates that temporality has an intersubjective dimension that structures our thinking and our actions (p. 237).[12] Lacan (2006) presents and analyses a problem requiring a new kind of logical solution – a solution that involves a temporal structure that includes movements, hesitations and interruptions that unfold over time, rather than the spatial structure of classical logic where the facts needed for the solution are static and are given 'all at once' (p. 166). Here is the problem: a prison warden, for unknown reasons, decides to free one of three prisoners and devises a test to determine which prisoner will be freed. He shows the prisoners five discs, three white and two black. He explains that a disc will be fastened on to the back of each prisoner such that the prisoner cannot see his own disc. Without speaking or communicating in any way to the others, the first prisoner who can formulate the colour of his disc as well as offer a logical explanation as to how he came to his conclusion will be freed (p. 162). In other words, the conclusion cannot be a good guess or based on probability.

The tripartite structure of the sophism's 'logical time' consists of 'the instant of the glance', 'the time for comprehending' and the 'moment of concluding' (Lacan, 2006). Lacan identifies the prisoners as Prisoner A, B and C. In the 'instant of the glance', each prisoner perceives the givens of the situation, i.e., the disc on the back of the two others, but not their own. In this time, the prisoners hope that the solution will be instantly revealed through passive perception of the other's discs (Stark, 2013, p. 1161). However, at this state of the deduction, there is not sufficient information to make a move to head for the door. Based on simple observation, each prisoner sees two whites and cannot know if they themselves are white or black based on this data. Additionally, there is no way to interpret the lack of movement towards the door; i.e., their immobility has not yet been (retroactively) given the meaning of a 'hesitation' (as they anticipate future moves). This mode of passive apprehension is the impersonal 'one sees' – there is no intersubjective dialectic.

The 'time for comprehending' follows and lasts as long as it takes for each prisoner to develop his line of reasoning regarding his disc's colour based on the prison warden's 'rules of the game' and what each prisoner can see of the others. In this time, each prisoner must put himself in the other's place to imagine their line of reasoning – which he can only do if he assumes, in an act of imaginary identification, that the other is *like* himself. In other words, during the time of comprehending, each prisoner must shift their focus from passive perception to realizing that the meaning of what they are apprehending must come from their own interpretation of the situation; each must form a hypothesis based on how they imagine they appear to the other. Since neither B nor C leave immediately, Prisoner A forms the hypothesis that he is white and not black, because he puts himself into the shoes of B and C and imagines that they are both thinking, 'If I too were black, the other would have necessarily realized straight away that he was white and would have left immediately . . . As they did nothing of the kind, I must be a white like them' (Lacan, 2006, p. 162). Lacan explains that during the time for comprehending, each prisoner begins to head for the door, and then hesitates two times (from indecision) before making his final move towards the door.[13]

The 'moment of concluding' is most significant, in that each prisoner's line of reasoning depends upon the double 'hesitations' (representing the doubts that stop them just as they begin to act) of the other two prisoners. As they contemplate their dilemma, the prisoners read the moments of waiting and hesitations as meaningful temporal 'signs' that they interpret as different possibilities regarding how the others are hypothesizing about their disc. Since all three prisoners are assuming that the others think like himself, each suddenly panics, realizing that the other two will have reached the same conclusion as he has. Lacan (2006) describes the 'moment of concluding' as that moment when – in his anguish – each prisoner *hastens* to act *before* the others *for the sake of* ensuring his freedom.

Although each prisoner cannot be certain that his reasoning is correct until he has rushed headlong to the door before the others, each must jump to a conclusion and act, closing the time for comprehending. Once they have declared the line of reasoning to the warden and been proven correct, Lacan (2006) asserts that the moment of concluding gives *retroactive* meaning to the earlier moments of comprehending, i.e., their line of reasoning. Although the prisoners are sure that it is *necessary* to act, they cannot be sure of the soundness of their thinking because there is not enough information to draw a certain conclusion. In Lacan's analysis, the haste – as part of the action – concludes the prisoner's line of reasoning in an act of *anticipatory certitude*. Lacan says that haste is 'the relation to time peculiar to the human being, this relation to the chariot of time, which is there, at our backs' (Lacan, 1991, p. 291). Though not using the term *Nachträglichkeit*, Lacan demonstrates that death, 'the chariot of time', pushes us towards the future in a way that retroactively confers meaning to past actions while we bear the doubts and uncertainties of the present moment.

A 'sophism' was originally a method of teaching and did not have the current meaning of a fallacious argument. Lacan's solution to the prisoner's dilemma is only a fallacious 'sophism' from the point of view of classical logic, which is static, timeless and spatial.[14] With classical logic, in the 'instant of the glance' if Prisoner A were to see two black disks on the back of the others, then Prisoner A could conclude with certainty that he is white. In this sort of instantaneous timeless logic, all other solutions would be impossible. However, as Lacan (2006) points out, the sophism 'maintains all the constraining rigor of a logical process, on condition that one integrates therein the value of the two *suspensive scansions*' (p. 165, original emphasis). In other words, when the solution takes into account the prisoners' inevitable *doubts*, which are revealed over time through the observable suspended movements that are *interpreted* as signs of 'hesitations', then the solution demonstrates a form of logical process based upon temporality as structured through our interactions with others (p. 165).

Through his 'sophism', Lacan (2006) is philosophizing about how the intersubjective aspect of time structures our actions; i.e., the ways in which we are always identifying with other people and imagining what they are thinking in order to decide what we want to do and how and when we want to do it (Verhaeghe, 2013). Lacan's (2006) analysis of the 'perfect solution' to the problem requires the integration of the time it takes for the prisoner's reasoning to make itself known and the 'temporal tension' experienced between the three prisoners (pp. 165–73). Lacan says 'temporal tension' is generated between people when the ego identifies with its alter-egos (little others)[15] and ascribes *meaning* to the others' actions (or inactions) based on their hesitation or urgency. Because there is no way to interpret the Other's intentions or actions with certainty, time-with-others is characterized by discontinuities and disruptions that generate a range of reactions including competitiveness, paranoia and aggression. Lacan locates these reactions in the 'Imaginary order' because they are linked to the ways we mistakenly base our identity on our (mis)identifications with the Other, imagining – like the prisoners in the sophism – that everyone is 'the same'. Our need for the admiring recognition of the Other is often the 'true' intention behind our speech and actions, and so we may wait interminably imagining we can figure out 'what does the Other want of me?' But this can generate fear that someone has *more* of the Other's love or enjoyment setting off our aggressive or paranoid reactions and triggering us to make hasty, impulsive decisions. It is not irrelevant that this sophism involves prisoners anxious to secure their freedom where the 'rules of the prison warden's game' allow only *one* of them to escape.

The critical idea of the sophism that I would like to stress rests in the *act* that puts an end to 'the time for comprehending', which has been punctuated by hesitations and interruptions and *retroactively* determines the 'truth' or 'error' of the prisoner's line of reasoning. The act pushes the subject into the uncertainty of future possibilities while at the same time conferring 'meaning' to events that have already happened, in the movement of *Nachträglichkeit*. For Lacan, an act is not defined by 'action' or 'locomotion' but an act is *signifying* (i.e., meaning-making) and includes speech acts ('I am white!'). In his later work, Lacan develops his notion of the 'act' as the use of signifiers in a way that changes the very structure of the subject and redefines the very coordinates of what the subject cannot do and what the subject *must* do (Žižek, 2007, p. 49).[16] In the 1960s, Lacan spoke about analysis ending in an act, because the subject who 'acts' (unlike the subject in relationship to 'fantasy') is no longer looking to the big Other for recognition or as the guarantor of truth (Pluth, 2007, p. 64). In contrast to mere animal 'behaviour' that is not free, the Lacanian act involves a subject who assumes responsibility for being the 'cause' of his or her own life. In other words, we no longer live from the position of trying to be the answer to the question *'What does the Other want of me?'* This grants us a small degree of freedom.

Doubt is an inherent condition of the situation the prisoners find themselves in, both because of the hesitations of the other prisoners and due to their own uncertainty (Stark, 2012, p. 1162). If the prisoner hesitates too long, he will no longer be able to determine whether he is black or not, and so the time of comprehending would lose its meaning if he does not act and *precipitate* the conclusion – 'temporal tension is reversed in a move to action manifesting to the others that the subject has concluded' (Lacan, 2006, p. 169). In order to break out of the prison of the big Other's hegemonic rules, we must act *without guarantee* if we wish to freely participate in life. Only retroactively, will the (future, anticipated) outcome, precipitated in an act, become the 'cause' of the earlier events. When we realize that the 'meaning' of our acts will be infinitely deferred through the process of *Nachträglichkeit*, we must face our existential limitations and our shame. Thus, an act requires modesty – for although the outcome of the act emerges *from* a line of reasoning, we lack foresight and can never guarantee whether the outcome of the act will match our intentions (Pluth & Hoens, 2004). Modesty serves as the veil that can cover the shame of our limitations.[17]

Fate as cause: *tuché* and *automaton*

So far, I have been claiming that via the dynamics of *Nachträglichkeit* we can become the 'cause' of our own lives and take responsibility for our fate. This is possible because Lacan calls into question the concepts of 'cause' and 'effect' when applied to the subject of psychoanalysis – i.e., the subject who recognizes that it is an ongoing ethical endeavour to decipher the symptoms of the unconscious – an unconscious that is constituted through our relationship to the Other.[18]

In our everyday understanding of 'cause' and 'effect', we assume that there is a fixed and stable relationship where cause precedes the effect. When the same cause predictably produces the same effect, a continuous chain is set up where you cannot locate the cause of the cause of the cause (Miller, 2013). This becomes a chain of necessity – i.e., determinism. However, as discussed above, Lacanian time is not deterministic. Rather, Lacan is interested in how we make sense of the contingent and accidental nature of our lives. In order to demonstrate a new way of positing the 'causality' of the non-determined subject, he borrowed (and revised) two concepts from Aristotle related to chance happenings in nature and chance happenings that we consider lucky or unlucky: *automaton and tuché* (Harris, 2017, p. 116).[19]

Automaton refers to the insistent movement of the signifying chain. The structure of the unconscious (which Lacan describes as 'structured like language') follows certain logical rules (similar to the way language is ordered by grammatical rules) and once these rules are set into motion, the structure itself 'remembers' chains of signifiers without the necessity for an intentional subject. Due to the possibility of the infinite repetition of a sequence of signifiers, *automatons* belong to the deterministic, mechanical model of existence (Harris, 2017; Hyldgaard, 2003; Miller, 2013; Verhaeghe, 1998). *Automatons* are chains of signifiers fixated or 'frozen' in a temporal loop where we endlessly repeat sterile or worn-out stories about who we are or what we want (De Kesel, 2009; Scarfone, 2006). The repetition of the *automaton* stops the process of becoming and constrains our existential choices to 'the same'. Fortunately, we are not condemned to an eternal return of the same, because *automatons* are interrupted by *tuché* – Aristotle's term for 'fate' or 'chance' – which Lacan (1998) reformulated as the non-determined cause or an 'encounter with the Real' (Hyldgaard, 2003; Miller, 2013; Verhaeghe, 1998).

The Lacanian 'Real' is not a substance and is not to be confused with socially constructed 'reality'. The Real is the unpredictable *excess* that escapes the signifying process – i.e., that which *cannot* be formulated in speech or represented in the language. Because the Real cannot be represented, it is experienced as trauma. Encounters with the Real include contingent events, accidents or bad luck – *dystuchia* – that erupt into our lives. When there is an 'encounter with the Real', the *automaton* – the automatic repetition of signifiers – is 'cut' by the Real. The laws of repetition and predictability fail. So in this sense, causality would be the unexpected, the surprise, the accident that is not inscribed in the signifiers of the *automaton*. For Lacan, the subject of the unconscious is involved in the very structure of causality because it is the 'lack-of-being' that disrupts the signifying chains of the big Other. *Tuché* (i.e., the Real) becomes the 'cause' of the subject of the unconscious, which emerges in the *gaps* of the signifying chain as a *disruption*. The 'subject of the unconscious' though represented by a signifier (I am white – that's me!) is *of* the Real, *a negativity* that only 'exists' as a temporal pulsation. The Real thus saves us from determinism because 'the Real' is the void that *precedes* all notions of causality (Shepherdson, 2008).

Lacan explains that the machine-like movements of the *automaton* endlessly return us to a primal traumatic event – an encounter with the Real as *tuché* that could not be assimilated into the chain of signifiers (i.e., the eruption of *tuché* could not be given meaning). However, as both Freud and Lacan demonstrate, it takes *two moments* to generate trauma. Through the temporality of *Nachträglichkeit*, there is always an (apparently) *a priori* choice of interpretation of the unexpected *tuché*:

> It is not so much that the Real imposes itself from an outside, as form on matter, but rather that the very arrival of the Real as cause is always-already prepared for by the Symbolic context upon which it impacts … it is only through the deferred action of triggering by a signifier that a prior repressed trauma might interrupt the mental life of a subject … it is only in retrospect that the encounter with the Real can be posited as an origin.
>
> (Eyers, 2012, pp. 80–1)

When there is an 'encounter with the Real' and *tuché* cuts the *automaton*, then the Real as the inassimilable *excess of the signifier* that escapes all attempts at understanding, retroactively becomes the Real as the '*absent cause*' of the subject, through the dynamic of *Nachträglichkeit* where an 'effect' precedes the 'cause'.

Tuché or the Real as non-determined 'cause' of the subject is the fateful configuration of our parents' desire, the senseless accident of our birth. The loss of eternal life, which is installed at the very instant we are conceived, is our originary trauma; it is the radical void at the centre of our being.[20] There are no answers to the questions of our birth and death, and so for Lacan, the 'fundamental fantasy' is our singular 'mythic' answer to these impossible questions. The most fundamental question we ask about our origin is '*what does the Other want of me?*' We try to become what we believe the Other wants of us; the 'fundamental fantasy' is how we position ourselves unconsciously as an answer to the desire of the Other. This *Urphantasie* lays the ground for how we interpret our encounters with the Real; it is our unconscious choice of interpretation of what is meaningless and accidental and becomes the filter through which the world is perceived (Hyldgaard, 2003, p. 240). Each time *tuché* disrupts our lives, our finitude is revealed and we feel the shame of our helplessness and vulnerability. However, by cutting into time-as-repetition, *tuché* – as the shame-inducing contingent or accidental event – disrupts our interpretations, allowing the process of *Nachträglichkeit* to free us by unsettling our past and opening our future.

Subjectivization and subjective destitution

Despite the unknowable mystery of our origins, we generate myths and stories in order to make life meaningful so that we can bear the difficulties of existence. We make a 'choice' (although not a conscious intentional choice) of interpretation regarding the original trauma of our existence. However, through the work of psychoanalysis – which is accomplished in 'ethical time' – we can change our stance towards the Real of trauma by assuming responsibility for our lives and seeing that 'we ourselves are fate' (Kertész, 2004, p. 260). As Lacan says, 'one is always responsible for one's position as subject' (Fink, 1995, p. 47).

This ethical stance is reflected in Freud's famous quote '*Wo es war, soll Ich wolden*', which literally translates to 'where *it* was, *I* shall be'. In his essay, 'The Freudian Thing', Lacan (2006) says that he wants the phrase to be understood as 'There where it was, it is my *duty* that I come into being' (p. 348, my emphasis). Lacan is stressing the ethical imperative that we take responsibility for our unconsciousness (the 'it') by becoming the cause of the subject (the 'I').[21] The future-perfect tense of *Nachträglichkeit* is implicit in this formulation: where 'it' has happened 'to' me, or where 'it' once ruled over me, once I have done the work of assuming responsibility for 'it', then I will have been the cause of my own life, even as I anticipate my duty towards the future (Fink, 1995; Harris, 2017; Neill, 2014). This does not mean, however, that becoming the cause of one's own life can ever be a final achievement:

> The ethical invocation of *Wo Es war, soll Ich werden* is not something that can be responded to once and for all in an attainment of subjective security. Rather it is momentary and perpetual. It is momentary insofar as it manifests in conscious thought only fleetingly. It is perpetual insofar as it is indicative of the unconscious processes which necessarily continue unobserved.
>
> (Neill, 2014, p. 20)[22]

Wo es war, soll Ich wolden can also be read from the point of view of two processes: 'subjectivization' and 'subjective destitution'. Subjectivization is the process of the ongoing subordination of the subject to a signifier – i.e., it is the ongoing process of narrating stories about ourselves and assigning attributes to ourselves. For example, at the moment Prisoner A in Lacan's 'Logical Time' essay concludes that he must be 'white', he moves from imaginary identification with his alter-ego to assuming his Symbolic identity when he declares, 'I am white – that's me!' The act of assuming a signifier precipitates subjectivity covering over the void of our radical lack and retroactively gives meaning to our earlier actions (Žižek, 1996, p. 135). In assuming a *symbolic* identity ('I am *that*'), the subject becomes an object and fades back into the chain of signifiers. Subjectivization is not a static moment but rather the process of perpetually subjecting ourselves to the signifiers of the Other. The subject-turned-object is mortified – murdered by the signifiers of the Other. For example, we feel humiliated, shamed or angry when someone labels us with attributes or tells us what we are 'really' like. In this case, the signifiers are coming from another person, and yet this is what we continuously do to ourselves when we unconsciously identify with the stories and messages that we have taken in from Others throughout our lives.

Žižek (1996) critiques the process of subjectivization saying it is 'a tragic/heroic gesture of *amor fati*' where the subject internalizes their fate and lives it 'to the bitter end' (p. 94). With subjectivization, the psychoanalytic subject fully assumes the guilt and responsibility for the meaningless and contingent events of their life by retroactively assigning meaning to them (Fink, 1995; Žižek, 1996). This reading of subjectivization coincides with the belief that there is a 'deeper meaning' we can find for contingent and accidental events.[23] *Tuché* – encounters with the Real – is seamlessly integrated into the subject's life narrative by making sense of the senseless. The risk of this involves creating an overly coherent narrative that generates a feeling of harmonious wholeness. This is problematic, because what is dissociated from the narrative in order to maintain an illusion of coherence inevitably makes its reappearance as 'a return of the repressed'. For example, in the Nazi narrative of a utopian future, 'the Jew' represented the imaginary obstacle to this vision and therefore had to be eliminated.

However, there is another more radical reading of *Wo es war, soll Ich werden.* Lacan posits that at the logical end of an analysis 'subjectivization' gives way to 'subjective destitution'. Subjective destitution involves the awareness that there is no 'Other behind the big Other'. When the big Other (as language, as authority, as culture) is revealed as lacking, the subject realizes that there is no *a priori* 'deeper meaning' to search for in the unexpected or accidental events that have shaped our life's trajectory. Encounters with the Real are recognized as entirely contingent and impersonal. *Tuché* is the unexpected 'it' that disrupts the signifying chain and our pre-existing interpretation of the world. It sets in motion the work of retranslating our understanding of self and world with no predetermined endpoint or goal, where a final meaning is indefinitely deferred (Laplanche, 1999). Lacan (1991) said, 'the game is already played, the die already cast. It is already cast, with the following proviso, that we can pick it up again, and throw it anew' (p. 219). Through *Nachträglichkeit,* we can remain subjects-in-process rather than staying stuck in the grinding machinations of our *automatons.* Where 'it' was, the ethical subject will have come to be.

With the realization that there is no foundational support to the Other, our state of destitution and our utter vulnerability are exposed. We experience a profound sense of shame when we realize that those persons we have looked up to and relied on are also finite and lacking (Copjec, 2004). There is no authority or institution or ideology that has 'the' answer to the problems of existence – all are as vulnerable and inconsistent as the subjects who look up to them. Despair is often the reaction to this realization that the Other is lacking, that there is *not* a subject-who-knows. However, despair implies that we are still assuming that there is something – a promise of happiness or wholeness – that we can find. For Lacan, despair is a 'sin' because it allows us to avoid working with our unconscious (Soler, 2015). Rather than despair, we must bear the shame of our limitations. Given that both the subject and the Other are lacking, what can guide us in our process of perpetual becoming? Shame.

Shame

At the end of Seminar XVII, Lacan (2007) tells his students, whom he is trying to shame, the story of Vatel, a servant in a noble house whose job was to prepare a magnificent feast for his master. Due to circumstances beyond his control, the necessary items for the feast did not arrive on time, and the event was a disaster. Vatel chose to literally 'die of shame' – he took his own life by falling on to his sword – because of his sense of honour. Lacan (2006) writes, 'Man's freedom is entirely circumscribed within . . . the sacrifice of his life that he agrees to for the reasons that give human life its measure' (p. 263). The 'reasons that give human life its measure' are the values we hold that make life worth living. Lacan was trying to shame his students because he sensed that we have entered an epoch where there are no longer any shared values that matter more than mere survival. When the meaning of death changes, life changes (Miller, 2006, p. 18). Life without honour is reduced to survival without meaning – *primum vivere*. Vatel's sense of honour mattered to him more than his mere life.

Mortifying shame is the affect evoked by the gaze that objectifies us. It is the gaze of the Other that unveils our ontological lack of being. But we cannot escape this shaming gaze, because the subject is 'extimate' – always already constituted by our relationship to the Other (Žižek, 1996). '*Extimité*' is a neologism Lacan created to express how the subject's most intimate 'interior' is the alien 'exterior' that resides inside like a foreign body (Miller, 1994). In other words, our unconscious is 'the discourse of the Other'. In order to emphasize the way in which shame is a primordial facticity of the temporal subject-as-lack, Lacan stated that the correct spelling for 'ontology' would combine shame and ontology into 'shontology' (Soler, 2015, p. 91).[24]

In his classic work *Shame and Necessity*, the philosopher Bernard Williams (2008) says that shame is the mortifying affect that alerts us that we are not who we imagine ourselves to be in a world in which we could actually imagine living. This definition of shame closely corresponds to the Lacanian concept of fantasy. Fantasy is the imaginary scenario where we position ourselves in relationship to an Other who matters to us in order to become the object of their desire. If there is shame, then there is still an Other whose gaze matters and whose recognition we desire. This gives a mooring to shame because there are then shared values we hold that demand more of us than mere life. This big Other is the one that mediates the social bonds formed by a culture's shared mores and values. In this sense, shame is historicized (Soler, 2015).

As discussed above, when we act, the situation in which we must act is always opaque and we cannot guarantee the outcome of our acts. This suggests that we must act with modesty to veil the shame of our lack. When we act with fanatic certainty, we are shameless. In addition to the act itself being opaque, there is no stable point from which to *assess* our acts (Žižek, 2007, p. 46). Williams (1982) explains, 'The standpoint of that retrospective judge who will be my later self will be the product of my earlier choices' (p. 34) and these earlier choices will have affected my future retrospective view through the wrinkled temporality of *Nachträglichkeit*. This 'retrospective judge' is our extimate Other whose gaze can serve as a barometer of our conscience by evoking shame if we have acted against the values we hold. This also implies that we have reflected upon these values and made a commitment to strive to uphold them.

Although we must take a leap of faith in order to act, what we do and the kind of life we lead condition our future possibilities, including our desires and judgements (Ruti, 2012; Williams, 1982, 2008). As demonstrated in the prisoner's dilemma, the act that concludes the 'time for comprehending' and precipitates the subject in 'moment of concluding' involves both other people (the three prisoners) and the big Other (the prison warden). With this act of anticipatory certitude, the big Other, who represents our retrospective judge, is *also* changed, because the Other is both 'out there', reflected in our cultural values, but is also 'internalized' as the voice of conscience. Like the subject, the extimate Other is always in a process of becoming.

When Lacan (2007) says to his students 'There is no longer any shame', Miller (2006) interprets this as saying 'we are at the time of an eclipse of the Other's gaze as the bearer of shame' (p. 15). In other words, we are living in a time when there are no longer shared values that matter to us. Values reflect our individual and collective history; they are of the Symbolic order and thus are inflected with the particularity of each historical epoch (Soler, 2015). In the late 1960s, Lacan linked the lack of shame to capitalism, which destroys social bonds, leaving only a relationship between the consumer and the object. Rather than being the gaze that shames, the Other commands us to 'Look at them enjoying so that you can enjoy!' (Miller, 2006, p. 15). Since Lacan's teaching, the social bonds that give a mooring to shame have only been further eroded. With the rise of neoliberalism, the forces of globalization and the emergence of the control state, our singularity is eliminated and our capacity for reflection dulled by the speed of technology (Miller, 2006; Stiegler, 2014). When we lose the time needed for reflection, the temporality of *Nachträglichkeit* is also lost. When there is no shame, we have lost that which can guide us back to the values that we have betrayed, and we are in danger of surpassing the limits of modest action.

Conclusion

Living in 'ethical time' means that we can allow the past to remain disturbed and unsettled rather than generating coherent narratives through the suppression of the traumas of the Real and the elimination of troubling truths. Rather than looking backwards with nostalgia and covering over the wounds inflicted and the injustices done to oneself or others, we gain the capacity to stay in touch with the shame of our lack and limitations, which can then serve as ethical guides. Then we can act with modesty – rather than with defensive and grandiose certainty – in our relationship with others. Living in 'ethical time' means the future can remain open rather than covered over with a utopian fantasy that there is some big Other who will offer the guarantee of happiness and wholeness – a guarantee that inevitably requires the elimination of some vital dimension of our being, e.g., our most closely held values, or the scapegoating of some actual other person(s) that we imagine pose an obstacle to our path forward. When there are no longer shared master signifiers (e.g., common religion, political aspirations, social causes) presiding over our cultural values and duties, we are left extremely vulnerable to the fanatic who purports to 'have the answers' and offers illusory promises and guarantees (safety, security, happiness). If we refuse responsibility for our own lives and fate – and instead succumb to the false promises of 'the one who knows' – the future is lost, because it is already overwritten by fantasies of wholeness. And yet we urgently need an open future, because the 'future' does not rescue us from the pain of the past – the future is the capacity and opportunity to re-translate what has already been in light of what may be (Hook, 2013; Ruti, 2012).

Notes

1 Imre Kertész was deported to Auschwitz at age 14. At the end of his first novel *Fatelessness*, his protagonist reflects on the nature of time and fate. Kertész was awarded the Nobel Prize for literature in 2002 for writing that 'upholds the fragile experience of the individual against the barbaric arbitrariness of history' (Nobel Diploma).

2 *Nachträglichkeit* has been translated into English as *deferred action* by Strachey and *afterwardness* by Laplanche. In French it is *après-coup*. The etymology of *Nachträglichkeit* derives from the verb *tragen* – to bear or carry – and the prefix *nach* – 'afterwards' or 'backwards'. '*Nachträgen*' conveys the paradox of our temporal condition – always arriving 'too soon' we look backwards at our actions 'too late' to change them. *Nachträgen* can also mean 'to bear a grudge' (Laplanche, 1999). Lacan's revised understanding of *Nachträglichkeit* is the process that allows us to retroactively become the cause of our lives *rather than* bearing a grudge against the world as a victim of 'fate'. This is why I am retaining the German word throughout.

3 Here is a very brief road map to the language of the Lacanian psyche for those unfamiliar: The 'big Other' designates the language, law and culture that a person is born into and as such it designates radical alterity (Evans, 1996, p. 133). The 'big Other' is also the group or the person that we believe guarantees the 'truth' of what we say when we speak and 'knows' what we mean and what we want. The 'big Other' is inscribed in the Symbolic order – the 'order' of the psyche that organizes human society and thought through language, laws, custom.

    The 'little other' is of the Imaginary order and is not really 'other' but a reflection and projection of the ego, our identifications with others who we imagine are 'the same' as we are (Evans, 1996, p. 132). The Imaginary is the realm of identifications and idealizations, which make up both fantasy and the ego.

The Imaginary order, the Symbolic order and the order of the Real are the three 'realms' or 'registers' of the Lacanian psyche that are in constant dynamic interaction with each other. The concept of the Real changes over time for Lacan, but it is never to be confused with socially constructed 'reality'. In his early teaching, the Real might be compared to the Kantian *noumenon* – the thing-in-itself. Like the Kantian thing-in-itself, the Real can never be directly experienced. In his later work, the Real emerges as that which is beyond symbolization and is therefore experienced as trauma.

4 In his later work, Lacan drops the term 'intersubjectivity' as it implies a dyad. Experience is always mediated through a 'third' – the Symbolic order.

5 The most well-known example of Freudian *Nachträglichkeit* appears in the 1895 Project, where Freud relates the case of his patient Emma who had developed a phobia of going alone into shops. See Boothby (2001) and Forrester (1991).

6 'Ec-stasis' means 'to stand outside'.

7 Heidegger's signifier for the temporal human being is *Dasein*, which means 'being there'; the use of *Dasein* is part of Heidegger's strategy for calling into question our everyday assumptions about what it means to be a person in the world.

8 Signifiers are the basic units of language and can be a syllable, a word or even a phrase. A signifier has no inherent meaning; it is only through its difference from other signifiers that it becomes a constituent in a process of meaning making. For example, 'cat' signifies a furry creature because (in a closed system) it is *not* a 'dog' and *not* a 'mouse' and *not* a 'goat' – i.e., there is no essential meaning underlying 'cat' that anchors these letters or this sound to the concept of a particular living furry creature. For Lacan, language is a system of signifiers, and the effects of the signifier on the subject constitute the unconscious and thus the field of psychoanalysis.

9 A succession of signifiers that produces meaning through their interaction is called a signifying chain or chain of signifiers. The production of meaning through the use of signifiers is referred to as 'the signifying effect' in order to emphasize that meaning results from the difference between the signifiers and is not inherent in the signifier itself (Pluth, 2007, p. 30).

10 The Lacanian 'subject of the unconscious' is also referred to as the 'subject *of* the enunciation' in order to stress that the *source* of speech is not the ego – in its mistaken belief that it is the master of its discourse and the agent of conscious intentions or actions, nor is it consciousness – but the source of speech is the *unconscious*, which is the discourse of the Other, i.e. the pre-existing cultural systems of language and ritual into which we are born.

11 Lacan (1986) calls this search for wholeness the fantasy of *das Ding*. *Das Ding* is not a substance – it is the retroactive yearning for an unmediated primordial bliss, which the subject never had (except in fantasy), but which he imagines can be refound. *Das Ding* offers a (false) promise of self-unity and completion. In his later work, the objects that we endlessly desire are represented by Lacan's concept of '*objet petite a*'—the 'object-cause' of desire.

These (non)-objects are both a little piece of the Real that escapes what can be put into words, setting desire into endless motion as the 'cause' of the subject as well as the ever-changing 'object' that the subject deploys to temporarily mask its ontological lack.

12 See Note 4 on intersubjectivity.

13 Fink (1996) demonstrates how the number of prisoners involved in the game dictates the number of hesitations needed for Prisoner A to conclude with 'anticipatory certitude' the colour of his disc. For more detailed explications of Lacan's logical problem, see Fink (1996), Forrester (1991), Johnston (2005), Pluth and Hoens (2004), Stark (2012) or Žižek (1996).

14 Lacan (2006): 'It is precisely because my sophism will not tolerate a spatialized conception that it presents itself as an aporia for the forms of classical logic, whose "eternal" prestige reflects an infirmity . . . namely, that these forms never give us anything which cannot already *be seen all at once*' (p. 166, original emphasis).

15 See Note 3 for definition of the 'the little other'.

16 Pluth (2007) points out that the signifying process that occurs during the analytic process can be taken as the major paradigm for the Lacanian act (p. 137).

17 *Aidos* is the Greek goddess of modesty and shame. She is the daughter of Prometheus, the god of foresight or anticipation. As mere mortals, our lack of foresight begets our ontological shame.

18 The subject of the unconscious, which is a product of unconscious processes, can also be considered a 'symptom' of the unconscious (Verhaeghe, 2013). In his later work, Lacan says that the goal of psychoanalysis is to come to recognize the 'symptom' that we are; in other words, we must come to recognize that we are never fully realized, always lacking, and yet responsible for our lives. Lacan (2016) calls this 'identification with the *sinthome*', borrowing the archaic French spelling for 'symptom' (p. 3).

19 For Aristotle, *tuché* is the unpredictable that happens even though the conscious agent intends to act in a purposeful way. *Automaton* refers to accidental occurrences in nature.

20 The 'myth of the lamella' is Lacan's '(anti) creation myth'. In it he explains that for creatures born via sexual reproduction (meiosis), immortal life flies away at birth, making individual death inevitable. 'Lamella' is the name Lacan creates for the 'organ' of eternal life that flies away.

21 In 'Subversion of the subject and dialectic of desire', Lacan (1966) offers another translation resonating with the *Nachträglichkeit* dynamic: 'There where it was just now, there where it was for a while, between an extinction that is still glowing and a birth that is retarded, "I" can come into being and disappear from what I say' (p. 300).

22 In the last stages of writing this chapter, I discovered Neill's book *Without Ground: Lacanian Ethics and the Assumption of Subjectivity,* in which he offers an in-depth analysis of how Lacan's understanding of the subject of the unconscious can serve as the 'groundless ground' of ethics in a way that saves

ethics from a type of 'anything goes' relativism as well as from any formulaic morality. Although this discussion is beyond the scope of this chapter, I refer readers to Neill's book (2014).

23 Lacan refuses any sort of 'depth' psychology where the 'unconscious' is conceived of as buried strata of meaning waiting to be discovered.

24 In French, Lacan (2007) writes this as '*hontologie*', which condenses *honte* [shame] and *ontologie* [ontology] (p. 180).

References

Boothby, R. (2001). *Freud as Philosopher: Metapsychology After Lacan*. London: Routledge.

Bowie, M. (1991). *Lacan*. Cambridge, MA: Harvard University Press.

Casey, E. & Woody, M. (2003). Hegel, Heidegger, Lacan: The dialectic of desire. In S. Žižek (ed.), *Jacques Lacan: Critical Evaluations in Cultural Theory*, Vol. 2, 192–220. London: Routledge.

Copjec, J. (2004). *Imagine There's No Woman: Ethics and Sublimation*. Cambridge, MA: The MIT Press.

De Kesel, M. (2009). *Eros and Ethics: Reading Jacques Lacan's Seminar VII*. Albany, NY: State University of New York Press.

Evans, D. (1996). *An Introductory Dictionary of Lacanian Psychoanalysis*. London: Routledge.

Eyers, T. (2012). *Lacan and the Concept of the 'Real'*. New York: Palgrave Macmillan.

Fink, B. (1995). *The Lacanian Subject*. Princeton, NJ: Princeton University Press.

Fink, B. (1996). Logical time and the precipitation of subjectivity. In R. Feldstein (ed.), *Reading Seminars I and II: Lacan's Return to Freud*, 356–386. Albany, NY: State University of New York Press.

Forrester, J. (1991). *The Seductions of Psychoanalysis: Freud, Lacan and Derrida*. Cambridge: Cambridge University Press.

Harari, R. (2002). *How James Joyce Made His Name: A Reading of the Final Lacan*. L. Thurston (trans.). New York: Other Press.

Harris, O. (2017). *Lacan's Return to Antiquity: Between Nature and the Gods*. London: Routledge.

Heidegger, M. (1962). *Being and Time*. J. Macquarrie & E. Robinson (trans.). San Francisco, CA: Harper & Row.

Hook, D. (2013). *(Post)apartheid Conditions: Psychoanalysis and Social Formation* (2013 edition). Basingstoke: Palgrave Macmillan.

Hyldgaard, K. (2003). The cause of the subject as an ill-timed accident: Lacan, Sartre and Aristotle. In S. Žižek (ed.), *Jacques Lacan: Critical Evaluations in Cultural Theory*, Vol. 1, 228–242. London: Routledge.

Kertész, I. (2004). *Fatelessness* (reprint edition). New York: Vintage.

Johnston, A. (2005). *Time Driven: Metapsychology and the Splitting of the Drive.* Evanston, IL: Northwestern University Press.

Lacan, J. (1966). *Écrits: A Selection.* A. Sheridan (trans.). New York: W. W. Norton & Company.

Lacan, J. (1986). *The Ethics of Psychoanalysis: 1959–1960.* J.-A. Miller (ed.), D. Porter (trans.). New York: W. W. Norton & Company.

Lacan, J. (1991). *The Ego in Freud's Theory and in the Technique of Psychoanalysis, 1954–1955.* J.-A. Miller (ed.), S. Tomaselli (trans.). New York: W. W. Norton & Company.

Lacan, J. (1998). *The Seminar of Jacques Lacan: The Four Fundamental Concepts of Psychoanalysis.* J.-A. Miller (ed.), A. Sheridan (trans.). London: W. W. Norton & Company.

Lacan, J. (2006). *Écrits: The First Complete Edition in English.* B. Fink (trans.). New York: W. W. Norton & Company.

Lacan, J. (2007). *The Seminar of Jacques Lacan: The Other Side of Psycho-analysis, Book XVII.* R. Grigg (trans.). New York: W. W. Norton & Company.

Lacan, J. (2016). *The Sinthome: The Seminar of Jacques Lacan: Book XXIII.* J.-A. Miller (ed.), R. Price (trans.). Cambridge: Polity Press.

Laplanche, J. (1999). *Essays on Otherness.* London and New York: Routledge.

Laplanche, J. & Pontalis, J.-B. (1974). *The Language of Psycho-Analysis.* New York: W. W. Norton & Company.

Masson, J. (ed.) (1985). *The Complete Letters of Sigmund Freud to Wilhelm Fliess, 1887–1904.* Cambridge, MA: Harvard University Press.

Miller, J.-A. (1994). *Extimité.* In M. Bracher, M. W. Alcorn, Jr., R J. Corthell, & F. Massardier-Kenney (eds), *Lacanian Theory of Discourse,* 74–87. New York: New York University Press.

Miller, J.-A. (2006). On shame. In J. Clemens & R. Grigg (eds), *Jacques Lacan and the Other Side of Psychoanalysis: Reflections on Seminar XVII.* Durham, NC: Duke University Press Books.

Miller, J.-A. (2013). To interpret the cause: From Freud to Lacan. *The Sinthome 15.* Retrieved from www.lacan.com/symptom15/?p=324.

Mulhall, S. (1996). *Routledge Philosophy Guide Book to Heidegger and Being and Time.* London: Routledge.

Neill, C. (2014). *Without Ground: Lacanian Ethics and the Assumption of Subjectivity.* New York: Palgrave Macmillan.

Pluth, E. (2007). *Signifiers and Acts: Freedom in Lacan's Theory of the Subject.* Albany, NY: State University of New York Press.

Pluth, E. & Hoens, D. (2004). What if the other is stupid? Badiou and Lacan on 'Logical Time.' In P. Hallward (ed.), *Think Again: Alain Badiou and the Future of Philosophy,* 182–190. London: Continuum.

Ruti, M. (2012). *The Singularity of Being: Lacan and the Immortal Within.* New York: Fordham University Press.

Scarfone, D. (2006). A matter of time: Actual time and the production of the past. *Psychoanalytic Quarterly, LXXV,* 807–834.

Shepherdson, C. (2008). *Lacan and the Limits of Language.* New York: Fordham University Press.

Soler, C. (2015). *Lacanian Affects: The Function of Affect in Lacan's Work.* London: Routledge.

Stark, R. (2013). 'The immanent logic of human experience': Reading Hegel's Phenomenology of Spirit after Lacan's 'Logical Time' essay. *Textual Practice, 27,* 7, pp. 1149–1175.

Stiegler, B. (1998). *Technics and Time, 1: The Fault of Epimetheus.* R. Beardsworth & G. Collins (trans.). Stanford, CA: Stanford University Press.

Stiegler, B. (2014). *Symbolic Misery – Volume 1: The Hyperindustrial Epoch.* Cambridge: Polity Press.

Vergote, A. (1983). From Freud's "Other Scene" to Lacan's "Other". In J. H. Smith & W. Kerrigan (eds), *Interpreting Lacan,* 193–221. New Haven, CT: Yale University Press.

Verhaeghe, P. (1998). Causation and destitution of a pre-ontological non-entity: On the Lacanian subject. In D. Nobus (ed.), *Key Concepts of Lacanian Psychoanalysis,* 164–189. New York: Other Press.

Verhaeghe, P. (2013). 'The function and the field of speech and language in psychoanalysis': A commentary on Lacan's 'Discours de Rome'. Delivered June 2013, Vancouver, Canada. Retrieved from: www.sfu.ca/humanities-institute/contours/paper1.html.

Williams, B. (1982). *Moral Luck.* Cambridge: Cambridge University Press.

Williams, B. (2008). *Shame and Necessity.* Berkeley, CA: University of California Press.

Žižek, S. (1996). *The Indivisible Remainder: On Schelling and Related Matters.* London: Verso.

Žižek, S. (2007). *The Parallax View.* Cambridge, MA: MIT Press.

Chapter 5

Abject bodies

Trauma, shame, disembodiment and the death of time

Angela Connolly

Introduction

If at first glance the relationship between shame and temporality is far from obvious, nevertheless they share certain characteristics which can allow us to begin to trace out possible paths of intersection. They are both uncanny concepts that tend to elude all our attempts to confine them within the boundaries of our human rationality. Emblematic is the famous phrase about time of St Augustine in *The Confessions*, 'If nobody asks me, I know: but if I were desirous to explain it to one who should ask me, plainly I know not' (1913, p. 239). As we shall see, however, shame is equally resistant to our attempts to encompass fully its meaning. Shame and temporality can both be seen as borderline concepts. On the one hand, they function to define and regulate boundaries and limits: the boundaries between body and world, self and other, good and evil, life and death. Indeed, *aidos,* the ancient Greek personification of modesty, respect and shame was considered one of the supreme ethical values governing individuals and society. Paradoxically, however, they are equally linked to the idea of transcending or transgressing boundaries. If, in a certain sense, temporality allows us to transcend the limits that chronological and bodily time impose on us, shame is intimately connected with the transgression of boundaries. We feel shame when we transgress a boundary and as such it has important regulatory functions, both in the personal and in the social sphere. When however, it is the boundaries of the body or the psyche that are transgressed, as is the case in trauma, shame becomes a devastating and de-structuring experience. Again, shame and temporality, the sense of living time, are intimately connected to embodiment, the process through which 'the live body, with its limits, and with an inside and an outside, is *felt by the individual* to form the core for the imaginative self' (Winnicott, 1988, p. 122, original emphasis). This body is the phenomenological body, *Leib* as opposed to *Körper*, which Mark Johnson describes as 'the living, moving, feeling, pulsing body of our being-in-the-world' (Johnson, 2007, p. 276). The aim of this chapter is to illustrate the way in which severe trauma and shame can lead to a loss of the sense of temporality. One of the problems, however, when we talk about trauma is that while exposure to trauma events has become almost ubiquitous, most of those who are exposed will not develop significant after-effects. As Verhaeghe and Vanheule comment, 'Whereas exposure to trauma is widespread—the majority of the Western population experiences a traumatic event during the course of life—only a minority of those exposed are likely to develop a clinically significant psychopathology' (Verhaeghe & Vanheule, 2005, p. 494).

This implies that not all kinds of trauma will have the same effects on temporality but the type of trauma which is relevant to my argument is intense, prolonged trauma, such as that suffered by the inmates of the Nazi death camps, both because of the numerous studies treating this theme and because it is the most extreme form of trauma human beings could undergo. The conclusions I draw, however, can be equally applied to other forms of intense trauma such as sexual abuse and severe relational trauma. The dehumanization carried out in these camps and the intense feelings of shame it created, led in many survivors to a progressive defensive dissociation between psyche and soma which, if sufficiently intense and prolonged, produced states of disembodiment. In turn, this disembodiment impacted negatively the capacity to use metaphors inasmuch as a metaphor is essentially an embodied practice. The creation of temporality, the sense of lived time as well as the sense of objective time depend, as I will show, on the use of metaphor, and if this capacity is lost, then temporality too breaks down, leading to what Elie Wiesel called the 'death of time'. As he so lucidly put it, 'Auschwitz means death . . . of language . . . and of time' (Wiesel, 1975, pp. 314–15). In this way, a vicious circle is created: trauma to shame; shame to disembodiment; disembodiment to the loss of metaphor; the loss of metaphoric capacity to the loss of temporality. As I have written earlier, this vicious circle leads to 'the creation of a rupture at the heart of the psyche such that a void is produced in which any representation of the experience becomes impossible' (Connolly, 2011, p. 608). The terrifying experience of this void is expressed in images such as the black hole or the 'empty circle that eclipses life and leads to a disorientation that cannot be overcome' (Laub & Podell, 1995, p. 1002).

Defining shame

One of the problems in any discussion of shame is that from all points of view – linguistic, psychological or neurophysiological – it is far from easy to define what we mean when we talk about it. Indeed, until the 1970s and the pioneering work of Helen Block Lewis (1971), psychoanalysis tended to conflate shame and guilt. The English word 'shame' comes from the Indo-European root 's(kem)' where 'kem' refers to covering up or veiling, but the term 'shame' has come to take on many layers of meaning, referring as it does to a series of emotional states that range from embarrassment to chagrin, dishonour, humiliation and mortification. In its essence, however, shame is linked to the idea that something which should have remained hidden has become exposed, the feeling that the confines between the inside and outside of the body have been transgressed. Sartre, in fact, in his analysis of the relationship between shame and the body in *Being and Nothingness*, speaks of 'my body as something that escapes me on all sides and as a perpetual outside to my most intimate inside' (Sartre, 2003, p. 375). Shame is both a noun and a verb, and other languages distinguish between two different experiences of shame, one related more to modesty and veiling sexuality such as the French *pudeur* and the Italian *pudore*, while the other is more related to feelings of being ashamed such as *honte* and *vergogna*. The Chinese language actually contains 113 shame-related terms and has specific terms for 'losing face', 'truly losing face', 'losing face terribly', 'being ashamed to death' and, finally, 'being so ashamed that even the ancestors of eight generations can feel it' (Edelstein & Shaver, 2007, p. 200).

There is still much uncertainty, however, about the psychological status of shame. Is it a primary affect, an innate affective motivational system which is potentially present from birth or is it a complex emotion which is above all culturally and socially constructed? Silvan Tomkins (1995) theorizes that affects are a biological motivation system with shame-humiliation as one of the four negative affect systems; he suggests that shame is expressed through facial clues which are cross-cultural and are easy to recognize. Michael Lewis on the other hand classifies shame among the social or self-conscious emotions such as embarrassment, pride and guilt, which involve interaction and blending between higher cognitive functions and more primitive affects such as disgust and separation-anxiety. According to Lewis, 'shame is the product of a complex set of cognitive activities: individuals' evaluations of their actions in regard to their standards, rules and goals and their global evaluation of the self' (Lewis, 2008, p. 748). For him, shame appears therefore only relatively late in children – somewhere between 18 months and three years – and it cannot be described by examining solely a particular set of facial movements but rather through the actions of the whole body.

From the phenomenological point of view, shame is intimately linked to embodiment, to the visibility of the body and to the way in which the bodily actions and appearance of the individual appear to, and are appraised by, the gaze of other humans. For Sartre, 'pure shame is not a feeling of being this or that guilty object, but in general of being *an* object; that is, of *recognizing myself* in this degraded, fixed and dependent being which I am for the other' (Sartre, 2003, p. 312, original emphasis). The experience of shame is triggered when one sees oneself as compromised in another person's eyes, when the subjective sense of *I* is 'fundamentally diminished, lost, dissolved, broken apart and exposed in a vulnerable state of being', as Wilson, Drozdek and Turkovic note (2006, p. 134). In this sense, shame is linked both to humiliation and disgust. Victims of sexual abuse and torture internalize shame within themselves; it is the humiliation created when the perpetrator treats them as an object, which can lead to severely paralysing psychological outcomes. Lindner (2002) has defined humiliation as:

> the enforced lowering of a person or group, a process of subjugation that damages or strips away pride, honour and dignity. To be humiliated is to be placed against your will, and often in a deeply hurtful way, in a situation that is greatly inferior to what you feel you should expect. Humiliation entails demeaning treatment that transgresses established expectations.
>
> (Lindner, 2002, p. 2)

Shame is also intimately related to the internalization of expressions of disgust on the part of the other. Rozin, Hardt and McCauley conceive of disgust as 'the emotion that is the guardian of the borders of both the bodily self and the social self' (2008, p. 761). If the other sees us in some way as less than human, then the risk is that we will feel that the boundary that separates us from the non-human is transgressed and that we will begin to experience ourselves as 'lowered, debased and mortal' (p. 762), thus provoking intense feelings of shame.

Trauma and shame

One of the most interesting things about psychoanalytical theorizing on trauma and shame is the way in which these two concepts gradually became excluded from early psychoanalytical discourse. As Jacqueline Rose notes, the attention Freud paid to shame 'dramatically declines as the question of morality and guilt become more and more the focus of his concerns. Shame, closer to disgust in terms of gut feeling, gradually refines itself out of the picture' (Rose, 2003, p. 6). There are many reasons for this, not least the personality of Freud himself, but one fundamental reason for the loss of interest in shame is Freud's increasing reluctance to recognize the shameful and shaming reality of the trauma of incest. In a sense, trauma can be seen as antithetic to psychoanalysis both because the traumatic neurosis poses a challenge to Freud's theories on sexuality and because severe trauma both fragments the ego and blocks the capacity for dreaming and for reverie, thus removing the conditions that were considered essential for psychoanalytical work to take place. As Christopher Bollas writes, talking about incest, 'the child not only cannot find true rest, but, dreading psychic processing of the elements of life, is therefore impoverished in the construction of the psyche and in the experience of reverie' (Bollas, 1989, p. 176). Jung too was deeply aware of the pernicious effects trauma exerts on the work of dreaming. In trauma, according to Jung, the dream is simply a reproduction of a real event which continually repeats itself without any metaphorical or symbolical transformation and any attempt at interpretation or at conscious assimilation thus proves useless. As he writes in the *Kinderträume*:

> The dream is never a mere repetition of previous experiences, with only one specific exception: shock or shell-shock dreams, which sometimes are completely identical repetitions of reality. The shock can no longer be *psychified*. This can be seen especially clearly in healing processes in which the psyche tries to translate the shock into a psychic anxiety situation.
>
> (Jung, 2008, p. 21, original emphasis)

It was only work with the pioneering work of researchers such as Silvan Tomkins (1995) on the neurophysiology and psychology of affects that brought shame once again into the consulting room. The year 1971 saw the publication of Helen B. Lewis's *Shame and Guilt in Neurosis*, and Heinz Kohut's *The Analysis of the Self* (1971), and gradually the focus of analytical work shifted towards recognizing the importance of shame. More or less contemporaneously, there was a revival of interest in trauma, linked both to studies on the survivors of the Nazi death camps and to a revival of interest in the work of Sàndor Ferenczi on the trauma of sexual abuse. One result was that the focus of interest in the effects of trauma gradually moved from an emphasis on guilt and identification with the aggressor to a renewed focus on the role of shame. Indeed Ruth Leys, in her 2007 book *From Guilt to Shame*, suggests that there has been a major paradigmatic shift in Western culture with shame now displacing guilt as a dominant emotional reference in the West. This paradigmatic shift can be seen both in works on the role of shame in sexual abuse and in the changes in the diagnostic criteria for post-traumatic stress disorder. Studies on individuals who have undergone sexual abuse have clearly shown that they suffer from profound feelings of shame and self-disgust. Michael Lewis (2008, p. 752) cites various studies of sexual abuse among children, such as Gold's study on women who had suffered sexual abuse in childhood. They suffered from psychological distress and low self-esteem and were more likely to blame themselves for negative events (Gold, 1986).

Again, in 1980, when the diagnosis of post-traumatic stress disorder (PTSD) was introduced into the American Psychiatric Association's *Diagnostic and Statistical Manual of Mental Disorders* (*DSM-III*) (APA, 1980), survivor guilt feelings were regarded as a characteristic symptom of the disorder and were included in the list of diagnostic criteria. In the revised edition of the manual of 1987 (*DSM-III-R*), however, the American Psychiatric Association, after considerable controversy, downgraded survivor guilt to the status of an 'associated' and non-criterial feature of the condition. With the disappearance of survivor guilt from the official list of criteria for PTSD, shame has come to take its place as the emotion that for many investigators most defines the condition of post-traumatic stress.

Embodiment and metaphor

It is becoming increasingly clear that 'most of the conceptual structures of a natural language are metaphorical in nature. The conceptual structure is grounded in bodily and cultural experience', as Lakoff and Johnson state (1980, p. 107). According to these authors, metaphor acts 'to provide a partial understanding of one kind of experiencing in terms of another kind of experience. This may involve pre-existing isolated similarities, the creation of new similarities and more' (ibid., p. 154). Through its capacity to allow us to understand one experience in terms of another, metaphor has a containing function allowing us to give shape to, and to communicate, experiences such as emotions, intuitions and feelings that are difficult to convey in conceptual verbal language. The most basic type of metaphors are primary metaphors which are 'learned unconsciously and automatically in childhood simply by functioning in the everyday world with a human body and brain' (ibid., pp. 256–7). Metaphor depends on the fact that human beings are both embodied and embedded in the world and it is for this reason that many primary metaphors are universal, as human beings basically share the same kind of bodies, and live and interact within the same kind of natural world. Primary metaphors arise when neuronal activation occurs simultaneously in two different parts of the brain, and therefore they depend on experiential co-occurrence or correspondences rather than on perceived similarities. Metaphor has also, however, a linking function that is at the basis of our capacity for abstract rational thinking and for imaginative creativity. Conceptual metaphors are the primary means for abstract conceptualization and reasoning and are based on 'the systematic mappings from body-based sensorimotor source domains onto abstract target domains' (Johnson, 2007, p. 177). They are usually complex combinations of primary metaphors and are mostly conventional in that they form part of the same linguistic and conceptual context of the individual.

Metaphor, time and personal identity

From the Greeks onwards, human beings have always tended to think of time in terms of the opposition between *kairos*, the subjective inner experience of time, and *chronos*, the experience of time as something external to the individual. *Kairos*, according to Elliot Jaques, in his 1982 book *The Form of Time*, denotes the lived experience of time, the time of human intentionality, purpose and goals in which past memory, present perception and future desire flow together, whereas *chronos* refers to the measurable time of succession, the conscious perception of the passage of units of time with its asymmetry of past and future and the idea of the irreversibility of 'the arrow of time'. The way in which we develop both the subjective sense of temporality and the capacity for abstract conceptualization of time is intimately linked to our embodied and embedded experience of the movement of objects and of our own movements through space. In a recent paper, I have described how infants learn to construct the sense of subjective inner time and abstract chronological time through the use of spatial metaphors (Connolly, 2017). Lakoff and Johnson (1999) in *Philosophy in the Flesh* have analysed these two principal spatial metaphors: the moving time metaphor and the moving observer metaphor. According to Johnson in *The Meaning of the Body*, 'The first spatialization understands discrete times metaphorically as objects moving towards a stationary observer, first in front of the observer, then passing her, and finally moving further and further away behind her' (Johnson, 2007, p. 29). In this way, the movement of objects allows the child to begin to construct a metaphorical understanding of the passage of time. In the second spatialization, the experience of an observer moving through space again facilitates the metaphorical understanding of the duration of time in which the distance moved becomes mapped on to the amount of time passed. These two different spatial metaphors are fundamental in the creation of our different experiences of time. In the first metaphor, we have the idea of chronological time as something that moves past us, something that we can only endure passively as the arrow of time moves us from birth to death. In the second, we move actively through time and the past is thought of as where I was, the present where I am now and the future where I am going, and in this way human intentionality becomes inserted into time. In any discussion on the relationship between personal identity and time, we need to be able to explain how the synchronic and diachronic unity of the self is achieved over time. Synchronic unity of the self refers to the experience of the unity of the self in separate moments of time whereas diachronic refers to the unity over time. The phenomenologist Shaun Gallagher has argued that:

> there is, implicit in the very nature of consciousness (no matter if it is perception, memory, imagination, a train of conceptual thought etc.) a binding of one moment to the next. This binding process is what Husserl calls 'retention' in regard to past moments of consciousness, and 'protention' in regard to the future. Husserl's model

explains not only how the perception of a temporal object such as a melody, is possible, given a changing stream of consciousness, it also explains how consciousness unifies *itself* across time.

(2007, p. 609, original emphasis)

Thus from the early stages of life, the time structure of the flow of consciousness permits some early intuition of the unity of past, present and future. From these premises, Dan Zahavi has suggested that before the individual achieves full self-reflective awareness of selfhood, there is already a pre-reflective experiential first-person subjectivity, an implicit first-order awareness of ownership of experience. In this reading, the continuity provided by the stream of consciousness is sufficient to guarantee, at least in part, the synchronic and diachronic unity of experiential self-identity over time (2012, p. 157). Ricoeur, on the other hand, suggests that identity is essentially narrative identity. Narrative identity is constructed through the stories we tell about our lives and, as Zahavi states, 'this identity can include change and mutation within the cohesion of our life' (2012, p. 146). Narrative identity, however, is not merely a question of individual authorship as it is both 'interwoven with the stories of others (parents, siblings, friends etc.), [and] it is also embedded in a larger, historical and cultural meaning-giving structure' (ibid., p. 147). Narrative identity is grounded in temporality but here it is neither the phenomenological time of the subjective consciousness nor cosmological time; it is human time, which for Ricoeur, bridges the gap between phenomenological and cosmological time: 'Human time is the time of our life stories. It is a narrated time, a time structured and articulated by the symbolic mediations of narratives' (Ricoeur, 1985, p. 439). Human time is the time of *kairos*, the time we create by inserting our intentionality, our imagination and our memories into chronological time in order to take possession of time. The construction of chronological, phenomenological and human time are all therefore grounded in metaphorical capacity which in turn is founded on embodiment, but equally it requires that we are embedded in the world. A story is always told to someone whether this is another human being or an inner 'other'. It necessitates a dialogical space, for, without the other, narratives become a mere chronicled, detailed, factual and historical account which, as Laub and Podell argue, are 'able only to convey the surface of the experience: they lose their power to impact on the present living world' (1995, p. 997). The loss of embodiment, the rupture of the primary empathic bond and sense of being embedded in the world, brought about by severe trauma, will profoundly impact the use of metaphor leading to a destructuring of temporality in all its aspects.

Dehumanization and disembodiment

In health we tend to forget that mind and psyche are born out of the body and we take for granted the lodgement of the psyche in the body. Embodiment, however, is not an automatic achievement and in cases of extreme trauma it can fail to develop or can be lost leading to states of disembodiment. From a phenomenological point of view, embodiment is linked to three separate and different psychological experiential phenomena: the sense of self-agency, the sense of body ownership and finally body image. The phenomenologist Shaun Gallagher distinguishes between self-agency, the idea that it is I that causes or generates an action, and body ownership, the sense that it is *my* body that is undergoing an experience. While, if all goes well, this sense of ownership is taken for granted, the attachment of the sense of self to the body or embodiment can fail to be fully established or can break down. As Gallagher writes:

> I do not need to reflectively ascertain that my body is mine or that it is my body that is in pain, or that is experiencing pleasure. In normal experience this knowledge is already built into the structure of experience. In some pathological cases, in contrast, the subject's relationship to his/her body is mediated by an observational judgement, and in some cases it is precisely a negative judgement about ownership.
>
> (2005, p. 29)

The body image, on the other hand, consists of a complex set of intentional states in which the intentional object of reflection is one's own body, whether on the perceptual, conceptual or emotional level. It refers to 'our reflexive and self-referential perceptions, attitudes and beliefs about our bodies' (Gallagher, 2007, p. 276).

The total powerlessness, the constant humiliation and the relentless process of dehumanization of the inmates of the death camps profoundly impacted both the sense of self-agency and the sense of body ownership until, finally, even the very image of an alive and fully human body became profoundly altered. In the face of the totally senseless world of the camps, where the actions of the executioners were totally unpredictable, it was impossible to take any action to avoid suffering or death. This had a devastating effect on the sense of self-agency and already led to feelings of shame. Levi in *The Drowned and the Saved* gives a poignant picture of the shame the inmate felt, 'because his will has proven non-existent or feeble and was incapable of putting up a good defense' (Levi, 1989, pp. 72–3). Even after the liberation, this feeling of shame persisted as we can see again from the words of Levi, 'When it was all over, the awareness emerged that we had not done anything, or not enough, against the system into which we had been absorbed' (ibid., pp. 76–7).

In the Nazi *lagers*, the bodies of the prisoners were at the complete mercy of their captors who exerted a total and sadistic power over them. The stark message of the captors was that 'If we so wish, and we do so wish, we can destroy not only your bodies but also your souls, just as we have destroyed ours' (Levi, 1989, p. 54). The only defence possible in these circumstances was to dissociate from the body. This loss of investment in the body led to a progressive loss of the sense of body ownership, which in turn led to states of disembodiment in which there is an alteration in the perception or experience of the self so that one feels detached from, and as if one is an outside observer of one's mental processes and body. Imre Kertész, who was sent to a camp when he was 15, gives a lucid description of this experience of disembodiment, 'My body was here, I had precise cognizance of everything about it, it was just that I myself somehow no longer inhabited it' (Kertész, 2004, p. 184). Disembodiment, therefore, has to do with not feeling real and fully alive to oneself:

> In the mildest cases disembodiment is manifested by vague sensations of lack of vitality and of emptiness but it can also lead to profound alterations of the body image and in more severe cases to pervasive and overpowering feelings of psychic deadness.
>
> (Connolly, 2013, p. 640)

The deliberate and intense process of dehumanization carried out in the camps further intensified these mechanisms, leading to profound changes in the very body image itself.

In a theoretical analysis of dehumanization, Haslam distinguishes between animalistic dehumanization which makes others less human by reducing them to the level of animals, and mechanistic dehumanization in which the denial of uniquely human emotions and traits renders the individual more like a machine. If the emotional reaction to mechanistic dehumanization is indifference, the emotional reaction in the face of animalistic dehumanization is disgust (Haslam, 2006, pp. 252–64). In intense trauma of the kind undergone in the death camps, the living human bodies of the inmates were exposed to an intense process of animalistic dehumanization.

Julia Kristeva in *Powers of Horror* describes how the borders and boundaries of the human body are mapped out by culture in order to separate out the human from the non-human, from the animal and from the inorganic. This cultural body is defined by the exclusion of the abject and anything that traverses the boundaries of the body, e.g. waste, body fluid and shit can be potentially abject although of course this will vary from culture to culture, for as Kristeva notes, 'abjection assumes specific shapes and different codings according to the various "symbolic systems"' (1982, p. 68). For Nazi ideology, it was the Jew who was construed as the source of defilement and a fount of abjection that not only had to be excluded from society but reduced to the level of something less than human, sub-human, animal, insect or worse. Giorgio Agamben suggests in *Remnants of Auschwitz* that Auschwitz must be understood as 'the site of . . . an experiment beyond life and death in which the Jew is transformed into a *Muselmann* and the human being into the non-human' (1999, p. 39). The aim of the death camps was not only to kill the Jews but, more appallingly, to transform them into abject bodies, bodies reduced to the level of the purely biological, something less than human, sub-human, animal or worse, which had to be disposed of. In the words of Liliana Segre, a survivor of Auschwitz, 'We were no longer human beings in the regular sense of the word. Not even animals, but bodies in stages of decomposition, that dragged themselves along on two feet' (cited in Consonni, 2009, p. 247).

The final stage of this process of degradation and dehumanization was the production of the *Muselmann*, the walking corpse described by Levi (1959, p. 103). Ataria and Gallagher suggest that:

> [t]he transformation from camp inmate to *Muselmann* occurs when the dissociative mechanism of the defence collapses as is expressed in a shift from complete body disownership (or a lack of sense of ownership) into an apathetic sense towards one's own body.
>
> (Ataria & Gallagher, 2015, p. 119)

The deep sense of shame that prisoners in the Nazi concentration camps felt after their release can be linked to this loss of body agency and ownership. They continued to feel humiliated for having allowed something horrible to happen to themselves and this feeling of perceived helplessness was projected on to the other and converted into shame as seen through the eyes of the other. Even more shaming, however, were the alterations in the body image, the sense that their bodies were and would remain in some way, abject, no longer fully human. Again, to cite Levi:

> Coming out of the darkness one suffered because of the reacquired consciousness of having been diminished. Not by our will, cowardice or fault, yet nevertheless we had lived for months and years at an animal level … we had endured filth, promiscuity and destitution, suffering much less than we would have suffered from such things in normal life, because our moral yardstick had changed.
>
> (Levi, 1989, p. 76)

This profound sense of shame meant that the sense of disembodiment was to remain; it weakened or destroyed the capacity to use metaphor, and inevitably led to profound alteration in temporality.

Trauma and temporality

To be able to experience subjective time, it is necessary therefore to be able to insert intentionality into time, to think in terms of projects and goals, and at the same time to be able, through imagination to create our own time. Intense prolonged trauma profoundly transforms the experience of *kairos*, of subjective time in which past memory, present perception and future desire flow together. In the camps, where it was always impossible to anticipate in any way the reactions of the executioners and to have any sense of being able to act or decide on one's fate, the subjective sense of human time was gradually destroyed; eventually, even the perception of external time became profoundly altered. Judith Herman in a 1992 article underlines that the dissociation which is common in individuals who have undergone severe and prolonged trauma, almost universally, led to characteristic disturbances in the sense of time. This disturbance 'begins with the obliteration of the future but eventually progresses to the obliteration of the past' (Herman, 1992, p. 381). In the extermination camps, in the words of Robert Antelme, one simply could not 'use the future tense' (1992, p. 95). The past too became foreclosed as it was simply too painful to recollect memories of things passed. In the end, the continuity between past, present and future was destroyed and all that was left was a series of dissociated and fragmented moments, an eternal timelessness in the face of imminent annihilation. Judith Kelly in an analysis of the temporal destructuring depicted by Levi in his romances notes that 'the normal human concept of time no longer prevails in a world where both past and future are negated by the spectre of annihilation. The victim is forced into a constant present' (Kelly, 2005, p. 7). In Primo Levi's own words in *The Drowned and the Saved*, 'we had forgotten not only our country and our culture but our family and our past, the future we had imagined for ourselves, because, like animals we were limited to the present moment' (1989, p. 57). The timelessness of this present moment impacted even the sense of chronological time. As Kelly puts it:

> Time in Auschwitz is meaningless because those factors that give a sense of shape and substance to everyday lives are subverted and no longer signify elements of human existence ... Annihilation renders the idea of time, whether cosmic, historical or existential, devoid of meaning because nothingness cannot exist within time.
>
> (Kelly, 2005, pp. 24–6)

Even when the survivors were liberated, this dissociation in temporality remained. The survivors on the one hand acted as though they had been able to return to ordinary time, while on the other they continued to act as though they were still immersed in the timelessness of their prisons. In the words of the Spanish writer Jorge Semprun, a survivor of Buchenwald, it is as if 'I never left, in spite of all appearances, and which I would never leave, despite the masquerades and make-believe or life' (Semprun, 1997, p. 153). So how can we work to interrupt this vicious circle between trauma, disembodiment, shame and time? How can we unfreeze the parts of the personality that have remained frozen in the timelessness of the traumatic event?

Opening up the circle

By way of conclusion, I will finish by looking at the dream of a woman with a history of severe relational trauma and physical and sexual abuse.

When we work with trauma, dreams offer the possibility of beginning to render 'psychified' the bare facts of the trauma, of transforming affects and sensations first into metaphoric images and then to connect the images to begin to tell a story that has a beginning and an end. Before this can happen, however, it is only the empathy of the analyst that can help the patient begin to get into touch with the unbearable dissociated affects. As Hessel Willemsen writes:

> Affect cannot be lost, yet is not accessible and may not be retrievable throughout a lifetime. A symbol can be formed when affects surface (like matter arising at the event horizon), felt through relating to oneself and another, and meaning is given only after the affect is first fully felt.
>
> (Willemsen, 2014, p. 708)

This dream illustrates graphically the devastating shame, the dissociation from the body and the fragmentation of the unity of the self brought about by trauma. At the same time, however, the dream shows how these partial selves become frozen in the timelessness of the trauma, unable to move forward until the dreamer is able to recognize, accept and integrate these fragments of the self into a life narrative:

> I meet a little girl of three years who is wearing a white dress, with a white bow in her hair. A girl in her late teens is holding her hand. I go up to them and see that the little girl is a Down syndrome child. I am confused. I hold the little girl's hand and say to her, 'I love you because you are kind and nice.' Then I am in a big hall full of important, rich people and there is a party. I sit with a girl I know who is very beautiful but who has a history similar to mine, as she comes from a poor social background and was abused. Her boyfriend brings us something good to eat. Then suddenly, the girl becomes a little girl of 11 who is epileptic. I take her by the hand and we go away into a dark place. She begins to cry and says to me, 'You don't know anything about a child like me.'

In the dream, the dreamer is beginning to come into contact with the split-off parts of herself that she had hidden away for so many years behind the carefully constructed mask of a beautiful, desirable and successful woman.

The patient is a replacement child, born after the death of a much-loved son and she was never accepted by her mother inasmuch as she was a girl. Both these dissociated partial selves are represented as handicapped, deficient and ill, and therefore a source of profound shame. It is this sense of shame that has led to disembodiment and a freezing in time of these partial selves. The little Down syndrome girl of 3 in the white dress is a metaphoric image that conveys the patient's desperate attempts to win her mother's love by being a clean, proper, good little girl, attempts that were destined to fail, for in the mother's eyes, her female body is deficient and handicapped, a poor substitution for the lost son. Here, however, the patient is beginning to be able to accept and show affection for this part, a sign that she is beginning to unfreeze this part self and to integrate it. The 11-year-old epileptic girl is an image of the patient's fear of losing control over her body and exposing her sexuality to the public gaze, a fear that is linked to her profound feelings of shame about a sexual body that was experienced as bad and dirty, feelings that can be attributed to the fact that her mother blamed the child for the sexual abuse. Freud himself in *The Interpretation of Dreams* traces out the associations between epileptic fits, falling down in the street and seeing oneself as a fallen woman in the dream of an elderly woman (Freud, 1976, p. 292). Here, the shame is still too strong to be able to overcome the dissociation as yet, although there is the beginning of an awareness of the refusal to accept this part. As Christian Roesler writes, 'The healing force of psychotherapy is contained in trying to create a new story about the life of the client which included the lost parts of the personality and which pays attention to the life of the soul' (Roesler, 2006, p. 583).

References

Agamben, G. (1999). *Remnants of Auschwitz: The Witness and the Archives.* Daniel Heller-Roazen (trans.). New York: Zone Books.

Antelme, R. (1992). *The Human Race.* J. Haight & A. Muller (trans.). Evanston, IL: Marlboro Press.

APA (American Psychiatric Association) (1980). *Diagnostic and Statistical Manual of Mental Disorders*, 3rd edn. Washington, DC: APA.

Ataria, Y. & Gallagher, S. (2015). Somatic apathy: Body disownership in the context of torture. *Journal of Phenomenological Psychology*, 46, 105–122.

Augustine (1913). *Confessions, Book 11.* London: Heinemann.

Bollas, C. (1989). *The Forces of Destiny.* London: Free Associations.

Connolly, A. M. (2011). Healing the wounds of our fathers: Intergenerational trauma, memory, symbolization and narrative. *Journal of Analytical Psychology*, 56, 607–626.

Connolly, A. M. (2013). Out of the body: Embodiment and its vicissitudes. *Journal of Analytical Psychology*, 58, 615–636.

Connolly, A. M. (2017). Broken time: Disturbances of temporality in analysis. Angeliki Yiassemides (ed.), *Time and the Psyche: Jungian Perspectives.* London: Routledge.

Consonni, M. (2009). Primo Levi, Robert Antelme and the body of the Muselmann. *Journal of Literature and the History of Ideas*, 7, 2, 243–259.

Edelstein, R.S. & Shaver, P. R. (2007). A cross-cultural examination of the lexical studies of self-conscious emotions. J.L. Tracy, R.W. Robins & J.P. Tangney (eds), *The Self-conscious Emotions: Theory and Research.* New York: Guilford Press.

Freud, S. (1976). *The Interpretation of Dreams*. Harmondsworth: The Pelican Freud Library, Vol. 4.

Gallagher, S. (2005). *How the Mind Shapes the Body.* New York: Oxford University Press.

Gallagher, S. (2007). *Phenomenological Approaches to Consciousness.* Oxford: Blackwell Publishing.

Gold, E.R. (1986). Long-term effects of sexual victimization in childhood: An attributional approach. *Journal of Consulting and Clinical Psychology*, 54, 471–475.

Haslam, N. (2006). Dehumanization: An integrated review. *Personality and Social Psychology Review*, 10, 252–264.

Herman, J.L. (1992). Complex PTSD: A syndrome in survivors of prolonged andrepeated trauma. *Journal of Traumatic Stress*, 5, 3, 377–439.

Jaques, E. (1982). *The Form of Time.* New York: Crane, Russak.

Johnson, M. (2007). *The Meaning of the Body: Aesthetics of Human Understanding*. Chicago, IL, and London: University of Chicago Press.

Jung, C.G. (2008). *Children's Dreams.* Lorenz Jung & Maria Meyer-Grass (eds). Ernest Falzeder (trans.). Princeton, NJ, and Oxford: Princeton University Press.

Kelly, J. (2005). *Primo Levi: Recording and Reconstruction in the Testimonial Literature.* Leicester: Troubador Publishing Ltd.

Kertész, I. (1989). *Fatelessness.* T Wilkinson (trans.). New York: Knopf.

Kohut, H. (1971). *The Analysis of the Self.* New York: International Universities Press.

Kristeva, J. (1982). *Powers of Horror: An Essay on Abjection.* Leon S. Roudiez (trans.). New York: Columbia University Press.

Lakoff, G. & Johnson, M. (1999). *Philosophy in the Flesh: The Embodied Mind & its Challenge to Western Thought.* New York: Basic Books.

Laub, D. & Podell, D. (1995). Art and trauma. *International Journal of Psychoanalysis*, 76, 991–1005.

Levi, P. (1959). *If This is a Man.* S. Woolf (trans.). New York: Orion Press.

Levi, P. (1989). *The Drowned and the Saved.* New York: Random House.

Lewis, H.B. (1971). *Shame and Guilt in Neurosis.* New York: International Universities Press.

Lewis, M. (2008). *Self-conscious Emotions: Embarrassment, Pride, Shame and Guilt.* Michael Lewis, Jeanette M. Haviland-Jones & Lisa Feldman Barrett (eds), *The Handbook of Emotions*, 3rd edn. New York: The Guilford Press.

Leys, R. (2007). *From Guilt to Shame: Auschwitz and After.* Princeton, NJ: Princeton University Press.

Lindner, E.G. (2002). Humiliation or dignity: Regional conflicts in the global village. *Journal of Mental Health, Psychosocial Work and Counseling in Areas of Armed Conflict*, 1, 1, 48–63.

Ricoeur, P. (1985). *Temps et récit III: le temps raconté.* Paris: Editions du Seuil.

Roesler, C. (2006). A narratological methodology for identifying archetypal story patterns in autobiographical narratives. *Journal of Analytical Psychology*, 51, 4, 574–587.

Rose, J. (2003). *On Not Being Able to Sleep: Psychoanalysis and the Modern World.* London: Vintage.

Rozin, P., Haidt, J. & McCauley, C.R. (2008). Disgust. In Michael Lewis, Jeanette M. Haviland-Jones & Lisa Feldman Barrett (eds), *The Handbook of Emotions*, 3rd edn. New York: The Guilford Press.

Sartre, J.P. (2003). *Being and Nothingness: An Essay on Phenomenological Ontology.* Hazel E. Barnes (trans.). London and New York: Routledge.

Semprun, J. (1997). *Literature or Life.* L. Coverdale (trans.). New York: Viking Books

Tomkins, S. (1995). *Shame and its Sisters.* Eve Kodofsky Dedwick & Adam Frank (eds). Durham, NC, and New York: Duke University Press.

Verhaeghe, P. & Vanheule, S. (2005). Actual neurosis and PTSD: The impact of the other. *Psychoanalytical Psychology*, 22, 4, 493–507.

Wiesel, E. (1975). For some measure of humility. *Sh'ma*, 5, 100, 314–315.

Willemsen, H. (2014). Early trauma and affect: The importance of the body for the development of the capacity to symbolize. *Journal of Analytical Psychology*, 59, 5, 695–712.

Wilson, J.P., Drozdek, B. & Turkovic, S. (2006). Post-traumatic shame and guilt. *Trauma, Violence and Abuse*, 7, 2, 122–141.

Winnicott, D.W. (1988). *Human Nature.* London: Free Association Books.

Zahavi, D. (2012). The time of the self. *Grazer Philosophische Studien*, 84, 143–159.

Chapter 6

Existential shame, temporality and cracks in the 'ordinary "filled in" process of things'

Sue Austin

Introduction

In this chapter I describe an approach that I have found useful when working with shame in general and especially when working with people whose inner lives are dominated by severe and chronic shame. A central aspect of this approach is how I have learnt to understand a number of my patients' unconscious use of subjective time to 'vanish' shame by living an internal life that is so speeded up that any thoughts, feelings, or images related to shame have no chance of registering in consciousness. In what follows, I will refer to this as a 'temporal defence' which can reveal the site of (basically) intolerable shame which is inseparable from states of helplessness and powerlessness. These states, in turn, point to the unresolvable instability of subjectivity and an enigmatic otherness at the core of subjectivity. As such, they also contain an opening towards an unknown and unknowable future, thus forming the basis of the analytic process.

Building on Kilborne (1997), I suggest that shame can reveal a window onto a crack in subjectivity and thereby, glimpses of the unconscious enigmatic otherness around which we are organized. In order to work with these aspects of interiority, I draw on Jung's and Laplanche's views of the unconscious as 'enigmatic', 'foreign', or 'other' to consciousness. Laplanche describes how analysis can offer a 'hollow' in which the patient can catch sight of this otherness (Laplanche, 1989, pp. 160, 190, 228–9); he also describes how the patient can use this hollow to make new 'translations' which preserve 'the sharp goad of the enigma' at its heart (Laplanche, 2002, p. 45). Such enlivening responses are in contrast to those which 'domesticate' this enigma, i.e., translate old translations of it (Stack, 2005, p. 68, referring to Laplanche, 1999, p. 65).

As a patient shifts towards making fresh translations of the enigmatic interiority pointed to by their temporal defences, their visceral sense of inner time changes, making it more possible for them to begin to experience, attend to, and reflect upon this interiority as it emerges, second by second. At times, this can become an almost still-by-still process and includes sitting with states of shame that had previously triggered high-speed escape responses, the horror of being stuck in tormenting shame for all eternity, or dissociation.

The approach I am describing has emerged from my clinical work with people with severe and chronic eating disorders, many of whose inner lives are dominated by self-hatred and shame. Accordingly, what follows is not a phenomenological analysis of the relationship between shame and temporality. Instead, it takes as its point of departure a clinical vignette drawn from my work with one of a number of patients with whom this approach has evolved. Theoretical ideas on temporality and shame are then used to discuss, in broad terms, some of what I learnt from working with this patient and from others with similar patterns of distress. This discussion is then linked back to the initial clinical vignette.

A clinical vignette

Leah (then aged 27) presented with a disorder of the self (borderline spectrum), bulimia nervosa, self-cutting, and body-dysmorphia, and she often described herself as 'feeling like a piece of shit'. After about four years of analysis, Leah's bulimia stopped, and after about seven-and-a-half years, she stopped cutting. In previous papers (Austin, 2016a, 2016b), I have described my work with Leah over a 14-year period. However, the vignette I want to take as a point of departure for this discussion is from a session towards the end of Leah's twelfth year of analysis.

Leah was now a couple of years into a stormy but warm relationship with a man. They had moved in together and sometimes feelings of intimacy and closeness were possible. When they were together on one occasion Leah heard herself think: 'You know, it's a shame you aren't pretty – it would be so much nicer for him if you were.'

Leah's attention was initially drawn to the tone of this inner voice, which she experienced as that of gentle regret. On further reflection, she was shocked to realize that this, one of the most comforting voices she had ever heard inside herself, was actually judgemental and shaming. She also became aware that it came from deeper inside her than her traditional, berating, self-hater voice that had previously raged at her endlessly, mocking her and telling her that she was useless, fat, disgusting, lazy, a piece of shit, and so on. Although Leah had come to know this painful self-hater voice well in analysis, the quiet, damning hopelessness of this new voice felt much harder to bear.

Any attempt to think (or even glance) in the direction of this new voice took Leah to a place that she described as 'disgusting' and 'squirmy', and she would often feel nausea and panic. Her mind and inner world would become blurry as she tried frantically to get as far away from these states as she could, preferably 'vanishing' them completely before they came anywhere near consciousness.

As I sat with Leah, I was trying to find somewhere in our engagement where these energetic, high-speed defences could risk slowing down enough for us to start to reflect on this new voice a little. A key point of reference was an intersection between the work of Jung and Laplanche which seemed to offer a space for what Leah had previously unconsciously defended against in this way. Although very different thinkers in many ways, both Jung and Laplanche understood the unconscious as unresolvably, non-pathologically foreign or other to consciousness. Before exploring the temporal dimensions of my work with Leah further, I need to elaborate on this intersection and the space it offers for working with the defensive use of subjective time.

Jung and Laplanche: the unconscious as inner otherness

Based on his word association test and psychogalvanic skin response researches, Jung theorized the unconscious as organized around pockets of highly affectively charged inner otherness which he called 'complexes' (1935, pp. 71–3). John Haule makes clear the extent to which the complex is other to consciousness through the following observations:

- it has a sort of body with its own physiology so that it can upset the stomach, breathing, heart;
- it has its own will power and intentions so that it can disturb a train of thought or a course of action just as another human being can do;
- it becomes visible and audible in hallucinations.

(Haule, 1992, p. 252)

Jung also located otherness at the heart of his concept of the symbol, as is evident in his comment that a symbol is dead when it does not have an unknown element (Jung, 1921, pp. 474–5). An important implication of this is that, for something to be a motivating factor in creating new psychic realities, it must contain an enigma.

Likewise, although post-Freudian, Laplanche saw the unconscious as organized around non-pathological, enigmatic internalizations/signifiers. Indeed, for Laplanche, a person's unconscious does not belong to them, rather it:

> comes inside through an act of miscommunication, a mode of unwitting seduction, in which the parental desire excites the child, without being understood ... What comes from the one to the other is something unknown to both, yet intense in its effect (and affect) ... however 'deep' we go, we find the other already there.
>
> (Frosh & Baraitser, 2003, p. 782)

For Laplanche, the vehicle for the intergenerational transmission of this inner otherness was the excess of the mother's desire (which stems from her own enigmatic other); for Jung it was the collective unconscious. Although very different in many ways, Jung's and Laplanche's work meet in the idea that we are organized around an unconscious that is hauntingly excessive and, although unresolvably foreign to our sense of self, affectively connects us to that which is other.

As Allyson Stack describes, Laplanche refers to these internal foreign bodies as 'enigmatic' (or 'enigmatic signifiers'), indicating that they are 'not puzzles or riddles that can one day be solved by learning and applying the proper codes (linguistic or otherwise)' (Stack, 2005, p. 65). Crucially, such messages harbour 'an irreducible, interrogative kernel - a question neither sender nor receiver can ever completely answer' (2005, p. 66).

Based on this view of the unconscious, Laplanche aims to provide an analytic 'hollow' in which:

> two, usually intertwined, types of transference come to rest. One is the reproduction of forms of behaviour, relationships and childhood images. This is the ... 'filled in' transference. The other dimension of transference concerns elements in the relationship that have an enigmatic

character. This latter is the … 'hollowed out' transference. In practice
these are usually mixed. The enigma is the means that enables 'analysis'
to take place—the 'lysis' part of analysis. The impact of the enigma may
create a kind of opening, a gap, a crack, a cleavage plane in the ordinary
'filled in' process of things. If not for the enigma, there would be no
analytic work and no dismantling of old patterns.

(Hinton, 2009, p. 643, referring to Laplanche, 1989,
p. 160, 1999, pp. 228–9)

The practical application of this meant that I often asked Leah to 'slow
down' and/or 'walk me back through' material she had described earlier in
sessions to offer her a space where the habitual, almost instantaneous,
processes which knitted a sense of herself as abject into the very act of
perceiving might become a little slower, perhaps more child-like, and a
little less concrete and impenetrable.

Slowing things down: the neuroscience of perception and the default mode network

This approach was also part of an alternative to interpretation and builds
on Laplanche's observation that our predominant response is to domesticate the enigmatic messages or othernesses around which we are
organized. When we do so, we are not translating the enigma of the message itself, rather we are simply 'translating our old translations' of it
(Stack, 2005, p. 68, referring to Laplanche, 1999, p. 65). In contrast, the
enlivening, engaged response 'preserves the sharp goad of the enigma'
(Laplanche, 2002, p. 45).

Part of my aim in encouraging Leah to slow down was to provide a place
where, instead of habitually domesticating her inner othernesses (through
her high-speed, unconscious temporal defences), she might encounter precisely what Hinton described earlier: a kind of opening, a gap or crack,
through which a more enlivening form of translation might become possible (Hinton, 2009, p. 643, referring to Laplanche, 1989, p. 160, 1999,
pp. 228–9). This approach also fits with Dominique Scarfone's observation that 'the past is not the passive container of things bygone. The past,
indeed, is our very being, and can stay alive and evolve; the present is the
passage where the retranscription and recontexualization [i.e., retranslation]
of our past continually occur' (2006, p. 814). Seen in this way, working
with the patient's experience of temporality and memory can offer access

to their self-hatred and the shame embedded in it which would often otherwise be, as described, impenetrable.

Emerging neuroscience research offers images and metaphors that I find useful for trying to imagine my way into these vital clinical processes.[1] This research identifies a neurological state between the brain registering incoming perceptual data, and its having organized that data into conscious perceptions. Using Laplanche's imagery, I imagine this in-between zone as offering a gap or crack in the ordinary, solidified, '"filled in" process of things' (and the 'filled in transference'). This crack or gap exists before we have domesticated incoming perceptual data by organizing it into familiar 'knowledge'.

In their research, Sid Kouider and colleagues (2013) have found that adults need to look at an image for 300 milliseconds before we are conscious of what we have perceived. Prior to that we are unconscious of what we are looking at and have yet to recognize perceptual data as something we can describe. Clinical experience suggests to me that the roots of a sense of one-self as abject (and the self-hatred and chronic, severe shame through which it expresses itself for the kinds of patients I have in mind) are to be found in these very early stages of experience of self and the world. It is as if the act of drawing perceptual data together into 'a something' (and this includes the experience of oneself as 'a something') is shot through with a deeply dis-tressing sense of badness or wrongness, which is simultaneously diffuse and cellular. As a result, consciousness itself is experienced as excruciatingly painful, and demands behaviours such as self-harm and eating disorder to manage it.

Kouider's team's research also shows that for infants between 12 and 15 months this delay between stimulus and the patterns of neural activ-ity that indicate conscious perception is about 750 milliseconds, and in 5-month-olds it is about 900 milliseconds (Kouider et al., 2013, p. 376). In the light of these images, I would say that, by encouraging Leah to 'slow down', I was trying to help her to intermittently 'drop down' or regress into an affect-based, almost light trance-like, younger state of consciousness where the fluid zone between stimulus and perception was longer. Again, the aim of this was to increase the likelihood of catching glimpses of the othernesses around which she was organized through cracks or gaps in her ordinary 'filled in', domesticated (and domesticating) patterns of perception.

This emphasis on slowing things down (within the patient's tolerance limits in any given moment) also came from Gary Hartman's observation that Jung allowed the time necessary for the characteristics and personality of the patient's 'Not-I' to emerge (Hartman, 1994). By inviting Leah to slowly take me back through seemingly trivial day-to-day life experiences or aspects of her interiority which she had 'rushed through' earlier, I was inviting her to let go of her high-speed escape defences a little and let her affective experiences emerge more. Over time, tiny cracks and gaps in her self-hatred's previously unquestionable tirades started to appear.

At the most basic level, working with Leah's temporal defences in this way meant that she became able to spend (microscopically) longer and longer periods of time in states of 'flow', i.e., states where she was engrossed in her moment-to-moment experience of feelings, sensations, images, thoughts, and so on. Occasionally she would find (to her surprise) that in her state of absorption, she had 'gone off script'. Initially, it fell entirely to me to notice such changes and comment on them. Over time, however, as part of her growing capacity to slow down and live from a less 'filled-in' place, Leah became increasingly able to notice these spontaneous changes herself and point them out so that we could then think about them and talk about them together. (I will return to a more complete discussion of the complexity of this process at the end of the chapter.)

For example, when Leah first brought her 'it's a shame you aren't pretty' inner voice to session, we both heard it as a new expression of her self-hatred. However, as we explored echoes and resonances around it, slowing down as we went, it became clear that it offered a glimpse of a deeper, pervasive shame which had become visible through something like a crack in her self-hatred. What also emerged was that this voice marked one of a number of important shifts from a very 'filled in', domesticating pattern of perception (associated with Leah's habitual attacks of self-hatred and longings for them to stop) to a slower, more gappy, more painful, shame-based experience of interiority.

Working with these dynamics with Leah and with a number of other patients led me to a way of thinking about shame which I will describe next; this will then be linked to my work with Leah and further discussion of her experience of, and use of, temporal defences.

Shame's existential function

Jungian analyst Peer Hultberg describes his work with a patient for whom shame was an all-enveloping state as follows:

> I was consulted by a girl of about 16 years ... She was in despair but was not able to give concrete reasons for it. Twice a week she sat before me, crying and repeating: 'I'm so ashamed, I'm so ashamed.' It would have been useless to question the girl; I could only stay with her, accompany her, inwardly avoid all kinds of false consolation, and take her seriously. I saw that the sessions were following a certain pattern: Shame was answered with shame of the shame until it became an almost global state which seemed to devour the girl's identity; its overwhelming power threatened to dissolve her psychically. I could only hope that she felt ... that I had respected her shame as a phenomenon which had an important function in her psyche.
>
> (Hultberg, 1987, p. 158)

I imagine that, drawing on Jung, Hultberg sees affectivity as the ground and basis of personality (Jung, 1907, p. 38) and emotion as 'the chief source of consciousness' (Jung, 1954, p. 96).[2] Through this, he recognizes the impenetrability of his patient's shame as an unconscious communication and therefore does not ask her questions or try to engage with it directly or 'heal' or 'cure' it. If the potential consciousness within her shame is to emerge, it needs to be attended to on its own terms (Redfearn, 1985, p. 111). Hultberg's capacity to sit with 'not-knowing' and bear his own and his patient's helplessness is essential for this.

Again, although from what seems a very different analytic tradition, Hultberg's post-Jungian position resonates with Laplanche's view that, when working with the transference:

> The analyst ... tends to be seen as 'the one supposed to know'. In order for the process to evolve it is crucial for the analyst to remain in touch with his/her own enigmatic core. By refusing to 'know'—or, more accurately, being aware that he/she does not know—the analyst provides a 'hollow' in which the process can evolve.
>
> (Hinton, 2009, p. 643)

Hultberg's description of his patient's shame as an 'existential mode' initially struck me as accurate (Hultberg, 1988, p. 110). However, I have since come to think of this kind of intense, chronic shame as performing an 'existential function' rather than being an 'existential mode'. Like the Greek idea of the *Pharmakon*, it marks something disavowed, something we cannot bear to know but must know – it is both cure and poison (Steigler, 2013). Without the necessary and irreducible ambivalence of this tension, we would become fixed in place, stuck in an eternal present with no future, no possibilities.

From a background in philosophy, psychology, and literature, Alba Montes Sánchez expands on this idea of shame as marking the site of necessary and irreducible ambivalence. Working with ideas from Levinas, she writes:

> Whatever the source of any judgement of inadequacy, whatever its causes or the norms that govern it, the genuinely private side of shame is … [the self-relation that nobody] but myself could feel riveted when realizing that I am *this* being, *this* body, *this* person; nobody else *is* riveted to it. Shame involves a sense of alienation and simultaneously an impossibility to be other, an indissoluble self-relation.
>
> (Montes Sánchez, 2013, p. 48, original emphasis)

Thus shame confronts us with our own unassimilable, inescapable foreignness which we cannot sublimate or transform through effort. But as Levinas points out, we are *riveted* to this alienness that we *are*: it is not just a gateway—although utterly foreign, it is who 'I am' (Levinas, 2003, p. 64). *Seen in this way, shame is a window on the inherently unresolvable instability of subjectivity that is always escaping our control.*

As part of this function, Hinton sees shame as a boundary emotion, a teacher of limitations, observing that if shame is 'endured consciously, a kind of *kenosis* – emptying – results. This "emptying" is a deeper openness without the ego's preconditions' (Hinton, 1998, p. 184). From this perspective, what shame offers is closer to Laplanche's view of psychoanalysis as a 'Copernican revolution', where the centre of the experience of selfhood moves beyond the ego, towards the unconscious (Hinton, 2009, pp. 639–40).

The hole in the paper sky

Drawing on Italian dramatist Luigi Pirandello's discussion of *Orestes* and *Hamlet*, psychoanalyst Benjamin Kilborne offers an image that expands this description of shame's broader psychological function:

Pirandello conveyed this point tellingly when he spoke of the differ-ence between Orestes and Hamlet. "Suppose that, at the climax, when the marionette who is playing Orestes is about to avenge his father's death and kill his mother and Aegisthus, a little hole were torn in the paper sky above him? Orestes would still want his revenge, yet when he saw that hole, he would feel helpless. [Overcome by indecision and inaction] Orestes would become Hamlet! That's the difference between ancient tragedy and modern: a hole in a paper sky." Descriptions of shame will inevitably fall short of the mark not only because this is the nature of the limitations of human description, but also because it is difficult to take into account the "hole in the paper sky". Shame can perhaps be said to be that hole in our paper sky, something that reminds us of our flaws, something that threatens our ability to communicate what we have in a way that can be taken seriously by others, something that punctures our image of ourselves and puts a rent in our experience of the social fabric, yet something without which human relationships and consciousness would be inconceivable.

(Kilborne, 1997, p. 266)

If shame offers a glimpse of the (unbearable but essential) inherent instability of subjectivity, it makes sense that (as one of the core struc-tures of subjectivity) our experience of time would twist, morph, and polarize into extremes when we approach shame. The corollary of this is that shame is partly an experience of these disturbing distortions in, or experiences of, temporality.

Kilborne offers us an analytic response to this hole in the paper sky of subjectivity through his work with Mark, who describes having been 'pushed out all his life' for making people's lives difficult. When Mark sneezes, Kilborne understands it as his need to expel his dangerous conflicts over potency and power before they become conscious.

In a subsequent discussion, Mark finds space to question his assump-tions about his own and others' power (Kilborne, 2002, p. 39). Kilborne writes that 'the clinical focus . . . needs to be the patient's difficulty in knowing what is real and what is fantasy, and how shameful such a difficulty feels to him' (p. 40). Although his theoretical orientation is 'phe-nomenological, drive-oriented, and conflictual' (p. xi), Kilborne's next comment resonates with Hultberg's earlier description of how he worked with his patient:

In terms of Oedipal conflicts, if I challenge [Mark's] sense of reality by attempting to explore his feelings of shame over not knowing what is real to him, this produces a crushing sense of Oedipal defeat. The task, then, is to allow him to feel the hole in the paper sky, so as better to grasp the illusion in his omnipotence and the reality of both his limitations and possibilities.

(Kilborne, 2002, p. 40)

By allowing Mark to feel the hole in the paper sky, Kilborne offers him space to find a changed relationship to limitation and places within where will and effort are to no avail. Hence, Mark can develop an awareness of the rent in subjectivity and, through that, come to be able to bear shame (2002, p. 40).

My sense is that, in addition to offering Mark space to question his assumptions about his own and the others' power, Kilborne (like Hultberg) is offering an analytic hollow in which his patient's temporal defences against shame can begin to break down. Through this, the 'sharp goad' of the enigmatic unconscious (which these defences point towards) can become more available, demanding new translations. This is part of how I understand Kilborne's image of allowing the patient to feel the hole in the paper sky. Although, as Montes Sánchez observes, shame remains a window on the inherently unresolvable instability of subjectivity which is always escaping our control, the patient may begin to realize that their defensive manoeuvres, including 'vanishing' shame through brutal but fragile temporal defences, must fail. While acceptance of this kind of inevitable failure (even to some small degree) may seem trivial or defeatist, it can, over time, give rise to powerful internal changes. If shame is worked with as these authors describe, it no longer needs to be so stuck and repetitive, so refusing of consciousness.

Shame: some further background comments

Before linking these ideas back to my work with Leah, a little more discussion is needed to draw out further temporal implications of Kilborne's image of shame as a hole in the paper sky of subjectivity.

Montes Sánchez observes that 'shame, as an experience of self-revelation and self-exposure, requires the social and the private to take place, and thus *can only appear in the intermediate spaces between them*' (Montes Sánchez, 2013, pp. 29–30; emphasis added). This structure is reflected in those languages which differentiate 'social shame' (scandal, criminality) from the inner personal experience of shame ('private shame') that has its roots in bodily experiences (Pines, 1995). Using German and French, Warren Kinston illustrates this:

> Shame-unashamed (German: *Scham*; French: *Pudeur*) refers to modesty, chastity, shyness, bashfulness. In Biblical usage it refers to genitals. The emphasis in this meaning is on inner personal experience.
>
> Shame-shameless (German: *Schande*; French: *Honte*) refers to disgrace, scandal, criminality (cf. deeds of shame). The emphasis in this meaning is on social customs and standards.
>
> (Kinston, 1983, p. 213)

Shame would be much simpler analytically if, by regarding social customs and standards as solely externalizations of internal phenomena, we could ignore social shame, viewing it as an external manifestation of the inner, personal experience of shame.

However, Montes Sánchez's image of shame as arising in the space or gap *between* 'the social and the private' suggests that although 'social shame' is a product of the inner lives and feelings of individuals, it *also* has a collective, impersonal element. Social shame may be made of the same 'stuff' as private shame, but, as indicated by the different word for it, it is so different in degree as to be almost different in kind, hence the 'gap' between the two terms for shame.

This formulation maintains the tension between these facets of shame, and offers a way of thinking about why it is often experienced as *two irreconcilable states at once.* Crucially, it is *unresolvably and simultaneously* deeply personal and private (perhaps the most personal and private of affects), *and at the same time*, totally impersonal and public (perhaps the most impersonal and public state of exposure possible).

The tensions and vulnerability that arise from this core structure, plus the contagious, usually hidden and private nature of shame is why we prefer to look away from it in ourselves (and the others), as quickly as possible (Lewis, 1987, p. 2), hence our high speed temporal defences and our attempts to 'vanish' it. Failure to look away/get away from shame risks falling into (and potentially getting stuck forever) in the nightmarish tensions and gaps in and around it. The terror of that provides the enormous energy and momentum of these defences.

Developing his metaphor of shame as a hole in the paper sky of our subjectivity, Kilborne points out the helplessness of this state and links it to the limitations of the human condition. He again quotes Pirandello, expanding on the image of shame as puncturing our illusory belief in the efficacy of the self:

> Still the thought of the puppet Orestes, disturbed by a hole in the sky, lingered for a long time in my mind—lucky marionettes, I sighed, over whose wooden heads the false sky has no holes! No anguish or perplexity, no hesitations, obstacles, shadows, pity—nothing! And they can go right on with their play and enjoy it, they can love, they can respect themselves, never suffering from dizziness or fainting fits, because for their stature and their actions that sky is a proportionate roof.
>
> (Kilborne, 2002, p. 38)

Kilborne is contrasting the contemporary, complex experience of subjectivity (which can never be 'complete' or feel 'right') with the certainty of '[t]he tragic virtues of honor, pride, and harmony so essential for the Greek theatre, [which] give way in our contemporary world to off-kilter shams and misguided attempts to seem intelligible' (2002, p. 38).

Understood like this, shame also puts us in touch with a rent in our experience of the social fabric. Since this social fabric is foundational to (and defines) what constitutes intelligible (i.e., 'sane') selfhood, this rent is, as Kilborne observes via Pirandello, fundamental to our livable experience of ourselves. I suggest that we experience it as a crack or gap in our subjectivity, giving rise to the kind of dizzying vertigo that Pirandello describes, and the kind of temporal defences and distortions I am exploring. This is also why shame is experienced as arising *simultaneously* from our separate, private self, *and* our social, field-emergent self, *and* the gap or crack between them.

Using Bachelard's description of human beings as 'half-open creatures', Malcolm Pines (1995, p. 346) notes our need to move between openness and concealment (i.e., social and private states). I read Pirandello's reference to dizziness and fainting fits (and again, I would add, temporal distortions) as images of what happens when the gap between our private, separate self and our social, field-emergent self suddenly opens up, flooding us with shame. We lose our proportionate roof and cannot continue to pretend that these aspects of our lives are seamless and continuous. Instead, our attention is drawn to the mad, maddening, mind-destroying crack between them. The harder we try to look away, the more our experience of ourselves becomes dominated by what we are trying to avoid, hence the nightmarish, amplifying shame feedback loop which Hultberg's case illustrates. Quoting from Virginia Woolf's diary in 1937 (as she was waiting for the reviews of her novel *The Years* to be published), Hultberg makes this experience and the urgency of our need to escape it or 'vanish' it through temporal distortions even more clear:

> I wish I could write out my sensations at this moment. They are so peculiar and so unpleasant ... As if something cold and horrible—a roar of laughter at my expense were about to happen. And I am powerless to ward it off: I have no protection. And this anxiety and nothingness surround me with a vacuum ... And I want to burst into tears, but have nothing to cry for. Then a great restlessness seizes me. I think I could walk it off—walk and walk till I am asleep ... And I know that I must go on doing this dance on hot bricks till I die ... I'm going to be beaten, I'm going to be laughed at, I'm going to be held up to scorn and ridicule—I found myself saying those words just now.
>
> (Hultberg, 1988, p. 120, referring to Bell, 1984, p. 63)

Hultberg's clinical vignette (quoted earlier) conveys the corrosive quality of this kind of shame which a colleague once described as 'like having had acid thrown on one's soul': it burns and burns and nothing can be done to stop it or distract oneself from it.[3] Such shame is felt as a permanent wound or visible scar, or a chronic running sore.

From this perspective, 'normal shame' is the capacity to look away from the crack in one's subjectivity, hoping that others will look away too, as they do in themselves. I take this to be Kilborne's point when he quotes H. L. Mencken's comment that '[s]elf-esteem is the secure feeling that no one, as yet, is suspicious' (Kilborne, 2002, p. 1).

Leah described 'normal people' as being able to 'paper over' this crack in themselves, reducing it to 'a flaw in the pavement'. In contrast, she could never fully distract herself from the knowledge that, at any moment, something could trigger an eruption/avalanche of shame, turning the crack into a chasm. At times, Leah found herself in a terrifying, mindless, endless free-fall into this chasm and again, Hultberg's description of sitting with his patient echoes this.

Linking these ideas to my work with Leah

At the start of analysis, Leah described her father as a hard-working migrant tradesman who had built his own small business and was rarely home. She experienced him as a profoundly disappointed, alienated man and she recalled how, as a child, she had felt overwhelmed and helpless around him. After several dreams, she developed a sense that she had tried to master these feelings by assuming that she was the source of his deep disappointment.

During the course of analysis, Leah began to wonder if she had taken her father's unlived and unlivable life into her body, feeling it as a failure of her flesh and her lovability. She also wondered whether living through the prism of her internalization of his unbearable loneliness and disappointment was the nearest (perhaps only) thing she had which felt like a relationship with or love for him. This made sense of how, at a deep level, she had *had* to see herself through that prism, hate herself accordingly, and enact that self-hatred through unconscious communications such as bulimia and cutting to have any sense of connection to him. What also emerged was that Leah experienced moments of well-being, delight, contentment, or feelings of worth as pushing her father deeper into isolation and his tormented inner world. For a long time, we sat with her grief at this unbearable dilemma.

Again, in Laplanche's terms, I was trying to offer Leah an analytic hollow in which her high-speed temporal defences could begin to fall apart. As Kilborne describes, this enabled Leah to feel 'the hole in the paper sky' of subjectivity and through this she became increasingly able to sit with the inherent and unresolvable instability of subjectivity and try to make fresh translations of her experience of it. Key to this was her developing capacity to 'drop down' into a slower internal place where her experience of herself and the world was less 'filled in', busy, urgent – a place/pace where she felt less (shamingly) out of control of time. Through that, she was able to feel something of the rent in her subjectivity, and in subjectivity itself. As she became increasingly able to bear these glimpses, the shame that had previously been so debilitating began to take on a different role in her psyche, urging her to find fresh translations of the enigmatic othernesses around which she was organized at depth. In particular, it demanded that she find new translations of her experience of limitation, powerlessness and helplessness.

Earlier in this chapter I gave a 'high-level' description of applying these ideas to working with Leah's temporal defences, so that (very slowly) she became better able to spend longer and longer periods of time in states of 'flow', i.e., states where she was engrossed in her moment-to-moment experiences and thoughts. In reality, even the tiniest shift towards experiencing her inner world as a process would, for many years into analysis, precipitate a violent attack of self-hatred and shame which would abruptly pull Leah back into the desperate, despairing, impenetrable experience of herself as 'feeling like a piece of shit'.

What emerged over time was that these eruptions/avalanches were actually her self-hater's way of acting like a guard-dog that had a number of essential, protective jobs. These included: 1) preventing Leah from drifting towards (what she experienced as the cruel fantasy of) the possibility of having a less relentlessly painful inner life, and 2) keeping her specifically in the state of feeling like a piece of shit because that held the best chance of drawing close to her father and 'loving him better'.

Thus moments of emersion in interiority were inseparable from a sense of impending catastrophe because, as described earlier, Leah experienced states where her inner world had a more emergent, emerging, and engaging quality as catastrophic abandonments and betrayals of her father. Over time we came to understand this as Leah's unconscious sense that any moves towards having a more bearable inner life would cost her the longed-for relationship with him forever. As the potential cause of this loss, states of aliveness and flow were experienced as irrefutable proof of her hateful, contemptible, selfish, shitty nature, hence it was imperative that (part of her) block or attack them ruthlessly.

From this perspective, the aim of offering Leah an analytic 'hollow' in which her temporal defences could come apart was not to facilitate her experience of flow. It was, instead, to sit with the parts of her *that blocked or attacked inner flow whenever it began to emerge, and learn about the worlds contained within those parts.* While this included developing some acceptance of the powerlessness, helplessness, and shame that drove her temporal defences, the intermittent sense of fluidity that emerged out of that acceptance remained alarmingly unravelling and exposing in its realness and instability.

As Hultberg's vignette indicates, this kind of shame often cannot be looked at or referred to directly. Engagement with it needs to be, as Warren Colman describes (in relation to the psyche in general), through whatever metaphorical analogy is available. This includes 'TV soap operas, pop music, sport, the daily news' etc. (Colman, 2009, p. 211). For Leah, a seemingly simple, but powerful example of this was that, at one point, she developed a strong sense that she needed to get rid of what she described as the 'pretty clothes and shoes' she had bought over the years and had kept for the day she 'finally became pretty enough and thin enough to wear them'.[4] In spite of her sense that doing this was really important and urgent, Leah found letting go of these things extraordinarily difficult, and we were both interested in the intensity of this tension. On reflection she realized that these clothes and shoes were part of a whole unconscious inner world in which, if she could not draw close to her father and 'love him better' through her self-hatred and self-harm, she might, somehow, be able to touch him by being 'pretty' and thus be the source of his pride and delight.

Leah's changed relationship to her experience of inner time and her capacity to slow down enough to notice the 'it's a shame you aren't pretty' voice she had heard inside was pivotal in this process. It had enabled her to notice a tiny, but important crack between her sense of self and something which had previously always 'run her' at an impenetrable, visceral level. By slowing down her experience of this voice even more and becoming able to 'drop down' into the worlds within it, she realized that it was saying that she should be ashamed of herself for not being pretty enough to delight her father and boyfriend, and, through that, 'heal them' in some magical, pre-verbal way.

These processes demanded that Leah find a different relationship to places within, where will and effort were to no avail. Again, however, through the approach described she was able to find what Hinton (summarizing Laplanche) describes as 'a kind of opening, a gap, a crack, a cleavage plane in the ordinary "filled in" process of things' (Hinton, 2009, p. 643). Previously, anything that aroused shame risked opening up the chasm in her subjectivity, causing her to go into a kind of high-speed temporal defence that is the focus of this chapter, scrambling blindly and desperately to escape as the ground under her feet crumbled away. These states had, themselves, always been enormously shaming and the shift in Leah's experience of temporality enabled her to explore different ways of translating the inner othernesses that offered glimpses of more life.

Conclusion

In Laplanche's terms, Leah's shame demanded the kind of 'Copernican revolution' offered by psychoanalysis (at its radical best), in which the centre of her personality could move away from her ego towards her unconscious (Hinton, 2009, pp. 639–40). Working with Leah's experience, and use, of subjective time was integral to this shift and one of its symbolic expressions was her increasing willingness to live from a place of unresolvable and irreducible complexity. This was expressed in numerous ways, including her day-to-day relationship to clothes and shoes, which we were able to use as one of a number of languages and families of images through which we could explore and discuss the core structural shifts occurring in her inner life.

Acknowledgements

I would like to express my gratitude to Leah for what I have learnt from our work together and for her permission to write about it. I also thank the people I have worked with who have taught me so much about self-hatred and shame.

My thanks to Giles Clark and Leon Petchkovsky for their depth of engagement, outstanding generosity, and stamina which have been crucial to my thinking and writing, Ladson Hinton for making his work on shame available to me and for his ongoing, sustainingly generous encouragement of my work, and Hessel Willemsen for his patient, much appreciated interest and support.

Thanks also to John Wiley & Sons, Inc. for permission to draw on sections of my previous papers published in the *Journal of Analytical Psychology* (2016a, 2016b, © 2016, The Society of Analytical Psychology) and to Susanna Wright (joint editor-in-chief at *JAP*) for her invaluable help with those papers.

Notes

1 I am using this neuroscience research as the basis of imaginative (and therefore psychologically useable) narrative rather than offering an evidence-based model of interiority.
2 Bear in mind that for Jung affect was synonymous with emotions (Samuels, 1986, p. 11). However, as Hinton (1998) points out, Jung said contradictory things about the affective spectrum. Despite his ideas about the affective basis

of personality, Jung made a great deal of the separation between emotion and feeling. He was very eager to preserve feeling as something conscious and rational, and rather different from emotion (Jung, 1935, pp. 25–6).

3 My thanks to Vivien Bainbridge for this image.

4 Leah's relationship to clothes and shoes had always been psychologically important and a 'live' (though painful) thread in her analysis – see Austin 2016a, p. 29.

References

Austin, S. (2016a). Working with chronic and relentless self-hatred, self-harm and existential shame: a clinical study and reflections (I). *Journal of Analytical Psychology*, 61, 1, 24–43. doi:10.1111/1468-5922.12193.

Austin, S. (2016b). Working with chronic and relentless self-hatred, self-harm and existential shame: a clinical study and reflections (II). *Journal of Analytical Psychology*, 61, 4, 411–433. doi:10.1111/1468-5922.12241.

Bell, A. (ed.) (1984). *The Diary of Virginia Woolf*, Vol. 5. London. Hogarth Press.

Colman, W. (2009). Theory as metaphor: clinical knowledge and its communication. *Journal of Analytical Psychology*, 54, 2, 199–215. doi:10.1111/j.1468-5922.2009.01770.x.

Frosh, S. & Baraitser, L. (2003). Thinking, recognition, and otherness. *The Psychoanalytic Review*, 90, 771–789.

Hartman, G. (1994). The Franco-Prussian War or Jung as a dissociationist. Available at: www.cgjungpage.org/learn/articles/analytical-psychology/139-the-franco-prussian-war-or-jung-as-dissociationist.

Haule, J. (1992). From somnambulism to the archetypes: the French roots of Jung's split with Freud. In R. Papadopoulos (ed.), *Carl Gustav Jung: Critical Assessments*, Vol. 1. London: Routledge.

Hinton, L. (1998). Shame as a teacher: "Lowly Wisdom" at the millennium. In M. A. Mattoon (ed.), *Destruction and Creation: Personal and Cultural Transformations*. Proceedings of The Fourteenth International Congress for Analytical Psychology, Florence. Einsiedeln: Daimon Verlag.

Hinton, L. (2009). The enigmatic signifier and the decentred subject. *Journal of Analytical Psychology*, 54, 5, 637–657. doi: 10.1111/j.1468-5911.2009.01811.x.

Hultberg, P. (1987). Shame: an overshadowed emotion. In M. A. Mattoon (ed.), *The Archetype of Shadow in a Split World*. Proceedings of The Tenth International Congress for Analytical Psychology, Berlin. Einsiedeln: Daimon Verlag.

Hultberg, P. (1988). Shame—a hidden emotion. *Journal of Analytical Psychology*, 33, 2, 109–126. doi: 10.1111/j.1465-5922.1988.00109.x.

Jung, C. G. (1907). *The Psychology of Dementia Praecox*. CW 3.

Jung, C. G. (1921). *Psychological Types*. CW 6.

Jung, C. G. (1935). *The Tavistock Lectures. CW* 18.

Jung, C. G. (1954). 'Psychological aspects of the mother archetype'. *CW* 9i.

Kilborne, B. (1997). The hunting of the red-faced snark. In M. Lansky & A. Morrison (eds), *The Widening Scope of Shame*. Hillsdale, NJ: The Analytic Press.

Kilborne, B. (2002). *Disappearing Persons: Shame and Appearance*. New York: State University of New York Press.

Kinston, W. (1983). A theoretical context for shame. *International Journal of Psychoanalysis*, *64*, 213–226.

Kouider, S., Stahlhut, C., Gelskov, S., Barbosa, L., Dutat, M., de Gardelle, V., Christophe, A., Dehaene, S., & Dehaene-Lambertz, G. (2013). A neural marker of perceptual consciousness in infants. *Science*, 340, 6130, 376–380.

Laplanche, J. (1989). *New Foundations for Psychoanalysis*. Oxford: Blackwell.

Laplanche, J. (1999). *Essays on Otherness*. London: Routledge.

Laplanche, J. (2002). Sublimation and/or inspiration. L. Thurston & J. Fletcher (trans.). *New Formations,* 48, 30–50.

Levinas, E. (2003). *On Escape*. B. Bergo (trans.). Stanford, CA: Stanford University Press.

Lewis, H. B. (1987). Introduction: shame—the "sleeper" in psychopathology. In H. B. Lewis (ed.), *The Role of Shame in Symptom Formation*. Mahwah, NJ: Lawrence Erlbaum Associates.

Montes Sánchez, A. (2013). Social shame versus private shame: a real dichotomy? *PhaenEx*, 8, 1, 28–58.

Pines, M. (1995). The universality of shame: a psychoanalytic approach. *British Journal of Psychotherapy*, 11, 3, 346–357. doi:10.1111/j.1752-0118.1995. tb00739.x.

Redfearn, J. (1985). *My Self, My Many Selves*. London: Karnac Books.

Samuels, A. (1986). *A Critical Dictionary of Jungian Analysis*. London: Routledge and Kegan Paul.

Scarfone, D. (2006). A matter of time: actual time and the production of the past. *The Psychoanalytic Quarterly*, 75, 3, 807–834. doi:10.1002/j2167-4086.2006. tb00058.x.

Stack, A. (2005). Culture, cognition and Jean Laplanche's enigmatic signifier. *Theory, Culture and Society*, 22, 3, 63–80. doi:10.1177/0263276405053720.

Stiegler, B. (2013). *What Makes Life Worth Living: On Pharmacology*. D. Ross (trans.). Malden, MA: Polity Press.

Chapter 7

Shame and evanescence; the body as driver of temporality

Hessel Willemsen

Introduction

In this chapter I shall address shame, the painful affect, well known but often neglected with regard to its ability to affect lived life, awareness of the other, and temporality. Shame makes us aware of ourselves, our bodies, our limitations, gaps, lacks, the care we did not receive, the privileges we did not have and the deprivation we suffered. Like Sartre (1984), I shall argue that shame is not, as many think, exclusively related to a conscious evaluation of activities, morality or superego, but also has an ontological dimension. It is deeply related to an existential emptiness lying at the core of every human being. This emptiness, or gap, involves our awareness of death, of ending, the unique human quality to know about the end, but this gap, or Nothingness, as Sartre would say, is also an intrinsic psychological deadness or a negation. Shame signals deficiency and deadness and can freeze us, or stop us short from living life and being aware of the continuum of experience, the sliding from one experience to another, from relating to others and to the world outside us. The irregular process of time passing is also observable in the unavoidable changes of the body, thereby making temporality ever present although not always consciously observed, and often denied. I will address the ability of the present to command the past and argue that hardly ever is the past past. Excitement to engage, and shame to protect and moderate, influence the quality of relationships in psychic reality.

Speaking literally, experiences are truly part of the past when we can no longer remember them, when there is no memory trace left, and perhaps it is more accurate to speak of a changing past when the affect cathected to memories loses intensity. Because we adapt to new experiences and trauma – experiences which conjure up the past to transform the present[1] – the past is endlessly moderated and can never be found as it once was. Past experiences, with their associated affects, are not entities in themselves but are actually parts of present experience. In a sense, there is no past, there is only temporality. As Lombardi would say:

> I can state on the basis of several clinical experiences that giving prominence to the subject's relation to temporality can facilitate change as a goal of the psychoanalytic process … and bring about alterations to the ways affects are experienced: not by acting directly upon them, but by working instead on the formal parameters which organize the mind, that is primarily on its spatio-temporal organization.
>
> (Lombardi, 2003, p. 1532)

Affects, arising from the body, need to be understood in the present tense, within the spatio-temporal configuration which organizes the mind,[2] including a relationship with the other and adaptation to environment and trauma. Working with temporality has significant consequences for the analytic process because the focus of the analytic intervention is not on past experiences, as a regressive revisiting, but on the here-and-now in which the past is processed as part of the present. The spatio-temporal organization holds the past in the present; the past, then, is never divorced from its current reality. Having said this, it may now appear as if the present is privileged as a focus of understanding temporality but the next sections will bring more complexity to the present and its connection with the past, future, loss and identity.

Temporality

Hawking (1988, pp. 161ff.) described three notions of time which each has a vector: psychological, entropic[3] and cosmological time, denoting that time has a direction and varying magnitude. The perception of time, psychological time, is ever fluctuating and progressing, and has the same direction as entropic time (ibid., p. 169), or in other words, we remember the past, not the future. When considering the forward vector of time, one may observe that the entropy of a homeostatic gas (a state of optimal order) is zero, and therefore entropy can be static. Could time be seen as static, or circular?

Agamben (2007) explained that Plato and Aristotle delivered a concept of time that is circular and has no direction. Time, according to the Greeks, 'is quantified as an infinite continuum of precise fleeting moments' (ibid., p. 102). In contrast, the Christian experience of time 'appears as a history of salvation, the progressive realization of redemption, whose foundation is in God' (ibid., p. 103). Augustine considered that there was no such a thing as a 'precise fleeting moment' because if the moment was severed in its smallest part of that moment, then is there, in fact, a present? It could be thought that the present has no length, that there is only process. It seems to me that the present is more complex than the definition of an infinitely small moment. To understand how future and past may take their place in this present moment, however long, consideration is given to the neuroscience work of Szpunar and Tulving (2011) who describe two brain-damaged patients. The patients were able to *know* that they had a past and a future but were not *aware* that their current self extended into their personal past and future. They lacked an ability to anticipate the future. Szpunar and Tulving write: 'The capacity to appreciate one's current self with the future (and past) reflects the functioning of a special form of consciousness awareness called "Autonoetic Consciousness"' (ibid., p. 3). The present is not without anticipation, the ability to plan, meander and indeed not without being melancholic about what *will* be missed after having suffered a loss. James (2010, p. 210) discusses a Husserlian phenomenology account 'according to which the passage of time . . . is constituted in and through a structure of retention and protention, according to which traces of an immediate past are retained and future elements anticipated'.

Awareness of future and past and the passage of time is perhaps the characteristic that most differentiates human beings from animals. Animals evolve and adapt to a changing world, but conscious awareness of past experiences, of the present we find ourselves in, and the active anticipation of possible future environmental shifts, is a capacity observed mainly in human beings. We are painfully aware of time passing, of excitement ahead and of the 'unbearable lightness of being' (Kundera, 1984), of living in the moment. Hinton (2015) aptly coined the term *Homo temporalis* to denote that every experience we have has a temporal dimension: experience is always subjected to process.

Time, evanescence and identity

Time as an experience is not linear or causal; instead, it is an experience that is progressive and can be slow, sudden, gradual, erratic, at moments perhaps timeless and frozen: awareness may disappear and unconscious timelessness as described by Freud (1916[1915]/2001) may prevail. Terr (1984) helps us to understand the distinction between a *sense of time* as 'the subjective feelings and meanings connected with the perception of time passage', observable in early development, and the *perception of time* which she defines as 'the conscious, and perhaps unconscious, sensory experience of time'. The perception of time, or what may be referred to as our temporal memory, usually developing around the age of 4 or 5, is a conscious awareness of time – yesterday, today, tomorrow – as some sort of a continuum, but our sense of time, the subjective experience of things coming and going, of warmth and coldness, of hunger and satisfaction, develops at a much earlier stage. Hartmann (1956) speaks of the ability to distinguish between the objective and the subjective as a way of reality testing which, according to Lombardi (2003), is an aspect of time.

When considering time as progressive, is there, as a fact, a history and a future? Einstein, for example, suggested that 'for those of us who believe in physics, the distinction between past, present and future is only a stubbornly persistent illusion' (Speziali, 1979). It could be thought that Einstein would have needed to anticipate a future for him to make this well-known statement. He would say that we are only able to live in the 'here-and-now' but as human beings, in this here-and-now, we are only too aware of time that has passed because of memory traces, scars, traumas, adaptations we made to trauma, and indeed our progressive ageing. The changing body denotes the existence of our biological make-up, a past that was, and contributes to the determination of who we are, the image we have of ourselves. Freud, discussing the beauty of Nature and the changing of the seasons, in a brief essay 'On Transience', said that '[t]he beauty of the human form and face vanish forever in the course of our own lives, but their evanescence only lends them a fresh charm'. Kristeva, Jardine and Blake (1981) considered that the manner in which we experience the evanescence of our body affects the accumulation of past experiences and referred to this accumulation as 'historical sedimentation'. The *Vergänglichkeit* (evanescence) of the body contributes to who we are and therefore, by implication, the temporal dimension will be different for men and women. Whereas men can be seen to be on a continuous hunt, women are aware of the monthly cycle, carrying their babies, and, certainly traditionally, the care they afford their growing children. Women are more directly in touch with nature, the cosmos, reproduction, the beginning of life and the child's development, a set of experiences captured by Jung when describing 'The archetype of The Feminine' (1952/1986, para. 514).

Time, loss and future

To return to Hawking and use his ideas metaphorically, entropy is generally not zero: there is process in the infinitely small moment, except of course that some traumas may cause a state of timelessness, characterized by an absence of chronological time in the unconsciousness, as Freud would say, or what Scarfone refers to as the *Unpast*: 'For what regards the unconscious, what we naively designate as the past is in fact still quite active; it may seem dead but still haunts the present and is commonly seen as a repetition compulsion' (2015, p. 515). The *Unpast*, neither past nor present, does not become past history, nor does it open a window to the future because there is no sense of loss. But the loss of the past and the present also exist when a person suffers extreme desolation. Primo Levi describes his state of mind two weeks after he entered Monowitz, or Auschwitz III: 'Here I am, on the bottom. One learns quickly enough to wipe out the past and the future if the need is pressing' (2015, p. 32). He continues to describe how the Italians in the camp met but that the meetings stopped because it was better not to remember and think.

Temporality is that process of passing from moment to moment where in the moment we can be troubled by our past only to press forward to our future. In the moment, past and future are forever merged. Because of our organic fabric, we will not manage the status quo of the homeostatic gas: one of humanity's predicaments, the return to the Greeks' circular unending time, to live longer and hold life at a standstill, is ultimately always a forlorn case, yet one of humankind's main obsessions. We try to avoid death. Freud grasped this determinist principle when he considered that the death drive was fundamentally biological; its purpose was to return the body to ashes: 'the task of which is to lead organic life back into the inanimate state' (1923/2001, p. 40). This inanimate state is death but is also the original inanimate state of our 'being': organic life originated from the inanimate. Freud goes on to say that 'the emergence of life would thus be the cause of the continuance of life and also at the same time of the striving towards death' and speaks of love and hate being blended, the dualism of the two instincts. Life, Eros, is only possible when there is interplay with death. The ancient emergence of burial rituals, an acknowl-edgement of death during life, is often seen as evidence of the first signs of awareness of futurity. This is echoed by Heidegger (2010) who thought that the awareness of death is the basis of futurity. Loss in general seems involved in development and awareness of temporality, as in Freud's description of the child who developed a ritual to deal with the temporary loss of his mother. The game of the reel which disappeared and returned was played by the child who found the loss of his mother painful. Why then did he repetitively have to play this painful game? Freud said that 'It may perhaps be said . . . that [the mother's] departure had to be enacted as a necessary preliminary to her joyful return, and that it was in the latter that lay the true purpose of the game' (Freud, 1920/2001, pp. 15–16): by mas-tering the loss, the child could anticipate his mother's return.

Heidegger, a philosopher of ontology, considered that the being of a person is linked to 'nothingness' in that the human being is distinguished from other beings and objects in the world through being uniquely con-scious of death. This awareness of 'nothingness' is an integral part of 'being' of the human being (Critchley, 2004). While facing this nothing-ness, either as a state of being, or as an endpoint to life, we are faced with the progression of time. The child in Freud's example lived the past, the mother's departure, in the present to deal with the painful loss and to anticipate her return. Might this knowledge help us understand how to work with patients? Talero, when considering the respective roles of the psychological past and present in psychoanalysis suggests that 'It is the patient's present situation that has in effect "summoned" the past to come forward' (2004, p. 166). She considered that 'in the phenomenon of transference what we see is the power of the present to embody the past.' Perhaps hope, fantasies of the future and enigmatic expectations are a more important motivation for the initial transference. The embodiment of the present, in my view, includes, also, if not in particular, the counter-transference. The past – memories and experiences – are summoned to be worked through in a process that Freud referred to as *Nachträglichkeit* (1896/2001, pp. 166–7, footnote 2).

The Other

Before we address how the past may transcend a present, we need to understand how past experiences may have affected us. Winnicott wrote that the original experience of primitive agony 'cannot get into the past tense unless the ego can first gather it into its own present time experience' (1974, p. 105). Something is happening in the future, whereas it has already happened in the past, he suggested. When considering the patient's fear of a breakdown, he drew attention to the possibility that the anticipated breakdown had in fact already happened, near the beginning of the individual's life (ibid., p. 105). The infant was let down due to a pattern of environmental failures leaving these babies to carry unthinkable or archaic anxiety. He suggested that there was no ego to process the affect that emerged in the mind of the infant. The past could only be captured in a later present, when the ego would function well enough. Ferrari went a step further by describing how anxiety is related to unmetabolized affect, which arises from the body, thereby introducing the concept of affect as originating in the infant's body (2004, see also Carvalho, 2012, and Willemsen, 2014, pp. 700–1). Through its 'vertical relation', the infant is in touch with affect arising from the body while through the 'horizontal relation', the infant relates to the mother. The ability to 'be in touch', with one's self or with another, depends on the presence of a mind, i.e., the child's own 'horizontal', which though present in incipient form in the infant, is very rudimentary and cannot develop properly without the avail-ability of the mother's 'horizontal' until the infant's own is properly developed and in place. The mother's presence of mind assists as an auxil-iary to help modulate the infant's unbearable distress and affects, a point also made by Winnicott (1974, p. 104), who referred to the mother as being the 'auxiliary ego-function'. The inference from Winnicott's and Ferrari's theories is that the infant's environment and the affect as it emerges in the body are reflective of the impingement of the Other, as Scarfone (2006, p. 821) would say. The infant is highly affected by the care that is given causing an awareness of time and difference. In addition it is possible to conceive of the idea that the infant needs to meet and has to deal with unconscious communications from the mother when its ego is still archaic and developing.

Laplanche

Laplanche gives consideration to the manner in which the maternal envi-ronment, and particularly its unconscious content, might impose itself on the infant. Although the notion of infantile sexuality is generally accepted, would the mother's sexual feelings and other unconscious motives, such as for example having a baby to compensate for feelings of emptiness, indeed affect the infant's early development? Laplanche thought so. He considered that mothers communicate sexually charged enigmatic messages to children. This is the 'norm', and these messages are also enigmatic to the mothers (Scarfone, 2013). He named this situation of being exposed to unconscious messages from the Other, the 'fundamental anthropological situation' referring to the primacy of the Other, the mother, who:

> while [she] is attuned, as well as possible, to the needs of the *infans*[4] in a state of *radical helplessness* [*Hilflosigkeit*], this Other is also, necessarily, the bearer of a repressed unconscious that somewhat interferes within the relation of mutual adaptation between adult and child.
>
> (Scarfone, 2013, pp. 549–50, original emphasis)

Freud referred to this original make-up of the mind as primal repression (1915/2001, p. 148). Whereas Laplanche emphasized the importance of the Other, Freud's introduction of the term *Hilflosigkeit* 'used to denote the state of human suckling which, being entirely dependent on other people for the satisfaction of its needs (hunger, thirst), proves incapable of carrying out the specific action necessary to put an end to internal tension' (Laplanche & Pontalis, 1973, p. 189). Laplanche emphasized *Hilflosigkeit* and thought this made the infant more permeable to the messages of the mother.

According to Freud, the state of helplessness, for the adult, is the prototype of the traumatic situation based on the need to be entirely dependent on other people for the satisfaction of their needs. The infant adapts to the absence of the breast by creating a hallucinatory reproduction of the experience of satisfaction and, at the same time, experiences the beginning of a sense of time. It is clear that the hallucination creates the beginning of an image, or representation, and therefore can be seen as spatial, as development of mind, but equally infants can await the breast and then ruthlessly take it. Freud focused on the self, a solipsistic approach and suggested that the infant creates a hallucinatory object which is repressed, whereas Laplanche suggests that the infant is exposed to the Other who stimulates the baby to create part of its own unconscious content.[5] The infant tries to compensate for the absence of the breast, as Freud suggested, or tries to translate[6] the Other's unconscious content with which it has to cope. 'Time steps in when the infant notices that there is a message from the Other', but, not having the ego apparatus available to make the necessary translations, the Other's communications are repressed (Scarfone, 2006, p. 823). Having established that the infant and the young child are inevitably subjected to the care provided by the Other and are exposed to the unconscious motivations of the parent to which the infant necessarily needed to adapt, the question remains how these past experiences then continue to affect our lives now.

Nachträglichkeit

It is worth considering that analysis addressing early trauma is not a reductive exercise but focuses on the reworking of the past in the present. *Nachträglichkeit*, or *après coup*, introduced in Freud's early writings (Laplanche & Pontalis, 1973, pp. 111–14; for a discussion of *après coup*, see Perelberg, 2006), refers to the endless, unconscious reinterpretations of affect released by the originating body, which could not be mentalized at the time during infancy, as well as memories and cognitively endowed affective experiences originating at later stages of development. The affects are coated with enigma because the mother's response to the infant was inevitably suffused with her unconscious motives. The body and mind carry memories of unmetabolized truths about gaps in care or more obvious traumatic experience, as well as the enigmatic messages to which the infant was exposed, leading to the necessary incompleteness of the self as the first object. The consequent shifts of memory following these reinterpretations also evoke shifts in our sense of time and its rhythms. Freud referred to 'psychical temporality and causality' as revisiting experiences, memory-traces and impressions at a later date to fit in with fresh experiences or the attainment of a new meaning, or stage of development (Laplanche & Pontalis, 1973, p. 111). Through the mechanism of *Nachträglichkeit*, memories and imprints can be reorganized to transcend the present and provide a different outlook on life which makes us, in turn, principally teleological beings; we have an apparent purpose in the anticipated future. A person may be endowed with psychical effectiveness, or, in other words, the experience of life, and the outlook on life, may alter due to a reworking of experiences in the present, a process Scarfone

(2006) referred to as 'the production of the past'. Sartre emphasizes this coming together of past and present in his work *Being and Nothingness* where he writes:

> Since the past is no more, since it has melted away into nothingness, if the memory continues to exist, it must be by virtue of the *present* modification of our being ... the body, the present perception, and the past as a present impression in the body – all is *actuality*.
>
> (1984, p. 160)

For Sartre there is no actual past, only imprints and memories of the past, which we carry with us organically. The presence of the past in the present is actual. Later Sartre repeats this point: 'My past never appears isolated in its "pastness"; it would be absurd even to imagine that it can *exist* as such. It is originally the past *of this* present' (ibid., p. 163). If the past is isolated in its 'pastness', we would have lost the memory of the event, the memory has then faded. The historical past is only found outside us, as buildings, bones and the paper I write but also through a collective passing on of cultural memory, or collective unconscious (see, for example, Jung, 1953) and the genetic blueprint we leave behind. I would say, however, that the body carries a past that is no more, which leads me to talk about evanescence.

Evanescence

F. Scott Fitzgerald's 'The Curious Case of Benjamin Button' (1923/2008) is a short fantasy story about a man who reversed in age; he was born an old man and died a baby. The slow vanishing of his wrinkled body makes it possible for Benjamin Button to become young and love Hildegarde whose body ages normally. Time is of the essence as he becomes younger and she older, making for a window of time in which they can be lovers. The story leaves us with awareness that our body is the concrete evidence of changing times, of time past, and this change takes place slowly, gradually, but surely.

Evanescence comes from the Latin *evanescere* meaning 'to disappear, vanish'. Something that possesses qualities of evanescence has the characteristic of disappearing or vanishing, like being gripped with the fear of losing feelings of love and memories after a painful separation. Evanescence would imply that there is a history, something that has vanished away and no longer exists. Throughout life, the body presents with evidence of the loss of youth, of time past, of what has been and of what never was. In contrast to loss, the body is also reflective of a healthy life, a life well lived and of time passed satisfactorily. The body, it could be said, carries historicity.[7] There is a biological past that is no more; the youthful body that once was is no longer part of the present. The passing of time expressed by the ageing body may reflect memories which can no longer be remembered and have truly become past. The awareness of the ageing body may imply a pre-existing time-consciousness. The demise of the body, of what has been, drives time, drives the perception of the future and makes us anticipatory in the moment, as Sartre suggested. The actuality of the body, denoting the liveliness of the present and a past that has been, stands in contrast with what has gone, the body that is no more. The psychological gaps and lacks we carry with us define who we are and are shielded from us and from others by shame. It seems to me that shame protects and helps contain insufferable trauma, but shame also makes us want to disappear and so we set up barriers and move away from others and ourselves.

Shame

Shame is probably one of the most difficult emotions we as humans have to deal with. Often described as a painful feeling of humiliation or distress caused by a conscious feeling of wrongdoing, shame is about being seen by the other, or about observing oneself. Shame can be defined at two levels. The first well-known definition is related to the superego, the feeling of failure related to demands we place on ourselves and judgements we consider others have of us, as discussed, for example, by Kernberg. He sees shame as a function of superego realizations, efforts to live up to newly incorporated aspects of the ego-ideal. In his view: 'Under ordinary circumstances, shame is gradually replaced by the development of guilt over unacceptable behaviour' (2015, p. 640). This level of shame is more easily conscious, accessible to awareness and readily seen by me, or somebody observing me. Shame at this level may be described as a feeling, an emotion that has some sort of judgement related to it; the emotion can, principally, be thought about.

A more profound level of shame relates to what Jacoby (1994) describes as shame and organizational forms of the sense of self. He refers to the biblical myth of Paradise (ibid., p. 49) which he considers is the opening up of consciousness, a dawning awareness concerned with the separation of self and others and from God, which results in the loss of Paradise and eternal bliss. Jacoby, influenced by the work of Stern and Lichtenberg, considered that the capacity to experience shame first appears in connection with the realization that the self can also be seen from the outside. An 'objective self' has been born that stands against the merely 'subjective self' of earlier phases. The origins of shame, however, lie in the 'subjective self' and have a connection with the psyche-soma at early stages of development. Feeling comfortable with oneself is also about feeling comfortable with one's body: 'we may be so ashamed of our bodies that we can hardly live with or in them' (ibid., p. 50). Shame, Jacoby argues, is at the core of the formation of self-esteem, an important organizational aspect of the sense of self as described by Stern (1985). Jacoby referred to shame as an innate affect, connected to feeling inferior when being aware of the other. Shame, according to Tomkins (1987), may be experienced as shyness when there is a wish to have an immediate intimate relationship with somebody else, but can also be experienced as guilt 'when positive affect is attenuated by virtue of moral normative sanctions experienced as conflicting with what is exciting or enjoyable' (Demos, 1995, p. 404). He also defines shame experienced as inferiority when 'discouragement is located in the self as an inability of the self to do what the self wishes to do'; shame supports the regulation of excitement.

In her search for the origins of shame, and acknowledging that our forebears hardly, or limitedly, addressed shame, Wharton concluded that 'shame is above all linked to a person's self-image or sense of self' (1990, p. 328). For her, shame involves the whole self, including the body, such that a person in the grip of shame has a sense of shrinking, of collapse, an overwhelming impulse to hide, related to a sense of inner deficiency or badness which must be kept hidden. Wharton, like Jacoby, considers the origins of shame to be innate and leads to an impulse to hide from the other who is looking at and observing us. When observing infants in the presence of the mother, and particularly the face of the mother with its all-important ability to respond to the baby, shame is observable. As Levinas noted: 'Meaning is the face of the Other, and all recourse to words takes place already within the primordial face to face language' (Levinas, 1961/1969, p. 206). Scarfone (2006), similarly, referred to 'the impingement of the Other'. It is of course the mother who provides meaning to the many affective states the infant experiences when relating to his mother and to his body. The mother inevitably cannot remain focused on the infant indefinitely and, even when focused, she misses out on interests, excitements and disappointments expressed by the infant who may respond, when the mother repeatedly misses out, with upset, anger or withdrawing into himself.

Shame can be understood as a response to the disappearance of the face of the Other, and also as a response to enigmas, the unconscious messages of the Other the infant is faced with but cannot translate. Shame can be seen as a response to unmetabolized affect, of the lacks and gaps which inevitably are part of the self when we live with the Other who at times is unresponsive, particularly in the early days of life. The face of the Other, either a person outside us, or our objective self, may help us embrace shame to reach a deeper openness without the ego's preconditions. It is the face of the Other as Levinas suggested, and the awareness of our limits, which reminds us of 'that little clod of earth that we are' (Hinton, 1998, p. 184, and Adler, 1973, p. 19, footnote. 8). Shame, Hinton argues, could be a teacher, 'an everyday guide to humble knowing' (ibid., p. 172) while bearing the painfulness of what might not have been received. As a fundamental feeling reflecting the unmetabolized past, shame lives with us through our times as an observer: we have an intangible sense of what we might have been deprived of, a conscious awareness which would not have been evident in a state of privation, but can only become apparent subsequently. In such moments of time, however much we can learn, shame is also a painful reminder of the finite self.

Temporality, shame and evanescence

We progress through time, while registering sensations, experiences and ideas, sometimes as a gradual process, sometimes disjointed or stilted, at other times as if there is no movement. We can open up to what feels unknown and troubling; when we need to adapt to everyday life and its traumas, we summon our memories to understand the actualities we find ourselves in. The past, processed in the present, was formed when affect could not be metabolized, unconscious fantasies of the Other could not be processed and enigmas not translated. The unmetabolized affects and enigmas resonate with Nothingness because we cannot be perfectly attuned to, and neither can we resolve nor dispose of, all that is lost or never was. This existential emptiness lies at the core of every human being.

By implication, shame closely linked to our self-esteem is, I think, ontological, indeed existential (Hultberg, 1988). Associated with the meaning of life, shame regulates excitement and lust, and serves to hide painful parts of ourselves, full of dark affect. Erikson spoke of two basic alternating moods as those of 'carnival' and 'atonement': 'the first gives licence and leeway to sensual involvement, to relief and release at all cost; the second surrenders to the negative conscience which constricts, depresses, and enjoins man for what he has left unresolved, uncared for, unatoned' (1958, p. 75). Shame negotiates a life between lust and reflection, between Enlightenment and Memento Mori. One cannot help but think of Narcissus and Goldmund: Narcissus's atonement complemented Goldmund's lust for life and neither could be without the other (Hesse, 2006).[8] Shame serves as an intermediate between the reality of the world outside us, the excitement we have available to relate, and the darkness that needs protecting. Significant levels of shame may prevent us from being in the moment, from living life and from unlocking the past to deal with current traumatic situations to which one need necessarily adapt. On the other hand, flight from shame, or its possibility, can also result in a frozen life without depth.

Shame is found in the subjective self, is part of the psyche-soma and influences our sense of self and our body-image. Acutely aware of the changing organic fabric of our body, we are confronted with the lacks and gaps early in life. Connolly speaks of the importance of the body, a psychic deadness that preserves all that did not happen: 'The result of this traumatic non-happening is that temporality which is part and parcel of possessing an alive body becomes excluded and the future is foreclosed' (2013, p. 651). She quoted Merleau-Ponty: 'The body is our general medium of having a world' (Merleau-Ponty, quoted by ibid., p. 637). Through the changing body, shame is observed, sometimes projected upon: the perception of the body can be a manifestation of unspeakable shame. Distastefulness or fear of our body causes temporality to be a painstakingly complex process and interrupts the enjoyment of being with others. Shame can truly be a stumbling block to further development because of the humiliation and the suffering that may become exposed. It is hard to imagine human development without the notion of shame.

However, humbly accepting the humanity of life may make it possible to observe the changes in mind and body to give meaning to shameful moments.

Sartre (1984, p. 174) speaks of the 'evanescent value of the past' when the past is used to transcend the present and quotes Hegel: '*Wesen ist was gewesen ist*', an allusion to the historical nature of essence (ibid., p. 175). Perhaps certain experiences can never be shrugged off, but I think that the intensity of affect may be reduced, so that the original experience, with its associated affect, will not be the same, certainly not in its intensity. Surprisingly we may find ourselves in more navigable waters and discover that '[t]he past is never where you think you left it', as Katherine Anne Porter said (1962). There is the possibility to move forward; purpose is found when we undo the past (Scarfone, 2006).

There may be implications for technique when the focus of interventions is on working through trauma, regression or repetition-compulsion as a way of repeating past trauma, or creating awareness from the perspective of the objective self. The focus of analytic work is not on the past, but on the actuality of the past in the present. Over the course of psychoanalytic history, the focus of technique has increasingly moved from analysing the repressed to working with patients in the present. The ability to be with the patient in the here-and-now, particularly being attuned to one's countertransference and accepting that there is a significant unknown, a Nothingness, makes it possible to reconcile with the patient's temporality: the slow, or sometimes rapid, perhaps stifling or disjointed progression through the felt experiences as a way of developing increasingly more contact with the outer world.

The importance of working in the here-and-now was, among others, expressed by Bion for whom 'psychoanalytic observation is concerned neither with what has happened nor with what is going to happen but with what is happening' (1967/1996, p. 17). The past is not something that is removed from us but is at all times part of us: 'The past is never dead. It's not even past' (Faulkner, 1951). Ogden (2015) critically addresses the interpretative method, the verbalization of what has just happened. When the interpretation is made, the state of shared affect has already taken place. Ogden prefers the intuiting psychic reality. This is elsewhere referred to as 'Moments of Meeting' coined by the Boston Change Process Study Group (BCPSG, 2010), acknowledging that intuiting psychic reality or being attuned to it is essentially a complex process, for the infant, but also later in life. An interpretation comes after 'the psychoanalyst's intuition of reality with which he must be at one' (Bion, 1967/1996, p. 17).

In summary, I would say that the inevitability of death is the driver of temporality marking the ineluctability of time. Temporality manifests itself in its most primal way during the moment when the past, the present and the future converge; Heidegger called these 'ecstacies' of time, a unity of these three dimensions (2010, p. 319ff.). Time moves as a gradient beginning some time *in utero* and ending at the final breath. These ecstases cannot be thought of without considering shame, so important in its onto-logical meaning, relating to the chronic incompleteness of the person, and therefore without considering the incompleteness of the body. This chronic sense of incompleteness and finitude creates a quality of shame in life, varying with particular circumstances. Temporality, shame and mortality are strongly interconnected.

Notes

1 New experiences and trauma, to which the individual needs to adapt, resonate with similar past experiences or trauma to accommodate particularly the affec-tive component of the present experience. The past and present experience may amalgamate to a new representation of the present while also altering the past. Going forward the present experience transforms, has gone beyond the actual experience, to include past memory and affect, making for a healthy adaptation.
2 Freud is helpful in understanding 'temporal-spatial configuration' when he introduces time as working through emotions when one loses a loved one (Freud, 1917/2001). The process of working through requires a space, or a mind, to represent memory and affect (Ferrari, 2004).
3 The measure of randomness and disorder in the universe is called 'entropy'. In chemistry, entropy (represented by the capital letter S) is a thermodynamic function that describes the randomness and disorder of molecules based on the number of different arrangements available to them in a given system or reac-tion (Smith & Van Ness, 1987, pp. 148ff.). The second law of thermodynamics states that the total entropy of an isolated system always increases over time, or remains constant in ideal cases where the system is in a steady state or under-going a reversible process (ibid., pp. 155ff.). Hawking said: 'there are always many more disordered than there are ordered ones' (1988, p. 162).
4 Scarfone uses the terms 'infans' helpfully in that the root meaning of the word 'infans' is not speaking, i.e., without words, or before words (Cresswell, 2010).
5 Laplanche reintroduced Freud's seduction theory, which he largely abandoned in favour of the structural model. About Freud's seduction theory, he said: '[M]y job has been to show why Freud missed some very important points in this theory. But before saying that we must revise the theory, we must know it. And I think that ignorance concerning the seduction theory causes people to go back to something pre-analytic. By discussing the seduction theory,

we are doing justice to Freud, perhaps doing Freud better justice than he did himself. He forgot the importance of his theory, and its very meaning, which was not just the importance of external events' (Caruth, 2001).

6 Translation is a term introduced by Laplanche. He said that an enigmatic message first needs to be translated because it does not have a factual context. Once translated, the message has become part of a communication and can be interpreted (see, for example, Caruth, 2001, para. 108).

7 Historicity is the historical actuality of persons and events, meaning the quality of being part of history as opposed to being a historical myth, legend or fiction. Historicity focuses on the truth value of knowledge claims about the past (denoting historical actuality, authenticity, and factuality). The historicity of a claim about the past is its factual status.

8 In *Narcissus and Goldmund*, the influence of Friedrich Nietzsche's theory of the Apollonian versus Dionysian spirit is evident. The polarization of Narcissus's individualist Apollonian character stands in contrast to the passionate and zealous disposition of Goldmund. Hesse, in the spirit of Nietzsche's *The Birth of Tragedy*, completes the equation by creating Goldmund as a wanderer (a Dionysian endeavour) balanced out by Narcissus, the structured and stable priest-monk (an Apollonian approach), and highlighting the harmonizing relationship of the main characters.

References

Adler, G. (ed.) (1973). *C.G. Jung Letters*. Vol. 1. London: Kegan Paul.

Agamben, G. (2007). *Infancy and History: On the Destruction of Time*. Oxfordshire: Marston Book Services.

BCPSG (2010). *Change in Psychotherapy: A Unifying Paradigm*. New York: W. W. Norton & Company.

Bion, W. (1967/1996). Notes on memory and desire. In E. Bott Spillius & M. Klein, *Today: Developments in Theory and Practice*. Hove: Brunner-Routledge.

Caruth, C. (2001). *An Interview with Jean Laplanche*. Available at: http://pmc.iath. virginia.edu//text-only/issue.101/11.2caruth.txt. Retrieved 9 January 2017.

Carvalho, R. (2012). A brief introduction to the thought of Armando B. Ferrari. *British Journal of Psychotherapy*, 28, 413–434.

Connolly, A. (2013). Out of the body: embodiment and its vicissitudes. *Journal of Analytical Psychology*, 58, 636–656.

Cresswell, J. (2010). *Oxford Dictionary of Word Origins*. Oxford: Oxford University Press, 2nd edn.

Critchley, P. (2004). *Martin Heidegger: Ontology and Ecology*. [e-book] Available through academia website: http://mmu.academia.edu/PeterCritchley/Papers

Demos, E. V. (ed.) (1995). *The Selected Writings of Silvan S. Tomkins*. Cambridge: Cambridge University Press.

Erikson, E. (1958). *Young Man Luther: A Study in Psychoanalysis and History.* New York: W. W. Norton & Company.

Faulkner, W. (1951). *Requiem for a Nun.* New York: Random House.

Ferrari, A. B. (2004). *From the Eclipse of the Body to the Dawn of Thought.* London: Free Associations.

Fitzgerald, F. S. (1923/2008). *The Curious Case of Benjamin Button and Other Jazz Age Stories.* Penguin Classics.

Freud S. (1896/2001). Further Remarks on the Neuro-Psychosis of Defence. *SE* Vol. III. London: Hogarth.

Freud, S. (1915/2001). Repression. *SE* Vol. XIV. London: Hogarth.

Freud, S. (1915/2001). The Unconscious. *SE* Vol. XIV. London: Hogarth.

Freud, S. (1916[1915]/2001). On Transience. *SE* Vol. XIV. London: Hogarth.

Freud, S. (1917/2001). Mourning and Melancholia. *SE* Vol. XIV. London: Hogarth.

Freud, S. (1920/2001). Beyond the Pleasure Principle. *SE* Vol. XVIII. London: Hogarth.

Freud, S. (1923/2001). The Ego and the Id. *SE* Vol. XIX. London: Hogarth.

Hartmann, H. (1956). Notes on the reality principle. *Psychoanalytic Study of the Child*, 11, 31–53.

Hawking, S. (1988). *A Brief History of Time.* Reading: Cox & Wyman.

Heidegger, M. (2010). *Being and Time.* Joan Stambough (trans.). Albany, NY: State University of New York Press.

Hesse, H. (2006). *Narcissus and Goldmund.* London: Peter Owen.

Hinton, L. (1998). *Shame as a Teacher: "Lowly Wisdom" at the Millennium.* Einsiedeln: Daimon Verlag.

Hinton, L. (2015). Temporality and the Torments of Time. *Journal of Analytical Psychology,* 60, 3, 353–370.

Hultberg, P. (1988). Shame – a hidden emotion. *Journal Analytical Psychology*, 33, 109–126.

Jacoby, M. (1994). *Shame and the Origins of Self-Esteem.* London: Routledge.

James, I. (2010). Bernard Stiegler and the technics of time. *Cultural Politics*, 6, 207–228.

Jung, C. G. (1952/1986). *Symbols of Transformation. CW* 5. London: Routledge and Kegan Paul.

Jung, C. G. (1953). The archetypes of the collective unconscious. *The Psychology of the Unconscious. CW* 7. London: Routledge and Kegan Paul.

Kernberg, O. F. (2015). Narcissistic defenses in the distortion of Free Association and their underlying anxieties. *Psychoanalytic Quarterly*, 84, 625–642.

Kristeva, J., Jardine, A. & Blake, H. (1981). Women's Time. *Signs*, 7, 13–35.

Kundera, M. (1984). *The Unbearable Lightness of Being.* Michael Henry Heim (trans.). London: Faber and Faber.

Laplanche, J. & Pontalis J.-B. (1973). *The Language of Psychoanalysis.* London: Karnac Books.

Levi, P. (2015). *If this is a Man*. In Ann Goldstein (ed.), *The Complete Works of Primo Levi*. UK: Penguin Classics.

Levinas, E. (1961/1969). *Totality and Infinity*. Pittsburgh, PA: Duquesne University Press.

Lombardi, R. (2003). Knowledge and experience of time in primitive mental states. *International Journal of Psychoanalysis*, 84, 1531–1549.

Ogden, H. O. (2015). Intuiting the truth of what's happening: On Bion's 'Notes on Memory and Desire'. *Psychoanalytic Quarterly*, 2, 285–306.

Perelberg, R. J. (2006). The controversial discussions and *après-coup*. *International Journal of Psycho-Analysis*, 87, 1199–1220.

Porter, K. A. (1962). *Ship of Fools*. Boston, MA: Little Brown and Company.

Sartre, J.-P. (1984). *Being and Nothingness*. New York: Washington Square Press.

Scarfone, D. (2006). A matter of time: actual time and the production of the past. *Psychoanalytic Quarterly*, 75, 807–834.

Scarfone, D. (2013). A brief introduction to the work of Jean Laplanche. *International Journal of Psychoanalysis*, 94, 545–566.

Scarfone, D. (2015). The time before us (*The Unpast* in W. S. Merwin, W. Benjamin & V. Woolf). *Psychoanalytic Dialogues*, 26, 513–520.

Smith, J. M. & Van Ness, H. C. (1987). *Introduction to Chemical Engineering Thermodynamics*. New York: McGraw-Hill.

Speziali, P. (ed.) (1979). *Albert Einstein, Michele Besso: Correspondence: 1903–1955*. Paris: Herman.

Stern, D. (1985). *The Interpersonal World of the Infant*. New York: Basic Books.

Szpunar, K. K. & Tulving, E. (2011). Varieties of future experience. In Moshe Bar (ed.), *Predictions in the Brain*. New York: Oxford University Press.

Talero, M. (2004). Temporality and the therapeutic subject: the phenomenology of transference, remembering and working through. In J. Mills (ed.), *Rereading Freud: Psychoanalysis through Philosophy*. Albany, NY: State University of New York Press.

Terr, L. C. (1984). Time and trauma. *Psychoanalytic Study of the Child*, 39, 633–665.

Tomkins, S. (1987). Shame. In D. Nathanson (ed.), *The Many Faces of Shame*. New York: Guildford.

Wharton, B. (1990). The hidden face of shame: the shadow, shame and separation. *Journal of Analytical Psychology*, 35, 279–299.

Willemsen, H. (2014). Early trauma and affect: the importance of the body for the development of the capacity to symbolize. *Journal of Analytical Psychology*, 59, 695–712.

Winnicott, D. W. (1974). Fear of breakdown. *International Review of Psycho-Analysis*, 1, 103–107.

Chapter 8

The pharmacology of shame, *or* Promethean, Epimethean and Antigonian temporality

Daniel Ross

Our institutions, corporations and communities today abound in unadorned shamelessness in a manner not only public but political. Whether it is the willingness of candidates to exploit popular fears in the naked pursuit of political office, or of desperate individuals to commit atrocious crimes of terror even at the cost of their own lives, or of financiers to engage in predatory practices following no economic principle beyond a frequently self-defeating logic of the shortest possible term, or the willingness of polluters, investors and ultimately consumers to contribute unceasingly to the disruption of the geophysical and atmospheric systems that are the first abode of all terrestrial inhabitants, a series of behaviours is on constant display virtually unparalleled in their depth and gravity. At the ordinary level of everyday madness, of familial relations, collegial relations, sexual relations and friendship too, sensational examples fed to us on a daily basis by the 'news' media and our own quotidian experience seem constantly to attest to the contemporary *weakness* of that fundamental characteristic, identified by Primo Levi and adopted by Gilles Deleuze, as the 'shame at being human' (Deleuze, 1995, p. 172). At every turn, ours appears to be an age in which increasing numbers of the souls who compose it act with an unprecedented absence of constraint.

In short, we find ourselves subsisting in a world that seems constantly shame-inducing, in so far as we remain capable of being induced. In so far as we are capable of *recognizing* this feeling, it places us in question and invites us to question ourselves, our understandings and the world around us. In other words, it functions as a 'reflexive act', calling us to enact a genealogy of our situation, in the hope, ultimately, not just of elaborating a critique, but of navigating an exit. In this sense, the experience of shame is the experience of a disruption, whether individual or collective, that urges us towards a readjustment.

But can all this be subsumed within one explanation? Are all these forms (or deformations) of behaviour of a single type? More pointedly, what is the relationship between the thirst for power and cynicism of the scaremongering and scapegoating politician and the absolute (and sometimes absolutely methodical) desperation of those who grant themselves licence to commit literally any crime in their own quest to produce terror and panic? Are these forms of shamelessness similar to or of a different kind from those that systematically but carelessly pursue courses that lead ineluctably to the disruption of economic or ecological systems?

In so far as these are questions addressed to *us*, they are not just psychological or sociological but *philosophical*. 'What is philosophy?' is a question that has not only received a plurality of answers, but whose clarity has never been more elusive. Nevertheless, we would argue that philosophy is always, and firstly, a question of the pursuit of the knowledge of *how to live*, as Kant himself suggested by recalling that the 'first meaning' of philosophy was 'scientific *wisdom of life*' (Kant, 2002, p. 431).[1] Today we must understand this knowledge of 'living' as referring not just to the disciplines concerned with 'life' (the realm of biology), or individuals and their relationships (psychology and its therapies), or even the mechanisms and processes of collective life (anthropology, sociology, politics), but to a *question* or a *problem* of living for the challenged and questioning beings that we are, encompassing each of these levels *without being reducible to any of them*. 'Without being reducible' means that the answers to the questions of how to live today exceed those that can be derived merely from the laws formulated by each of these domains. These laws themselves derive from the *abstraction* from the 'facts' defining the contours of these fields of knowledge. Philosophy pursues or ought to pursue such problems *systematically* but *speculatively*, which is to say that the outcome ought never be the elaboration of a system.

By my title, however, I purport to pursue something that is not quite or not only a philosophy, but a 'pharmacology'. This should be heard as an allusion to the thought of the *pharmakon*, and so as an invitation to recall, *firstly*, what writing was for Socrates in the *Phaedrus*, namely, both a poison and a remedy, since writing's relationship to memory consists in being both a crutch and a threat. Writing, that is, the exteriorization of living memory in dead matter, enables *practices* of writing and reading to *shore up* memory, but also to become that on which living memory becomes *dependent*, deadening it, constituting the possibility of knowledge but also of its loss: it is for this reason that Plato has been called the 'first thinker of the proletariat' (Stiegler, 2010, p. 28). It is an invitation to recall, *secondly*, that Jacques Derrida, as a late reader of Plato and a foresighted writer of 'Plato's Pharmacy' (Derrida, 1981), advanced his deconstruction by showing that, *in fact*, this opposition of living to dead memory is strictly speaking impossible, and ought instead to be rearticulated as a 'dynamic composition', that is, as a process (Stiegler, 2006, p. 18). For Derrida, the name of this process was *différance*: both a spatialization of time and a temporalization of space (see Ross, 2013).

But it is *mainly* an invitation to situate the problem of shame within the orbit of the 'pharmacological' philosophy elaborated by Bernard Stiegler, for whom the deconstruction of the *who* and the *what* constitutive of and constituted by *différance also* means that the proto-human *invention* of the *what* (the artefact, that is, technics) *required* both the opening-up of horizons of anticipation and was the *condition* of such opening. Furthermore, for Stiegler, every artefact is a *pharmakon*, and is always also a *mirror*, opening up what he calls an 'instrumental maieutics' *between* this *who* and this *what*, in which each (say, the evolving cortex and the primordial flint tool), observing itself in the other, is formed and deformed by this process (Stiegler, 1998, p. 128). The technical artefact is thus always already a mirror and a clock, exposing time and opening up every horizon of specularity. Hence specularity is always also the *speculation* of temporal horizons, looking forward by looking back into those *already* manufactured objects through which alone something like a 'reflexive act' is possible. To think shame pharmacologically would then be to do so on the basis of this constitutive and instrumental maieutics, and with a view to its formative and deformational characteristics.

Shame is epochal, and very old: recall Freud's suggestion that repression may have originated in the olfactory repugnance and corporeal shame provoked by the naked proto-human's conquest of the upright stance (Freud, 1985, p. 279). Yet, however ancient or originary, shame is always a question of *our* shame, the shame of our *time*: it always raises, before anything else, the question of how to live 'today'. And the question of 'today' is always a question of technics, in so far as the latter is both the maker and the marker of time.

Today, confronted with a world whose systemic problems threaten to 'end up being a world without us', the reflex of shame raises questions that exceed the confines of the personal, the psychological or the socio-logical, or even the political, in the direction of what we are tentatively presuming can still be called the philosophical. But before descending more deeply into Stiegler's pharmacology, we will begin with Günther Anders, another thinker for whom the myth of Prometheus (the 'first philosopher') will allow consideration of the temporality opened up by the relationship between shame and technology, and from there, and via Peter Sloterdijk's concept of 'disinhibition', arrive at the problematic of shame and contemporary shamelessness that prompts Stiegler to formu-late what he refers to as the 'Antigone complex'.

The shock of the contingent

Sixty years ago, Günther Anders – the son of psychologist William Stern, cousin of Walter Benjamin, ex-husband of Hannah Arendt, stu-dent of Martin Heidegger and doctoral candidate of Edmund Husserl – linked shame and technics in the first volume of *The Obsolescence of Human Beings* (published in 1956, but not available in English, due apparently to Don Ihde's dislike of its 'pessimism' [Babich, 2012–2013, p. 46 and n. 103], until a portion was published in 2016). With his notion of what he calls 'Promethean shame', that '*shame when confronted by the "humiliatingly" high quality of fabricated things*' (Anders, 2016, p. 30), Anders introduces an account of the affective consequences of technological acceleration that can be usefully compared and contrasted with Stiegler's own approach. By briefly examining this idea, forged as it was out of Anders's experience as an exile in the consumerist California of the 1950s, it will be possible to pinpoint more precisely the specificity of Stiegler's own analysis.

Twenty years earlier, Anders had already argued that the relationship of humanity to its environment differs from that of animals in two respects: firstly, the world is not there as a given and man 'instead must learn to know it [*connaître*] "after the fact", *a posteriori*; he needs *experi-ence*'; and secondly, he 'transforms the world and builds over it' (Anders, 2009, p. 279). Hence the relationship of humankind to its milieu is here already portrayed by Anders in terms of both its Promethean and Epimethean moments: without pre-given qualities thanks to the forgetful-ness of Epimetheus, the shamefully naked human must perpetually protect, clothe and equip its body with prosthetic supplements through a capacity granted by Prometheus's theft and gift of fire, and must discover the world through the experience made possible by these prostheses. Anders summarizes: *'artificiality is the nature of man and his essence is instability'* (p. 279). Originarily obsolescent, the essence of the human is to have no essence, its 'nature' prosthetic. This prosthetic quality, setting the world before it, corresponds to what Anders calls the 'abstract' character of human existence: part *of* the world, in part excluded *from* it.

Anders, however, does not go as far as Stiegler, for whom the human capacity for exteriorizing itself *in* the world (in the form of artefacts) is what *opens* the world *as* world (as Heidegger would also say, but on a different basis), thereby opening up the space for the becoming-symbolic of existence, and for what Stiegler will call our 'exclamatory soul' (Stiegler, 2011, pp. 133, 155). Through the possibilities afforded by this unfinished, indeterminate character of human being, which Anders calls its pathological freedom, what the human being learns is its own *contingency*, which it encounters as shock and experiences as shame:

> The state of shock of the contingent, as an attitude within life ... is called *shame*. Shame is not originally shame of having done this or that, [for] this special moral shame itself already requires that I am at the same time identical and non-identical with myself as a formal condition ... In shame the self wants to free itself.
>
> (Anders, 2009, p. 287)

This fundamental form of shame, more primordial than that concerning one's *acts*, is temporal: it derives from the discovery that there was a past before me, from which I emerge, nakedly, in all my accidentality. Shame is thus above all the discovery of having an origin (p. 288), and of oneself 'as a being that was already there before the act of self-experience', and which is also the tragic, mortal insight that 'I will have been', when one sees one's death as already past (pp. 290–1). The temporality of shame is this shock that requires another shock, which learns (from experience), in its freedom and through its acquired knowledge, to *adopt* its freedom. But what is it that really provokes this shock through which the human being experiences the shame of contingency that will be the spur of Prometheanism? Anders goes as far as to say that 'Space is the *Principium individuationis*' (p. 293), but we find no hint that what enables the discovery of contingency is the access to the already-there granted by the materialization of existence, that is, its technologization.

Promethean shame

After Auschwitz and Hiroshima, and the rise of consumer capitalism, the shock that provokes shame is unquestionably technological, and radically so. Although an oppositional residue remains in *The Obsolescence of Human Beings*, in which the human and the technological stand apart as the natural to the artificial, Anders explicitly states that our contemporary problem is not that technology is changing 'us', for 'alteration . . . is not fundamentally new'; rather, it lies in the fact that 'we are undergoing this transformation of the self for the sake of machines' (Anders, 2016, p. 48). For Anders, then, the shame of being human that he calls Promethean is not due simply to a technologically produced transformation of humankind amounting to a dehumanizing denaturalization, even if its originary source is the Epimethean neoteny for which we are perpetually striving to compensate. What, then, is *new* in this new Promethean shame whose explicit symptom is the feeling that it would have been better to have been born a machine, or, in other words, *not* to have been 'born' at all?

What is new is, firstly, speed, that is, the relation to time. Anders talks of the *slowness* of evolution: our corporeal form is still virtually indistinguishable from that of our distant ancestors, and the extreme gradualness of biological change forms an immediate contrast with the acceleration of technological advancement. The result is that the body eventually comes to seem 'obsolescent'. He immediately sees in this a reversal of conventional moral categories, for it is the human being who, constrained by seeming unchangeability, is therefore unfree, freedom being reserved for the constant changeability of modern *objects* (Anders, 2016, p. 38). This in turn makes evident, to those human beings who hitherto considered themselves the operators of technology, that this technological dynamic advances in a quasi-autonomous manner with respect to those it is purported to serve – this is the very meaning of Heidegger's *Gestell*. Biological and social evolution have thus been outstripped and overtaken by a rapid acceleration of non-organic change occurring since the Industrial Revolution compared with which biology is *as if* fixed and invariable, and society *seemingly* impotent. This connection between speed and freedom already hints that what is really at stake here is knowledge, at least if one recalls Amartya Sen's account of freedom in terms of *capabilities* (Sen, 2000).

This question of knowledge is raised by Anders against the objection that 'we', the producers of this acceleration, ought to feel pride in having created these machines and devised this system of proliferating objects. But since '99 per cent' of 'us' did not make, and are not the masters of, this envelope of machines, we do not feel this achievement as 'ours', which on the contrary confronts us as something strange and disconcerting (Anders, 2016, p. 33). But what is it that is now 'ours' only for the one per cent? The change is that the worker is no longer then one who possesses the *knowledge* through which work constitutes a process of individuation, including the possibility of enacting a technical individuation of tools themselves, or of their uses. The 'human' role in the technical process is reduced to the conduct of 'one single, specialised task' (p. 45), or, as Henry Ford described it, 'exactly one operation which the most stupid man can learn within two days' (Ford, quoted in Stiegler, 2016, p. 162).

To do just exactly one operation, however, workers are 'required to *exercise the strictest self-control* in order to start *an automatism*' and 'to extinguish what they are *as* acting individuals, and *transform* their actions into *mere processes*, heteronomous and automatic ones at that' (Anders, 2016, p. 82). The machine trains and untrains us at the same time, through a dependent relationship, and this extends beyond our life as labourers and into our life as consumers. For example, the machine trains us, all on its own (autonomously), and, today, without need even for instruction manuals, how to take direction from Google Maps, while at the same time *untraining* our capacity to *navigate*, by conditioning us to submit to, and *rely* on (like a crutch), the benefits of Googlian automatisms. Anders recognizes what this means: our problem is less our obedience to the automatism than the loss of that *knowledge* by which the operation of an instrument is also potentially its and our individuation – or in other words, the problem is not instrumentalization but the reduction of the instrument to a mere means (cf., Stiegler, 1998, pp. 205–6). As Anders says:

For sure, the violin player has to become attuned to their instrument. He or she has to adjust the strokes of their bow as the instrument and the movement of the music require, and must even make sure that this becomes 'natural and intuitive'. In comparison with the induction of factory workers, however, this task is still perfectly human. It is free from contradiction in as much as the violin player is allowed to be unambiguously active while learning to master the instrument, thus transforming the violin into a part of their body (which increases its field of expression), incorporating it as a new organ into the organism.

(Anders, 2016, p. 83)

Leaving responsibility for the 'perfectly human' to Anders, his account of technology succeeds in demonstrating that: (1) the artificiality of the human amounts to its perpetual entanglement with instruments; (2) the instrumental condition of human existence always requires one or another kind of becoming-automatic (just as biological existence is suffused with corporeal automatisms, often called *rhythms* – cf., Stiegler, 2015); (3) to learn the instrument involves internalizing the automatisms associated with that instrument; and (4) it is *on the basis* of such automatisms that we can learn truly to play and master the instrument, and ultimately compose with it.

In short, our relationship to the instrument is fundamentally a matter of knowledge and practice. The loss of such knowledge results in what Anders calls dehumanization, which is here another name for what Stiegler calls proletarianization, a loss of that knowledge on the basis of which behavioural bifurcations, that is, decisions, become possible. For Anders, the culmination of this loss was signalled when the responsibility for launching a nuclear strike was removed from General MacArthur and placed into the 'hands' of computers (Anders, 2016, pp. 58–62). It is the automatization of even this decision, where worldwide destruction and human existence itself are at stake, that justifies referring to this, as did Jacques Derrida, as the 'absolute *pharmakon*' (Derrida, 2007).

Phenomenotechnics of shame

Shame, for Anders, follows directly from the prosthetic entanglement that *abstracts* the human. His Promethean shame ultimately relates to the Epimethean absence of 'natural' qualities that *sets off* human existence, or rather what Gilbert Simondon called a process of psychic and collective individuation (Simondon, 2007): it sets it off *in pursuit* of (technical) perfectibility. In what we might dare to call Anders's phenomenotechnics of shame (cf., Bachelard, 2005), it is this originary incompleteness of existence that forms the condition of possibility of shame, and for which shame is the perpetual accompaniment, just as the Promethean theft of fire empowered (or weaponized) human beings, yet necessitated the further gifts (delivered by Hermes) of *aidōs* and *dikē* by exposing their lack of means for resolving conflict *peacefully*. For Anders, shame is a 'reflexive act' conducted before an 'authority', involving a *'reference to self'*, but where this reflexive act *fails*, and does so because *'those who are ashamed encounter themselves at once as identical and as not self-identical'*, this being, therefore, an *'act that never comes to an end'*. It is a reflexive act in which the reflection fails to reach its destination, where it 'permanently fails' (as email servers sometimes inform us), setting off an endless state (no longer an act) of *'disorientation'* (Anders, 2016, p. 63).

The reflexive act that shame provokes amounts, therefore, to a temporal act composed of two stages, in which the *I* [*das Ich*] finds within itself something not itself, which Anders calls the *it* [*das Es*], which is 'not only' Freud's id but something 'more general', and which he immediately refers to as 'everything pre-individual' (Anders, 2016, p. 66). The pre-individual, for Anders, is the *it*, 'everything that the self is a part of without being able to do anything about it'. The possibility of Promethean shame therefore lies in the primordial possibility of discovering, through an act of self-reflection before an authority, that the individual is perpetually incomplete, arising as it does from a pre-individual milieu that is always the wellspring of any process of individuation. The possibility of being an *I* is therefore a perpetual *problem* for the individual, and in a footnote Anders relates this *it* to Heidegger's *das Man*, interpreting *Being and Time* as an account of the 'systematic fight against shame' by which the *I* strives 'to overcome the disgrace of being an "it" and to become "itself"' (p. 93). As Anders states, '[s]hame erupts because one is simultaneously "oneself" *and* something else' (p. 67).

The *'quintessential'* form of shame may be sexual, he argues, but this is only because primordial sexuality amounts to 'the pre-individual sphere *par excellence'* (Anders, 2016, p. 67). Promethean shame, however, is something other than sexual shame: it 'was not without a good reason that the term "it" was left utterly unqualified' (p. 75). For, beyond that psychic pre-individuality which we might call primordial sexuality, beyond that collective pre-individuality which we might call *das Man*, Promethean shame is a question of 'the machine or technological device that is encountered as the "it"', the '*it of the technological device* (das Apparat-Es)' (p. 76). Promethean shame thus arises from the emergence of the *it as such*, exposed by a globally extended and constantly transforming apparatus that turns our Promethean hubris (Anders draws a link between hubris and hybrid) into the melancholic realization that 'human beings are no longer a match for what they have produced' (p. 47), when the originary 'defect' or '*flaw*' that sets off the individuation of the individual is experienced as a '*malaise of being singular and unique*' (p. 55). At this moment, which is ours, we experience the *conjunction* of the corporeal pre-individuality of sexuality and the collective pre-individuality that is *das Man*: 'Instead of the rift between the body on one side and the self on the other there is now only the rift between the machine . . . and the old residue. This residue is made up of body and self in an undifferentiated manner' (p. 85).

Biological automatisms and sociological automatisms are today all placed on 'one side' of a struggle, confronted with technological automatisms operating more rapidly and more powerfully than either nature or culture, overtaking them and outstripping them. It is the temporality lying behind this failure that forms the root of Promethean shame, an affective experience that amounts to a kind of *shock*:

> The effect of this actual failure is not limited to highlighting the different levels of perfection between humans and machines, that is, between the producer and the product. The failure rather 'ejects' (*wirft heraus*) the one who fails. Throwing him or her back onto themself so that their old residue of self now suddenly stands there without a world, inept, 'rejected and disproved' (*verworfen*), no longer knowing what to do with itself.
>
> (Anders, 2016, p. 86)

No longer *knowing* what to do: this motivational failure corresponds to a loss of world and amounts to the loss of the knowledge of what to do or how to live, the loss, we might say, of the feeling of existing. To the shock produced by the acceleration of technological automatization, the only adequate response would be a kind of dis-automatization amounting to a hermeneutic, that is, to the possibility of new interpretations, a possibility originally granted by Hermes, and on the basis of *aidōs* and *dikē*. Anders puts this in the following terms at the beginning of the second volume of *The Obsolescence of Human Beings* through an inversion of the eleventh of Marx's theses on Feuerbach, insisting that an Epimethean moment is always required after the Promethean moment that each technological advance represents:

> It is not enough to change the world. Humans do this anyway ... We also need to interpret this change, in order to change it. So the world no longer changes without us, and does not end up being a world without us.
>
> (Anders, in Müller, 2016, p. 106)

I, we and it

Such would be the phenomenotechnics of Promethean shame and the Epimethean hermeneutics that would alone constitute its adequate response. Epochality, understood in relation both to Husserl's 'suspension' and to the decision enabled by technological disruption, is defined by the possibility of such an Epimethean counter-shock that responds to the shock of being ashamed by elaborating new interpretations, enabling decisions that turn a technological state of fact into a new technological state of law. Promethean shame derives from our becoming incapable of the second moment of this temporality, and consequently our submission to what Stiegler calls the 'electronic Leviathan' (Stiegler, 2016, p. 13) and Anders calls the 'calculating robot', the latter signifying the fate of General MacArthur with respect to the nuclear *pharmakon* (Anders, 2016, p. 59). As already indicated, this is how Anders *interprets Being and Time* – as the *problem* of the relationship between the *who* and the *it*: '*Being and Time* is about the attempt of the "I" (which is ashamed-of-itself) to overcome the disgrace of being an "it" and to become "itself"' (p. 93).

This *it*, which is the origin of the prosthetic incompleteness of the human being and the originary source enabling the later development of its Promethean shame, has for Anders three dimensions: the Freudian *Es* of primordial sexuality, *das Man* of quotidian sociality and *das Apparate-Es* of our fundamental technicity. As we have already hinted, this three-dimensionality of the *it* can be translated into the language that Bernard Stiegler adopts (and transforms) from Simondon: the threefold inextricability (or transductivity) of psychic individuation, collective individuation and technical individuation, as three perpetually unfinished processes defining the mortal beings that we are, and resulting from the originary default of origin defining our Promethean/Epimethean being-as-becoming. Such a translation offers the best chance at making an advance on Anders's diagnosis of the contemporary symptomatological and affective consequences of our originary technicity. The account of Promethean shame offered by Anders might then form the basis not just of an interpretation of Heidegger, but of a *critique*, in such a way that it rebounds upon Anders's own analysis while leaping out beyond it.

Stiegler's critique of Heidegger is indeed congruent in many ways with Anders's account of Promethean shame. The originary default of origin, which amounts to the *feeling* of a lack of origin or propriety, also corresponds to that originary and Promethean mortality that for Heidegger was the fundamental characteristic of *Dasein*, as the lack of knowledge of my mortal future. For Heidegger, as Anders well knows, it is in fleeing from this *indetermination* that *Dasein* is tempted to fall prey to the attitude of *das Man*, which for Heidegger determines the indeterminate, calculates the incalculable and in general behaves as a crowd in order to evade its mortal singularity (see Stiegler, 2003, p. 159). But if we interpret the existential analytic of *Being and Time* as describing the struggle of the *I* to *overcome* the *it* of *das Man*, as Anders does, then, even if this is a perpetual struggle without a victor, we risk entering into an oppositional logic of the genuine *I* and the fallen *das Man* – that is, and despite all the Heideggerian qualifications that would need to be acknowledged in the letter and the spirit, if not in the word and the deed, it would be to regress from an ethics founded on tragic finitude to a morality founded on guilt.

What Heidegger could not think, as Stiegler points out, is the positivity of collective individuation: not just *das Man* as the *collapse* of psychic individuation, but a genuine process of collective *individuation* occurring *through* and *with* the psychic individuation processes of the *Is* that compose it. If the history of being that Heidegger tried to think after 1935, and that ends in the thought of *Gestell* as the system of objects outstripping us, *might* be thinkable in this way, the problem remains that *with* this history of being, Heidegger abandoned the existential analytic: he cannot join the *I* and the *we* as processes, because he cannot see that the technical *it* is the *condition* of this conjunction. The technical object may be what contains the possibility of fleeing to *das Man* by reducing singularity to calculability, but it is *also* what, 'abstracting' the human from the world, as Anders says, *opens access* to the incalculable via, for example, the possibility of *returning to* a text we have written, and so *reinterpreting* it, whether individually or collectively (as for instance when a philosopher returns to the text of a poet or a tragedian, or when a judge returns to the text of a written law), that is, giving it and giving us a *future*. Heidegger's nadir, his attempt to think Germany as an 'historical-spiritual people' (Heidegger, 1990, p. 13), exposed this failure to think the conjunction of the individual and the collective as processes: he confounds them. This failure is for Stiegler the very source of Heidegger's great *Dummheit*: 'That is why there is no politics in Heidegger, because politics is precisely this: to join the "I" and the "we".' And he adds: 'Isn't this what *Antigone* tells us?' (Stiegler, 2003, p. 162).

Digression on the end of ulterior motives

Does an echo of this inability not remain in Anders? For all the subtlety and complexity of his account of originary artificiality, does it not in the end leave us with the feeling that it is, today, a question of *saving* the human *from* the power and 'authority' of the machine? We may indeed have entered into an age where what Dominique Janicaud called the 'power of the rational' (Janicaud, 1994) seems to have turned, paradoxically, into the impotence of the irrational (Stiegler, 2013, p. 8). But in Anders any rise of irrationality figures less than the passive hyper-rationality of Weberian disenchantment, even if Anders does indeed admit that this de-motivation brings with it, in a quasi-automatic way, a '*shame of being ashamed*', resulting in 'an attitude diametrically opposed to shame, brazenness, for example, or one that declares "I couldn't care less"' (Anders, 2016, pp. 34–5).

Can the present age, then, really be encompassed with a concept such as Promethean shame, or is what requires critique not rather this brazen counter-tendency – the growth of what Peter Sloterdijk (2013) calls 'disinhibition'? For the latter, what characterizes 'modernity', that is, the world following the Industrial Revolution (or, the advent of the Anthropocene), is a change in *motivation*: what enables *action*, or the 'transition from theory to practice', is decreasingly a matter of external *authorities* and increasingly an *internalization* of *reason(s)* (Sloterdijk, 2013, p. 57). Hence Sloterdijk's account of the rise of subjectivity owes more than a little to Nietzsche's account of the genealogy of morality as the internalization of guilt (Nietzsche, 1994).

Nevertheless, for Sloterdijk, the 'organization of disinhibition' proper to the modern subject is precisely not some *'passage à l'acte'* but rather 'obeying sound self-understood reasons and sensible interests' (2013, p. 57), and so this is also not without relation to Foucault's 'disciplinary society'. But the collapse of the modern subject does not amount, for Sloterdijk, to a regression to inhibition, to some new technologically induced sense of shame, but to a new phase of disinhibition, at first mandated by the ideology of creative destruction under the banner of 'innovation', but where 'what spirals out of control' in consumer capitalism is 'an end use devoid of ulterior motives' (p. 209), a process that culminates in terrorism without reason(s). This requires consideration, not in terms of a *'new, second level in the history of the reification of human beings'* in which they feel *'shame at not being a thing'* (Anders, 2016, p. 35), but through an account of the way the hijacking of the libidinal economy by the productive economy leads not to a reification of desire but to its liquidation, resulting not just in the passivity of shame but, precisely, in new, systemically induced passages to the act of shamelessness.

The shame of being human

Fifty years after the Andersian account of Promethean shame, Stiegler described what he refers to as the Antigone complex in *Uncontrollable Societies of Disaffected Individuals*, the second volume of his series on *Disbelief and Discredit*. The first volume, *The Decadence of Industrial Democracies*, described the historical and technological basis of capitalism as lying not just in Watt's steam engine but in Jacquard's loom, which inscribed the *gestures* of the craftsman in a machine capable of reproducing them, depriving workers of the knowledge they hitherto possessed, *proletarianizing* them (Stiegler, 2011) – that is, leaving us with a situation in relation to which '99 per cent of today's population' do not feel like 'proud creators' (Anders, 2016, p. 33). The mechanical loom is in *this* sense *mnemotechnical*: an invention that produces a new epoch of exteriorized memory, following that of alphabetic writing and enabled by that of the printing press.

The *Grundrisse* contains elements of such an analysis (Marx, 1973), but what Marx could not foresee, and what Marxists (and others) have tended not to see clearly, is *how* in the twentieth century this loss of knowledge was *generalized beyond* the worker – to the consumer. Capitalism may indeed have found a solution to the decline in the rate of profit, in the form of mass market production (embodied in the Ford Model T), but this solution depended for its success on the capacity to *anticipate* consumption: not just to *calculate* but to *condition* and thereby *control* consumer desire. The transformation of capitalism from the dictates of what Foucault called a disciplinary society to the modulations of what Deleuze called a control society depended on another set of mnemotechnical inventions: the mass broadcast analogue media (radio, then television), which, through all the techniques of marketing, has systematically interfered with the *intergenerational* transmission of the knowledge of how to live by undermining every authority.

For Stiegler, the pre-individual milieu suffusing the Epimethean being that we ourselves are is technology, that environment, medium and support which is so intimate and ubiquitous that it withdraws into the background of existence so as to remain almost unthought, and, for most of human history, unthinkable. Nevertheless, from the moment proto-humans began to manufacture and use tools, this envelope has tended to form itself through a process of technical individuation into more or less stable systems, in relation to which societies and individuals have adjusted themselves, in so far as they are processes of psychic and collective individuation. Hence to say that the pre-individual milieu is the 'wellspring' of processes of individuation is also to say, in less quasi-natural and more quasi-technical terminology, that, for *us*, 'the artefact is the mainspring' of human evolution (Stiegler, 2016, p. 9).

But 'relatively stable' also means 'relatively *un*stable', and the introduction of new tools inevitably disrupts the technological system, hence the individual and collective systems that operate in relation to it. If we are the questioning beings for whom being is a question, this is because we are thrown *into* question (and projected into our mortality) by the disruption that results from these new technological introductions, and, thus challenged and questioned, we must constantly *readjust* to these disruptive dis-adjustments by *adopting new practices* through which the disruption is 'socialized'. Between these two moments of disruptive introduction and invariably late adoption, the mortal beings that we are find ourselves within a temporality perpetually caught between the leap ahead and the step back, between Prometheus and Epimetheus, foresight and hindsight, advance and delay. All the stages of proletarianization (that is, loss of knowledge), from that first identified by Socrates with respect to writing, to that identified by Marx and Simondon with respect to the gestures of the manual worker, to that identified by Stiegler with respect to ways of life proletarianized by consumerism, are consequences of new technological introductions (alphabetic writing, printing press, mechanical production, analogue audiovisual technology), where each of these stages leads to what Stiegler, like Anders, calls 'disorientation', and so to the struggle for a *reorienting* adoption of new practices.

The second volume of *Disbelief and Discredit* concerns the *consequences* of this generalized proletarianization, that is, the systematic production of 'stupidity' resulting from the combined loss of work-knowledge and life-knowledge. 'Stupidity *inspires* shame': it confronts us with what Stiegler (following Levi's 'shame of the world' [Levi, 1989, p. 65]) calls 'the shame of being human' (Stiegler, 2013, p. 24). Here the reference is also to Deleuze, for whom shame was something we feel 'in the face of too great a vulgarization of thinking, in the face of TV entertainment, of a ministerial speech, of "jolly people" gossiping' (Deleuze, 1995, p. 172): in short, in the face of *das Man*. For Stiegler, this originates from our Epimethean default of origin, that is, our mortal condition. Knowledge, then, as itself a process of individuation, is not only what is acquired: it is what is always on the way to being transformed or amended, or lost. Knowledge, the accumulation of which is perpetually threatened by proletarianization, is always a *not-yet-knowing* 'towards which we must raise ourselves' (Stiegler, 2013, p. 25). Knowledge in *this* sense is the very thing that makes life worth the effort of being lived.

For Stiegler, this is a matter of the difference between what exists and what does not exist, yet consists. Law, for instance, as the set of rules *materialized* in written form, positively exists. But justice, *dikē*, which forms the *basis* for the *interpretation* of law (by, for example, a judge), does not exist, except at 'infinity', yet it consists – we cannot give it up as an idea. This is also a way of orienting our existence, even if law, *as* written, retains a perpetual tendency to substantialize into dogma, when authority regresses into authoritarianism and the thirst for power, which is the very reason for which justice is constantly *needed*. In this, *aidōs* plays the same role with respect to morality:

> This is why ethics is not morality: it is what, as shame, assigns to those susceptible to justice, to the justiciable, their place (their *ethos*), precisely insofar as they are subject to the difference between existence and consistence, which is also to say, to the experience of shame, to the intimacy of stupidity – insofar as they are neither of the gods, who purely and simply consist ... nor of beasts, which merely subsist. Ethics, like justice, is what must be interpreted, and can thus never be codified. This is why it is Hermes, who is both the god of *hermeneia* and the god of writing (of *hypomnemata*), who brings these two feelings [*aidōs* and *dikē*] to mortals.
>
> (Stiegler, 2013, p. 25)

This raising of knowledge towards what does not exist yet consists (in short, towards the *ideas*) is always, then, a kind of striving – that is, a matter of desire, and more particularly of the sublimation of desire. In so far as this is the case, all knowledge depends on an authority that *authorizes* it, that is, on those processes of superegoization that define the process of sublimation as what contains (in both senses) and binds the drives. But as conceptual knowledge is the so-called 'rational' knowledge of the scientific disciplines that emerge from ancient Greece, and as social knowledge is the 'political' knowledge that likewise has a Greek origin (although this 'origin' is undoubtedly *complicated*), this 'authority' has a peculiar form: what this authority authorizes somehow *includes* the undermining of its own foundations and formations. Hence Stiegler opens his chapter entitled 'The Antigone Complex' in the following terms:

> A society without authority, that is, without super-ego, is inconceivable. The point is not to *destroy* the super-ego – which would be to destroy society – but rather to *critique* the super-ego ... The *political* age – as the epoch of the psychic, collective and technical individuation process that characterizes ex-sistence, that is, the way of life proper to those who are called human beings, and as the typically Western epoch of this process – is the age that has *instituted* ... the critique of the super-ego, that is, of *authority*.
>
> (2013, p. 30)

From this strange conjunction of authority and critique, an even uncannier link emerges between sublimation and transgression – but where, as critique or as politics, this transgression 'is in some way legal'. Both rational and political knowledge thus *include* the potential for transgression, and to this extent the transgressive moment is peculiarly 'lawful'. Whereas Sloterdijk tends to place on opposite sides the actions of the reasonable subject and the *passage à l'acte* of transgressive behaviour, for Stiegler these are intimately related: 'a sublime acting out [*passage à l'acte sublime*] that expresses a desire – the desire for justice . . . which means, precisely, the will of the *demos* insofar as it is entitled and qualified to critique the super-ego' (2013, p. 31). For all forms of desire, of whatever kind, share the *anticipatory* structures of a libidinal economy: they are so many forms of *elpis*, all those blind hopes released last of all from the jar of Pandora, given by her as a gift to Epimetheus, the forgetful one whose crime was precisely to have failed to reserve any gift for humankind.

For Stiegler, politics is itself a process of individuation, that is, a temporal process, which begins with the *written* law of the Greek *polis* that initiates the process of publication, interpretation and publicity. With this idea of politics as a sublime form of transgression, its generational character is already manifest: the will of the *demos* of the succeeding generation is inherently bound, by the authority of its education in political knowledge, to in one way or another critique the established order of the previous generation. But the sublimity of this transgression is also perceived as a threat, as a dangerous openness to the risk of the indeterminate: hence Anders's description of the 'thirst for power' as a symptom of the *shock* of contingency that strives to 'neutralize' its *fact* (Anders, 2009, p. 293). This is exemplified and idealized in tragedy as the struggle between the gerontocracy of Creon and the revolt of the youth, embodied in Antigone (who is herself also, as Sophocles says, the 'crutch' of her father, Oedipus, who together *with* Antigone is, of course, the child of Jocasta and as such the very symbol of the confusion of the generations).

What is it that enables this movement to inaugurate another form of authority, which corresponds to the general movement from *muthos* to *logos*? For Stiegler, the answer can *already* be located in the Prometheus myth: the Titan, exposed in shame to the suffering brought by naked exposure to the elements, is also condemned to have his liver consumed, according to a rhythmic temporality (an automatism) operating as regularly as clockwork. The liver is not only the 'mark of mortality' but a kind of 'organic *mirror* in which divinatory hermeneutics is practised, in which, during the sacrifice, divine messages are interpreted', and which secretes the black bile of melancholy (Stiegler, 1998, p. 203). But when myth becomes *logos*, it is tragedy that bears witness to the melancholic struggles to which this gives rise, for this is the entrance into another age, the dawn of a new temporality in which the exactitude of *alphabetic* writing enables a repeated return that opens the possibility for 'an interpretation that is no longer a divination', signified by a de-divination of Hades and Dikē that nevertheless preserves the primordiality of these feelings (Stiegler, 2013, p. 32). It is through writing that youth can, through scholastic practice, access and accumulate the knowledge of the first geometers, the first philosophers, the first historians and so on – reproduce it intergenerationally, and so transform it.

Only on the basis of scholastic practice founded on writing does it become possible to aim at those *rational* objects of desire that do not exist, yet consist, and more precisely those proper to collective individuation processes, such as justice. If the feeling of shame is the condition of possibility not of *achieving* justice (which can never *be* achieved) but of *striving* for it, and where to exist without such striving is merely and unsustainably to subsist, this is because shame is the awareness of our originary faultiness: shame is '*the knowledge of that which signifies the situation of mortals* between beasts and gods, between pure subsistence and pure consistence, as knowledge of this condition' (2013, p. 34). This faultiness is not a lack but that which forms the seed of individuation that grows out of the pre-individual milieu, even if this growth can also become deformed. Through the mnemotechnics of writing, through which scholastic practice becomes possible, the singularity of the object of desire pursued by the individual can *become* rational and collective. And it does so precisely as the *sublimation* of the desire of the psychic individual, a sublimation that is on the one hand founded in this awareness of the *limits* of our mortal situation in pursuit of what does not exist, and on the other hand in an excess that *goes beyond* the individual in pursuit of a *collective* singularity that is no more (and no less) existent.

Antigone and *Antigone*

Antigone, and the tragic situation depicted in *Antigone*, that Sophoclean tragedy whose ode to the uncanny excessiveness of human being formed the hinge of Heidegger's turn from the existential analytic to the history of being (Heidegger, 1996, 2000), depicts and stages this strange situation and this tension between the individual and the collective, and between the archaic and the critical. This is not just a matter of the difference between the 'state' and 'religion', or between 'human' and 'divine' law. Nor is it just the *fact* of the generational difference between the old and the young. For this difference is not strictly chronological: while Creon may indeed be the uncle of Antigone, and as such belongs to the ascending generation, yet, in so far as he is the embodiment of 'human' law, he represents that which is more 'recent', and ultimately finds himself forced to learn wisdom from the younger Antigone, who, *in her very youth*, stands paradoxically and unbendingly as the representative of the most 'archaic' law.

What injunction compels Antigone? Surely she is outraged at the corporeal shame to which her brother's corpse is condemned, left lying naked and exposed to the city, without the socio-technical rituals of burial. Yet Heidegger insists it is neither blood (kinship) nor some death worship that drives Antigone (Heidegger, 1996, pp. 116–17). Counter to some standard translations (but congruently with Lacan), for Heidegger Antigone states clearly that the wellspring of her actions consists in the dictates *neither* of Zeus nor of Dikē, but rather beyond *both* the 'upper' and the 'lower' gods. This is not to deny that Antigone acts from a feeling for justice, for what Heidegger is addressing is precisely the process of de-divination to which Stiegler will refer. The 'beyond', here, is precisely that consistence which exists only infinitely. So, if the injunction to which Antigone responds is bound to remain *agrapta*, unwritten, this involves 'a certain legality which is . . . an invocation of something that is, in effect, of the order of law, but . . . not developed in any signifying chain' (Lacan, 1992, p. 278). A 'certain legality', 'in some way legal': here lies the whole *problem* of Antigone. Her *youthful* libidinal economy is organized around her love for her departed brother, yet irreducible to it, because Antigone's desire is sublimated to a collective individuation process that she nevertheless exceeds. If Antigone acts on the basis of the unwritten, nevertheless *Antigone* is written, and remains, to transform our cities, and this is why, even if Antigone is without *graptus*, without the materiality of the inscribed trace, Heidegger will state that '[s]he is the purest poem itself' (Heidegger, 1996, p. 119). The temporality of Antigone's shame thereby stretches across more than two millennia, to touch us – through the *text* of Sophocles.

If Antigone acts beyond the finitude of law, and in her shame that unwritten justice has been forgotten, she remains, for the *polis* constituted by the temporality of written law, anything but an embodiment of Kant's *'wisdom* of life'. Her vehement, hyperbolic shame marks her as a figure of excess, of *hubris*, and in that sense a *hybrid*, set off by the shameless-ness of Creon's deformed authoritarianism. Outraged by the city and thirsting for justice, Antigone desires *to excess*, through a *passage à l'acte* in which life and death are confounded. Hence Heidegger's quotation of Hölderlin to characterize the Antigonian injunction: 'Life is death, and death is also a life' (Heidegger, 1996, p. 118). Antigone grants herself a self-sacrificial right, if not a suicidal willingness to die, that suicide which, according to Anders, has always been forbidden by the 'highest authori-ties' on the grounds of constituting an act of '*arrogant self-degradation*' (Anders, 2016, p. 49). Or as Stiegler spells it:

> [I]f this *preferring to die* is not simply wanting to die, if it is, on the contrary, the sublime affirmation of a *wanting to live in death* – but *in shame* as the highest expression of life, and very close to death, where life *is* dying … then this *preferring to die* can appear in the *eyes of those who are without shame* only as a refusal of life, as acting out, as the passage to the act of someone who is desperate, who has lost all reason, and who has sunk into excess.
>
> (Stiegler, 2013, p. 37)

'*The eyes of those who are without shame*': are these the optical organs of a public constituted by the publicity of the written word, then the sensational-ism of the hypocritically moralistic tabloid press, and later still what Deleuze called 'TV entertainment' – three stages of the temporality of shame? For Anders, what is *not* true is that machines lack eyes: we behave *as though* we are seen by a technological panopticon, and it is before *these* very eyes that we are exposed to our Promethean shame of being human (Anders, 2016, p. 74). It would thus be the seizure of the law by the apparatus, by *Gestell*, that today invokes a sense of our own comparative limitations and at best inspires us to some kind of passage to the act of resistance.

For Stiegler, the digital technical system that has given rise to the data economy sees us and knows us only in the calculability of the informa-tion we provide 'voluntarily', as we labour (in our 'work' or our 'leisure') at our screens for *it*, supplying this information on which it feeds accord-ing to a rhythm (an automatism) operating as regularly as clockwork (but so much faster than anything merely mechanical, let alone biological), leaving us to secrete, in our secret shame, the malaise and melancholy of whatever remains of our singularity. What is reflected back to us on the platforms of this economy thus tends constantly to foreclose any potential for some future instrumental maieutics that would form the mainspring of any process of psycho-social individuation. In short: 'The tyrant who seizes the law is thus no longer Creon; it is the market that no longer knows any limits, having forgotten the meaning of shame' (Stiegler, 2013, p. 39).

What requires critique is less the authoritative or authoritarian superiority of a more perfect and infinitely perfectible technocracy than a weaponized broadcast media and digital data economy whose target is precisely the relationship between the generations itself. In other words, marketing aims to interfere with the process of psychic and collective individuation as a whole, by utilizing the fruits of technical individuation to interfere with the generational transmission of knowledge, in all its authoritative and transformational complexity. With *generalized* proletarianization, that is, the conjoined loss of work-knowledge and life-knowledge, the systematic and systemic destruction of the capacity for attention and memory, we find ourselves disoriented *in time* that, as Kant and Husserl understood, must be the *basis* for the *I* in so far as it is a process of individuation that *aims*, infinitely, to unify itself.

What Stiegler understands and Kant, Husserl and Heidegger did not understand is that this *basis* is historically conditioned, and more specifically by the epochs that form the successive ages of the mnemotechnical *pharmakon*, where such *pharmaka* are both the condition of access to the consistence beyond existence that is the individual, and the threat to that access. The temporality of the psychic individuation process can occur only *through* the processes of collective individuation to which it is joined (and which it in turn enables), and this entanglement of the psychic and the collective is in turn possible only because *between* them, there is a mediating process of technical individuation, and more specifically of mnemotechnical individuation. *Dikē* and *aidōs* arise within us only because technical individuation opens up the possibility of desire for what eventually comes to be called the idealities, which are accessible only through the becoming-symbolic of the world, or as Anders says, our 'abstraction'. By targeting the processes of psychic and collective individuation, what the technical individuation processes of consumer capitalism and the data economy ultimately threaten is the capacity for singularity, that is, our capacity to be temporal beings as such.

The Antigone complex

Stiegler's account of the disorientation wrought by contemporary hyper-industrial society is thus even more radical than Anders's. The three crucial elements of this radicality are:

1   the recognition that technical individuation unfolds across a series of epochs, in which each new invention disrupts the psycho-social programmes organized as the forms of practice that make some particular stage of this process liveable and more or less stable;
2   the recognition that crucial to all these processes are more specifically the mnemotechnologies that are all those stages in the development of communicative media, as the basis for the mediation of the relationship within and between the individual and the collective, from cave painting to alphabetic writing, the printing press, radio, cinema, television and now digitalization;
3   that if these technologies and mnemotechnologies are each inherently disruptive, that is, a *shock* to the systems of psycho-social organization, nevertheless it is only through a second moment, a *counter* to this shock, that new practices can be developed capable of leading to another more or less stable and livable epoch.

Today's disorientation results from systematic interference in the inter-generational transmission of knowledge, authority and consistence that has obstructed the formation of any such livable, more or less stable, new epoch. This disruptive obstruction of collective individuation amounts to the prevention of the process of synchronization that is our very possibility of constituting a *we*, while the obstruction of psychic individuation amounts to the prevention of the process of diachronization that is our possibility of constituting an *I* in its *différance* from the *we*, including through transgressions 'in some way legal'. Or in other words, the synchronic and the diachronic are names for those negentropic *orders* by which individuals and collectives reproduce society while changing it – so long as these 'orders' are thought of not as states but as processes, that is, temporally. But even as processes, they operate within limits, thresholds that can be crossed or forgotten through excess (hubris) or rigidification (repression), either sexual or technical. Shame would then be a reflexive act that responds to this failure or this reaching of limits.

What threatens today, however, is some permanent failure of the synchronic and the diachronic. Consumer capitalism and now the data economy replace these processes with hyper-synchronizations in which all differences tend to be eliminated in favour of the calculability of mass market audiences or hyper-segmented market niches. But the outcome is less the passivity of indifference than the advent of 'hyper-diachronizations', forms of acting out in which there is a fundamental 'rupture with the symbolic milieu, a decoupling of individual and collective time, a de-composition of the diachronic and the synchronic' (Stiegler, 2009, p. 50). Or, more simply, 'the decomposition of the social' (p. 82). This is less a problem of repression by an authority than of regression *from* authority, even if it in turns gives rise to desperate authoritarianisms (which are unauthoritative because without knowledge). Beyond thresholds crossed and forgotten, what accompanies such de-symbolized hyper-diachronizations when the very possibility of synchrony and diachrony seems on the way to being eliminated is a feeling perhaps better described as 'hyper-shame'.

The hyper-diachronization engendered by the hyper-synchronization of consumer capitalism is relatively new, but the *possibility* of such obstructions of the psycho-social individuation process is as old as the process itself. This is so precisely *because* our potential for synchronic and diachronic *orientation* has *always* been dependent on mnemotechnical exteriorization, such as the system of written law, which in the eyes of Antigone had become shamefully rigidified, that is, deadened. *Antigone*, as the tragic representation of the struggle between archaic and critical authorities, is already the product of a demythologizing world of writing in which, as Sophocles says, the divine 'draws away'. This crisis of authority is ultimately replaced by the authority of monotheism, founded no longer on the tragic sense of human existence as occupying that tense, limited space between beasts and immortals, but on the law of guilt, itself destined to be intensified after the appearance of the Lutheran bible (enabled by the printing press that in turn enabled mass literacy) that leads to the founding of a new spirit that will become that of a new technical system called capitalism. But this new spirit will prove to be dedicated to undermining spirit as such, and hence the Industrial Revolution leads to what Nietzsche called the 'death of God', that is, to his prophecy of the nihilistic unfolding that would characterize the 'history of the next two centuries' (Nietzsche, 1968, p. 3). *This* crisis of authority, combined with an exacerbation of guilt, will lead at the end of the nineteenth century to the burgeoning of those hysterical symptoms afflicting young minds the study of which will set Freud on his singular path of thinking and therapeutics.

Today, this destruction of the authority of preceding generations in the eyes of youth has been exacerbated, not just because parents lack knowledge *in fact* but because what knowledge they may possess seems constantly to be outstripped and outdated by the shocks of a perpetually accelerating process of technical individuation. At the same time, the multiple limits that are being reached by consumer capitalism mean that this younger generation remains increasingly dependent, economically, on the preceding generation. They find themselves in a world that seems populated by those only too willing to declare they 'couldn't care less', or else to conceal this nevertheless undeniable nihilistic fact. As a result, youth today:

> suffer from a psychological situation in which they have lost confidence in themselves, no longer believe in the authority of their parents, and are confronted with the *structural cynicism of the society* in which they live, a society that produces a world without shame.
>
> (Stiegler, 2013, p. 44)

In this situation, denial is indeed a constant temptation and tendency, and for Stiegler this nihilistic refusal is the fundamental character of *das Man* today (2013, p. 45). But another tendency is that of the Antigone complex properly speaking, in which, like Antigone herself, there can be a wish to hyper-diachronically leap back beyond the law without law of a society without shame, in the name of some long-lost archaic principle that can *make* law (great) again. Hence fundamentalisms of all stripes, and their sudden and extreme converts, ready to act out in ways that are sometimes *literally* suicidal.

Such highly energized actions, vehemently enacting a desperate relation to the end (of time) where 'life is death, and death is also a life', are always undertaken in some way in the name of the best, however much they embody the worst. This is so because of the transparently suicidal tendencies of a society that seems willing to sacrifice every genuine possibility of psycho-social individuation on the altar of a market that, as Sloterdijk noted, is even prepared to dispense with the dogma of innovation, that is, of Schumpeter's creative destruction (Sloterdijk, 2013, p. 65). Such hyper-diachronizations need not always be founded on a search for a new or archaic authority of consistence: they may simply amount to a desperate response to the feeling of having no place, hence no *ethos*, in a world that, in other words, has ceased to reflect back to them the feeling of *existing*. But even in these cases, Stiegler finds a sense that, *through* these acts, desperate individuals bear witness to their desperation, *testify*, as Levi himself felt bound to do (and in the shame of being able and not able to do so), to the shamelessness of a world that no longer offers them the feeling that there is a *future*, hence eliminating all *elpis*, other than that sometimes dark and horrifying possibility of confounding life and death by occupying the position of the martyr.

What could ameliorate this socio-psycho-pathological condition that we are proposing to call *hyper-shame*, however brazen the representatives of this situation may (already have) become, and which can lead only to disunity and war, both economic and military? Avoiding such wars is possible only if disagreement can be socialized in the form of a new, peaceful conflict of interpretations, which was the very notion behind Hermes's gift of *dikē* and *aidōs*. This would constitute, perhaps, the key political task of our time, because it harbours the possibility of political continuation itself, given that politics amounts to a sublime form of transgression through which the singularity of each of us, and of our collectivities, depend on finding ways, not just of opposing one another, but of composing. It is in order to write such a new composition that today we require new practices with which to play (and work), new instruments, or as Deleuze said, new weapons (Deleuze, 1995, p. 178).

This amounts to the injunction to practise, thoughtfully and therapeutically, a positive pharmacology, even if this comes late, as scientific wisdom of life tends always to do. If we wish to avoid concluding that this comes (always) *too* late – for a shape of life grown old, but *immediately* old, because this world shamefully fails to grant to the youths to whom it gives birth any feeling for or belief in a future – then we must nevertheless not deny that this pharmacology, and whatever rejuvenation its therapies might bear, may well take flight along lines that are becoming legible only at the onset of dusk (Hegel, 1991, p. 23).

Note

1 All emphases in this chapter are from the original.

References

Anders, G. (2009). The Pathology of Freedom: An Essay on Non-Identification. *Deleuze Studies*, 3, 278–310.

Anders, G. (2016). On Promethean Shame. In Christopher John Müller, *Prometheanism: Technology, Digital Culture and Human Obsolescence*. London & New York: Rowman and Littlefield.

Babich, B. (2012–2013). *O, Superman!* Or Being Towards Transhumanism: Martin Heidegger, Günther Anders, and Media Aesthetics. *Divinatio*, 36, 1, 41–99.

Bachelard, G. (2005). Noumena and Microphysics. *Angelaki*, 10, 2, 73–8.

Deleuze, G. (1995). *Negotiations*. New York: Columbia University Press.

Derrida, J. (1981). Plato's Pharmacy. In *Dissemination*. Chicago, IL, & London: University of Chicago Press.

Derrida, J. (2007). No Apocalypse, Not Now: Full Speed Ahead, Seven Missiles, Seven Missives. In *Psyche: Inventions of the Other*. Stanford, CA: Stanford University Press.

Freud, S. (1985). *The Complete Letters of Sigmund Freud to Wilhelm Fliess, 1887–1904*. Cambridge, MA, & London: Harvard University Press.

Hegel, G. W. F. (1991). *Elements of the Philosophy of Right*. Cambridge: Cambridge University Press.

Heidegger, M. (1990). The Self-Assertion of the German University. In Günther Neske & Emil Kettering (eds), *Martin Heidegger and National Socialism: Questions and Answers*. New York: Paragon House.

Heidegger, M. (1996). *Hölderlin's Hymn 'The Ister.'* Bloomington & Indianapolis, IN: Indiana University Press.

Heidegger, M. (2000). *An Introduction to Metaphysics*. New Haven, CT, & London: Yale University Press.

Janicaud, D. (1994). *Powers of the Rational: Science, Technology, and the Future of Thought*. Bloomington & Indianapolis, IN: Indiana University Press.

Kant, I. (2002). *Theoretical Philosophy after 1781*. Cambridge: Cambridge University Press.

Lacan, J. (1992). *The Ethics of Psychoanalysis, 1959–1960: The Seminar of Jacques Lacan, Book VII*. London: Routledge.

Levi, P. (1989). *The Drowned and the Saved*. London: Abacus.

Marx, K. (1973). *Grundrisse: Foundations of the Critique of Political Economy (Rough Draft)*. London: Penguin.

Müller, C. J. (2016). *Prometheanism: Technology, Digital Culture and Human Obsolescence*. London & New York: Rowman and Littlefield.

Nietzsche, F. (1968). *The Will to Power*. New York: Vintage.

Nietzsche, F. (1994). *On the Genealogy of Morality*. Cambridge & New York: Cambridge University Press.

Ross, D. (2013). Pharmacology and Critique after Deconstruction. In Christina Howells & Gerald Moore (eds), *Stiegler and Technics*. Edinburgh: Edinburgh University Press.

Sen, A. (2000). *Development as Freedom*. New York: Alfred A. Knopf.

Simondon, G. (2007). *L'Individuation psychique et collective*. Paris: Aubier.

Sloterdijk, P. (2013). *In the World Interior of Capital: For a Philosophical Theory of Globalization*. Cambridge: Polity.

Stiegler, B. (1998). *Technics and Time, 1: The Fault of Epimetheus*. Stanford, CA: Stanford University Press.

Stiegler, B. (2003). Technics of Decision: An Interview. *Angelaki*, 8, 2, 151–68.

Stiegler, B. (2006). Anamnēsis and Hypomnēsis: The Memories of Desire. In Arthur Bradley & Louis Armand (eds), *Technicity*. Prague: Litteraria Pragensia.

Stiegler, B. (2009). *Acting Out*. Stanford, CA: Stanford University Press.

Stiegler, B. (2010). *For a New Critique of Political Economy*. Cambridge: Polity.

Stiegler, B. (2011). *The Decadence of Industrial Democracies: Disbelief and Discredit, 1*. Cambridge: Polity.

Stiegler, B. (2013). *Uncontrollable Societies of Disaffected Individuals: Disbelief and Discredit, 2*. Cambridge: Polity.

Stiegler, B. (2015). Bernard Stiegler on Automatic Society: As told to Anaïs Nony. *Third Rail Quarterly*, 5, 16–17. Available at http://thirdrailquarterly.org/wp-content/uploads/05_Stiegler_TTR5.pdf

Stiegler, B. (2016). *Automatic Society, Volume 1: The Future of Work*. Cambridge: Polity.

Chapter 9

Justice, temporality and shame at the Khmer Rouge Tribunal

Alexander Laban Hinton[1]

Does justice for mass murder have meaning 32 years after the fact? This question was a hot topic of discussion in Cambodia in June 2011 when I attended the initial hearings that launched the trial of the four surviving, most senior leaders of the Khmer Rouge, which finally got underway at the Extraordinary Chambers in the Courts of Cambodia (ECCC). At this UN-backed international hybrid court, more commonly known as the Khmer Rouge Tribunal (KRT), the scales of justice appeared to be set before an hourglass, one that was quickly running out of sand.

After more than 25 years of delay, it took roughly three years after the June 2006 launch of the court for the first trial to begin. Only in February 2012 was the verdict finalized after the Supreme Court Chamber issued its decision on appeals, sentencing the accused, former commandant Duch of the regime's central prison and interrogation centre (S-21), located on the grounds of a high school, to life imprisonment. That was supposed to be the quick case, one that was more or less straightforward, since the accused admitted his guilt and cooperated throughout the trial.

Meanwhile, the second case, involving the four most senior, surviving leaders of the Khmer Rouge – a group of Maoist-inspired revolutionaries who enacted policies leading to the deaths of almost two million of the country's eight million inhabitants from April 17, 1975 to January 6, 1979 – had only more recently got underway, now more than thirty years after they were overthrown by a Vietnamese-backed army.

On June 27, 2011, the first morning of the initial hearing, I sat with 66-year-old artist Vann Nath, one of a handful of survivors of S-21, the Khmer Rouge security centre where over 12,000 inmates perished, many after being interrogated and tortured. We were positioned just yards away from the defendants: 'Brother Number Two' Nuon Chea (aged 85), Pol Pot's brother-in-law and Foreign Affairs Minister, Ieng Sary (86), Ieng Sary's wife and Minister of Social Affairs Ieng Thirith (79), and Head of State Khieu Samphan (80). There was also an unspoken absence, as their leader, Pol Pot ('Brother Number One') and other high-ranking officials such as General Ta Mok and Minister of Defence Son Sen, had passed away or had been killed.

Too much time had passed. By the look of things on that morning in court, it appeared questionable that the octogenarian defendants would all be able to participate fully or even live long enough to see the conclusion of the trial, which could last for several years.

As we gazed at the enfeebled defendants, who suffered various ailments and at times needed help to stand, it was hard to imagine them overseeing one of the most radical experiments of social engineering in human history. Upon taking power after a brutal civil war that had led to hundreds of thousands of deaths, devastated the economy, and resulted in massive population displacements, the Khmer Rouge set out to build a new revolutionary society: one that would be purified of, as they put it, the 'corrupting' influence of capitalism, feudalism and neo-imperialism (Chandler, 1999; Kiernan, 1996; Hinton, 2005).

Money, markets and traditional community life were replaced by cooperatives where people worked day and night in a constant state of fear and terror. Freedom of speech, movement and assembly were severely curtailed. Buddhism, which infused the daily life of the majority of Cambodians, was banned. Family members were forced to live and work apart for long hours and often on starvation rations. And then there were the purges and mass executions. In just three years, eight months and twenty days, the Khmer Rouge enacted policies leading to the deaths of almost a quarter of the population.

Several years later, as I write this chapter, I consider this moment when I sat by Vann Nath and the conjunction of juridical, revolutionary and Buddhist temporalities, two of which are secular (justice and revolution) and one religious (Buddhism). Each provides an orientation to the world, parsing time and providing maps for lived experience, including the emotions. Each is enmeshed with the rubrics of this book – temporality and shame – in different ways even as they share concerns, including the relationship of self and other, the social good, moral being and the crosscurrents of truth, knowledge and power.

The introduction to this volume provides an overview of some of the philosophical and psychological debates and histories regarding the relationship of temporality and shame. My goal is to bring an anthropological lens to bear on these issues, one that explores the intersection of temporality (the lived experience of duration that is mediated in part by discourses about and categorical maps of time) and shame (the lived experience of self-diminishment due to the awareness and exposure of one's lack) through a focus on thick description, local knowledge and the experience-near (see, for example, Geertz, 1977, 1983). In this sense, it differs from many of the other chapters in this volume in its wariness of categories – including 'temporality,' 'shame' and related theoretical rubrics – that have the potential to universalize and lead to broad but relatively 'thin descriptions' (see Geertz, 1977). These or more abstracted concepts deflect attention away from the everyday, lived experience and understandings that may diverge from Western philosophical and psychological ideas in places like Cambodia.

More broadly, and here I turn from an anthropological frame to one that is more philosophical even as it resonates with Buddhist understanding of the self and being, all scholars ultimately face this sort of paradox: we communicate through concepts and categories that inevitably simplify, edit out and erase. We articulate and we redact (Hinton, 2016). Justice, revolution and religion provide maps for doing so and as such provide the seeds of violence – even genocide – in terms of how they parse difference and assert moral purity. History provides many examples to support this point, ranging from the Crusades to the Nazis to the actions of ISIS today.

If this chapter takes up the issue of temporality and shame in relationship to issues that emerged at the Khmer Rouge Tribunal, it tries to do so in a reflexive manner, raising questions about authority and voice (who speaks and how, and who remains silent and why?). How, as scholars, do we write about such issues? In anthropology, much has been written about dangers of ethnographic authority and how writing and analysis assert power and a hierarchy of being.

Indeed, scholarly analysis articulates and redacts, asserts a moral order, and constructs self and other – including the 'others' who are the subject of our analyses, our 'audience' of readers and the discussions deemed as 'relevant' within any given disciplinary communities. Our analyses implicitly assert an authority and mastery – in part through our ability to invoke theoretical mastery – even as they dance around a lack, the danger of falling short, of being revealed as lesser. In other words, scholarship itself is enmeshed in temporality and shame as it provides a map for lived experience (the act of writing in which I am now engaged) including the relationship of self and other, moral hierarchies of being and degrees of purity.

If this predicament is inescapable – alas, writing also contains an implicit violence and even genocidal potentiality of a sort – it may also be raised directly. One way to do so is through acknowledgement and openness. Another route is through the way we write. As opposed to obfuscating language and theoretical invocations, scholarship can strive for clarity: defining terms and seeking to render ideas in ways that will be clear to readers. This may not always be appropriate, as others, including Derrida (1990) who embodied his deconstructionist ideas and methods in his writing, have pointed out, but it often is.

Along these lines, I have chosen to write this chapter in a narrative style. I do so intentionally to raise questions about scholarly writing, to seek a somewhat more engaging style, and to, at times, make points using literary techniques such as juxtaposition and metaphor (see Hinton, 2016). In the end, scholars are archaeologists of a sort, excavating ruins (our topic) with an authority (theoretical and conceptual 'permits') and a sort of fiery light (passions and desires that 'drive' the project forward). In the end, as I have argued about critical genocide studies (Hinton, 2017), scholars must directly and openly grapple with related questions, including what authorizes such excavations and what is, as the etymology of the word 'excavation' suggests, 'hollowed out.'

Vann Nath at the Khmer Rouge Tribunal

Roughly two years earlier during the trial of Duch, Vann Nath had told the story of how he became swept up in the violence. It was a story that he had told before to me and others in interviews and in a memoir, but, as he told the court that day, he was happy to do so. He wanted his testimony to serve as a 'mirror' upon which the younger generations could reflect and in order to attain 'justice for [the dead],' a justice that would be 'seen by everybody' (Trial Chamber, 2009, pp. 55–6; see also Vann Nath, 1998). On the first day of Duch's trial, Vann Nath had told journalists, 'I couldn't sleep last night. I was dreaming about my time at S-21' (Letisinger, 2009).

Vann Nath told the story of how he and his family and the rest of the population of Battambang City had been relocated to the countryside, where they, like Cambodians throughout the country, were forced to perform agricultural labour for long hours on increasingly meagre rations. In the Khmer Rouge imagination, the creation of a mass agrarian work force would catalyse a 'super great leap forward,' one that would surpass China and Vietnam. The plan failed miserably and the population suffered the consequences, both through diminished rations and from purges the Khmer Rouge leadership launched to track down the 'traitors' who were subverting the revolution. For it was inconceivable that the 'all-knowing' Party Centre had a deficient party line.

If all modern states are predicated on a uniformity of imagined belonging (Anderson, 2006; Taylor, 2003), they accommodate differences to varying degrees. While the reasons vary, lack of tolerance often arises in times of upheaval and change, including the desire to implement a project of social engineering and transformation (Bauman, 1991; Scott, 1998) and fear that threatening others seek to subvert the utopian visions. This, at least, was an aspect of what happened during Democratic Kampuchea (DK) – as has been the case for other radical and genocidal regimes – as the high-modernist drive for uniformity and revolutionary utopia instead generated a long list of subversive enemies.

Perhaps we might consider this an 'aporia of genocide' as the perpetrator regime is bound to fail since the utopian vision it seeks always remains 'to come' (Derrida, 1990). In other words, the regime is caught in an 'impassibility,' to invoke the etymology of aporia, unable to create a uniform social order filled with uniform beings out of the complexity of particular and pluralistic human beings that inhabit society.

As it strives for such limits, extremity is normalized and mass death and suffering ensue in the inevitable failure and 'lack' it causes, dynamics that speak to revolutionary temporality (the pursuit of an imagined future utopia and the rewriting of history and biography to fit this vision) and shame (the 'lack' of the revolution, the state apparatus, its followers and the imagined enemies on to whom the shaming 'lack' is displaced).

This aporia of genocide is also haunting. The 'impassibility' of attaining utopia results both in a lack (the inevitable failure of the universalizing aspiration for pure uniformity) and an excess (the particularity of distinct humans who can never be moulded into uniform revolutionary beings). This excess is 'redactic,' pushed out of sight until it dehisces (Hinton,

2016). It is such a sudden eruption of that which has been pushed out of sight that haunts the revolutionary regime, helping to catalyse action to destroy the threatening 'double' and 'enemy' that appears and reappears despite the regime's best efforts to efface them at places like S-21.

Vann Nath was caught in this spiral of violence on December 30, 1977, as DK purges were well underway, with executions taking place at the cooperative, district, provincial and national levels. Upon his arrest, Vann Nath was taken to a pagoda that had been converted into a detention centre, where he was accused of being a traitor and tortured by electric shock.

Eventually Vann Nath was trucked to S-21, located in Phnom Penh. He said that after arriving at S-21, he lost all hope upon seeing how the guards:

> degraded us. It's indescribable, the way they treated us, the prisoners. Sometimes … while we were asleep they suddenly woke us up and if

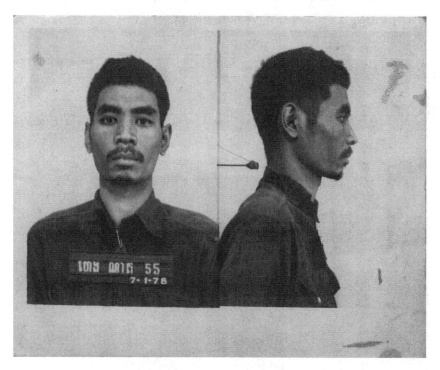

Figure 9.1 Vann Nath, aged 32, at S-21 in 1978. Courtesy of the Documentation Center of Cambodia (www.dccam.org)

we could not sit up on time then they used their rubber [tire] thongs to kick our heads.

(Trial Chamber, 2009, p. 64)

Vann Nath was shackled in a communal cell, where the prisoners sub-sisted on a few spoonfuls of rice gruel each meal. They rapidly began to weaken, which made them more susceptible to rashes and ailments. Due to infrequent bathing, they began to smell. Over time, they barely looked human, living in a state of shame and suffering.

The starving prisoners would eat grasshoppers or other insects if they could catch them, a difficult task since they were closely watched and would be beaten if they moved about or spoke to others. The prisoners 'didn't care' if a companion died because 'we were like animals.' Vann Nath thought only of thirst and hunger, a deprivation that was so extreme that he recalled thinking 'that even eating . . . human flesh would be a good meal' (Trial Chamber, 2009, p. 23). Meanwhile, the guards kicked and beat them without hesitation. Many inmates were interrogated and tortured; almost everyone was executed soon after arrival.

Figure 9.2 S-21 prisoner in cell (Tuol Sleng Museum of Genocide Crimes), painting by Vann Nath. Courtesy of the Documentation Center of Cambodia

Vann Nath survived because he could paint. In 1980, he was shown an execution list that included his name, crossed out in red ink with the annotation 'keep for use' (Trial Chamber, 2009, p. 68). While conditions were much better in the small artisan workshop where he began to work, Vann Nath frequently heard the screams of prisoners being tortured (one 'got used to it') and caught glimpses of the suffering and violence that took place at S-21, such as prisoners shackled in cells and a man strung to a pole like an animal.

After the fall of the Khmer Rouge, Vann Nath returned to work at S-21, where a genocide museum was being built. His contribution was to paint pictures about what he had seen or heard or what other former prisoners had related to him. During his testimony, his paintings were displayed, which included scenes depicting a prisoner being tortured by having his fingernails pulled out, waterboarding, and a baby being taken from a mother. These paintings are among the most powerful and iconic images at the museum that has been constructed at S-21.

* * *

As Vann Nath and I sat together at the initial hearing before the proceedings had begun, I asked him why he had come to the court. 'For justice,' he told me, 'and to see their faces.' When Nuon Chea, wearing a black and white ski cap and sunglasses, complained that he was 'not happy' with the proceedings, Vann Nath just shook his head, perhaps recalling how he was imprisoned by the Khmer Rouge without rights, counsel or due process.

As Vann Nath departed after the first morning session, he was surrounded by a large flock of journalists, eager to hear the impressions of this de facto spokesperson for Khmer Rouge victims. It would be the last court session Vann Nath attended. He died, after suffering from kidney disease for many years, on September 5, 2011.

* * *

Vann Nath's death brought the issue of justice and time into stark relief. An obituary by civil society leader Youk Chhang stated that Vann Nath's passing illustrated:

> the high cost that the simple passage of time can inflect on the pursuit of justice. Sadly, this tragedy repeats itself silently throughout

Cambodia, as each day victims of the Khmer Rouge pass away
without having been provided any measure of justice.

(Chhang, 2011; see also Shapiro, 2011)

This sentiment was echoed by others, including civil party lawyers,
donors, monitoring groups, and survivors who underscored the importance of moving the proceedings forward without further delay (Kong
Sothanarith, 2011; see also Di Certo, 2011).

After the weeklong initial hearings in June 2011, the case had stalled
once again due to a host of complications ranging from a sudden surge in
civil party applications to numerous appeals by the four teams of defence
lawyers. Meanwhile, it became increasingly doubtful that the ageing leaders would all be able to participate fully or even live long enough to see
the trial, which could last for several years, conclude.

On October 24, 2011, Ieng Sary's lawyers notified the court that Ieng
Sary, who had trouble focusing and had to relieve himself frequently,
would not testify during the proceedings (Ieng Sary Defence Team,
2011). He died in 2013, before the trial ended. On November 17, 2011,
the Trial Chamber found that Ieng Thirith suffered from progressive
dementia and was not fit to stand trial. They ordered her release, a decision that again highlighted the urgency of moving forward with the trial
even if it was reversed on appeal on December 13, 2011 (Trial Chamber,
2011d). She would later die in 2015. Nuon Chea and Khieu Samphan
continued to complain of ailments, with the latter having suffered a
stroke in 2007.

In response to such concerns, the Trial Chamber decided to split the
complicated case into parts, the first of which focused on population
movements and crimes against humanity. This was done 'in the interests
of justice' so that a shorter initial verdict could be rendered, one that
would thereby safeguard 'the fundamental interest of victims in achieving
meaningful and timely justice, and the right of all Accused in Case 002 to
an expeditious trial' (Trial Chamber, 2011c). To this end, the evidentiary
proceedings began on November 21, 2011. Nuon Chea and Khieu
Samphan were convicted of Crimes Against Humanity, including extermination and other inhumane acts, in the 2014 judgement in the first segment
of Case 002. The second part of their case, which includes the charge of
genocide, is ongoing at the time of writing.

Juridical temporality

Time. It is a central motif at the ECCC. If, outside of the court, the tribunal has been criticized for its glacial pace, the notion of time also figures prominently in the proceedings themselves. Here, time is directly bound up with fair trial rights, as the importance of upholding the due process rights of the defendants sometimes come into tension with the concerns of the civil parties. In this tribunal, civil parties have procedural rights almost on a par with those of the prosecution and defence, including the right to see the accused tried in a timely fashion. Even so, civil party lawyers frequently complain that their clients need additional time to speak in court or that they need more time to cross-examine witnesses. Meanwhile, in the first trial, a monitoring group timed each session down to the minute, noting how long the court spent in session on given matters. Here, the concern is trial management, as an efficient court presumably operates in a timely manner.

Time, however, constitutes a much bigger backdrop at the ECCC and is directly linked to the ways in which truth and knowledge are produced in the court. One of the most obvious illustrations of this point is temporal jurisdiction. The ECCC is authorized to examine mass human rights violations that took place while the Khmer Rouge were in power – not before and not after. As opposed to seeking a deeply historicized understanding of the genocide, the court provides a temporally limited one.

This was evident in the first case, the trial of Duch, who ran S-21 while Vann Nath was imprisoned there (Hinton, 2016). The judges did explore Duch's work at M-13, a detention centre Duch operated during the civil war, where he developed some of the techniques he would later employ at S-21. There was brief mention of the complex histories that enabled the Khmer Rouge to rise to power, including the Vietnam War and the carpet-bombing of Cambodia, but this information was deemed relevant only insofar as it bore upon establishing the guilt or innocence of the accused. Indeed, the trial verdict devotes a mere two pages to the discussion of the historical background of the genocide.

Nuon Chea's defence team picked upon this issue as part of a larger strategy of challenging the integrity of the court. On the first morning of the initial hearing, Nuon Chea's international co-defence lawyer, Michael Pestman, rose to explain why Nuon Chea was 'not happy with this hearing,' arguing that 'the proceedings should be terminated' due to investigative failures, political interference, lack of transparency, judicial incompetence and temporal bias (Trial Chamber, 2011a, pp. 11, 13).

In rapid order, he picked up on a series of controversies at the court, including accusations that the Cambodian judges were controlled by the government, the failure of the Office of Co-Investigating Judges to properly investigate Cases 003 and 004 and the subsequent resignation of the international co-investigating judge, and the unwillingness of the current Cambodian government officials who were themselves former Khmer Rouge to be interviewed.

'A trial is like building a house,' Pestman explained. 'It needs solid foundations, solid judicial investigation. Without a proper foundation, the trial will sooner or later collapse' (Trial Chamber, 2011a, p. 15). To avoid creating a 'show trial' like the 1979 People's Revolutionary Tribunal that was 'completely orchestrated and controlled by the Vietnamese,' Pestman continued, the court needed to 'start showing its teeth . . . It is time for transparency, not for sealed envelopes' (Trial Chamber, 2011a, p. 16).

Time was a central backdrop of Pestman's comments. He asked:

> Why were the terrible American bombings of Cambodia … and their lasting impact … on the people in this country [not investigated]? And why not the dubious role played by Vietnam, the Vietnamese in this country, in Cambodia, before, during and after the Khmer Rouge years. Is this Court trying to bury history? And why?
>
> (Trial Chamber, 2011a, p. 14)

Cambodians deserved 'a fair trial, a proper trial aimed at establishing the truth and not simply at rubber stamping history books written in Vietnam or in America' (Trial Chamber, 2011a, p. 16).

Pestman's remarks played upon a long-standing debate about what the function of a trial should be. On the one hand a large group of people, ranging from lawyers to diplomats, have argued that such legal proceedings have an important expressive component, a claim echoed in proclamations that such transitional justice mechanisms bring a host of positive results, ranging from healing to reconciliation to revealing 'the truth' (see, for example, United Nations, 1999). The Duch trial, for example, did reveal new things about the operation of S-21. But, by focusing on the years of Khmer Rouge rule in Cambodia, the case ultimately produced a 'truth' bleached of historical process and an understanding of the factors that enabled the Khmer Rouge to rise to power.

This was precisely the point Pestman sought to make as part of his larger strategy of calling into question the legitimacy of the court. For, if one key objective of a tribunal is to reveal the truth that has been hidden by the politics of memory, then why not explore the structural and historical roots of the genocide and the ways in which it is linked to geopolitics? Indeed, the 1999 'Group of Experts' directly invoked this truth-seeking function of the court, expressing the hope that 'the United Nations and international community can assist the Cambodian people in establishing the truth about this period and bringing those responsible to justice. Only in this way can this tragedy be brought to a full and final conclusion' (United Nations, 1999). The reason for this historical elision, Pestman directly implied, was politics.

The Cold War and Cambodia's attempt to find peace in the late 1990s meant that a trial only became a reality almost thirty years after the genocide had ended (United Nations, 2003). The agreement to form the ECCC, which took years to broker, included a limited temporal jurisdiction ('17 April 1975 to 6 January 1979') that would satisfy the US and China, superpowers implicated in the origins, dynamics and aftermaths of the conflict, and a personal jurisdiction ('senior leaders' and those 'most responsible') acceptable to Cambodian officials who wanted to avoid an expanding series of investigations that could imperil peace or even implicate current leaders, many of whom were former Khmer Rouge.

Besides eliding sociohistorical dynamics linked to the rise of the Khmer Rouge, like the Vietnam War and the US bombing of the Cambodian countryside, this temporal jurisdiction erases other key events, such as the fact that, after being deposed, the Khmer Rouge were rearmed by the United States, China and other powers due to geopolitics. Indeed, the Khmer Rouge were even given Cambodia's seat at the United Nations. It was only after the 1993 UN elections in Cambodia that many foreign government officials began to speak of the mass violence committed by the Khmer Rouge – as opposed to using euphemisms (for example, 'the unfortunate events of the past') as they had often done during the Cold War. Such events are too often omitted in juridical temporality, which prefers discrete intervals (the time and place of criminality), efficiency and parsimony (in terms of juridical process), and progress (toward a verdict with its attendant qualities, closure and evidentiary truth).

* * *

Counterposed to those who argue for expressive importance of tribunals are those who foreground legalism. This position was directly laid out in Hannah Arendt's (1994) *Eichmann in Jerusalem*, which argues that a court is first and foremost about the law. If a trial reveals something about the past, then that is fine. But a trial is ultimately about legal justice.

At the initial hearing, this position was staked out by Ieng Sary's defence team. Responding to civil party lawyer Moch Sovannary, who had argued on the first day that the 'victims need to understand the truth, the truth that they have been long waiting for, so that they can really move on with life' (Trial Chamber, 2011a, p. 109), Ieng Sary's international co-lawyer, Michael Karnavas, stated simply that 'the historical truth will never be found in this courtroom or any courtroom for that matter because courts are not designed for the historical truth' (Trial Chamber, 2011b, p. 3). Because of the temporal jurisdiction of the court, Karnavas noted, 'the whole picture, the whole truth will never be revealed' (ibid.).

Instead, Karnavas would argue repeatedly, the court needed to focus on the law. During arguments, Karnavas noted that he was:

> a fundamental believer in the power of the law. And the law has to be applied whether we like it or not. It is not a technicality. It is not something that we can just ignore when it's convenient or when difficult decisions need to be made.
>
> (Trial Chamber, 2011b, p. 82)

Later, during the press conference that followed the initial hearing, Karnavas explained that his team had made numerous submissions and jurisdictional challenges in the hope that the trials would constitute a 'civics lesson' on judicial procedure, one that, after the case had ended, would demonstrate how the Cambodian people should expect a court to work and thereby 'contribute to the betterment of Cambodia's future court system.'[2]

During the initial hearings, the Ieng Sary defence team's challenges related directly to the issue of time and justice. First, Karnavas and his Cambodian co-counsel, Ang Udom, argued that Ieng Sary could not be tried since the People's Revolutionary Tribunal (PRT) had already convicted him in 1979: to do so would violate the international legal principle of double-jeopardy (*ne bis in idem*).

Second, Karnavas and Ang Udom argued that, because Ieng Sary had been granted an amnesty and pardon in 1996, one that was critical in leading to the demise of the Khmer Rouge, who were still, at the time, waging war in the Cambodian countryside, he was immune from prosecution. Finally, Ieng Sary's defence lawyers argued that the statute of limitations had run out on their client's crimes and that to *ex post facto* apply international human rights law to the situation in 1979 would violate his fair trial rights.

These issues raised fundamental questions about juridical time, ones with which courts in other countries have grappled. Are some crimes so heinous that they transcend temporal limits? Relatedly, is it possible to try someone for crimes that are viewed as universal even if they were not formally codified at the time? And can an amnesty given to promote peace be nullified?

Running in the background of these questions were other issues about Cambodian history itself. Why wasn't an international tribunal held immediately after the Khmer Rouge were deposed? The answer, of course, was largely tied to Cold War politics. Why did the Khmer Rouge remain a viable fighting force until the late 1990s? This was partly due to geopolitical machinations that led the United States, China and others to support the Khmer Rouge for many years after they had fallen from power. And why was the Cambodian judiciary so incapacitated until the 1990s? Geopolitics, social instability and international sanctions were among the reasons.

* * *

If Karnavas stressed legal process, fair trial rights and the technicalities of law, civil party lawyers did not just support prosecution claims that the arguments of the defence teams were legally untenable; instead, they asserted that their clients also had fair trial rights, including the right to justice, truth and reparation (Trial Chamber, 2011b, p. 59f). For victims of mass human rights violations, international civil party co-lawyer Silke Studinsky argued on the second day of the initial hearing, effective remedy meant 'fair, effective and prompt access to justice' as well as 'prosecution and punishment' (Trial Chamber, 2011b, pp. 69–70). The victims had a right to truth, including 'obtaining adequate answers to the important questions – why crimes happened and why they happened to them and their families' (Trial Chamber, 2011b, p. 71). A pardon or amnesty clearly denied the victims such access to the truth and was 'an affront to the pain, suffering and damages done' to the victims (Trial Chamber, 2011b, p. 75).

The day before, Studinsky's international civil party lawyer colleague, Martine Jacquin, had framed these issues more broadly, asking 'Can justice heal or manage the suffering – or mitigate the suffering of victims?' Answering her rhetorical question, Jacquin stated:

> Justice can only restore whatever harm is reparable and whatever injury for which the victims can claim compensation. But justice cannot restore that which is beyond reparations, the physical and psychological wounds and scars that [are] borne by the victims for an entire life-time.
>
> (Trial Chamber, 2011a, pp. 115–16)

'But,' she continued, 'at the very least this trial can ascertain the truth, acknowledge facts, provide a sense of tranquility for victims and bring closure to their process of grieving' (ibid.).

Vernacular temporalities and the transitional justice imaginary

Can justice bring such closure to people like Vann Nath after so much time has passed? There is little doubt that the path to something like 'closure' or 'reconciliation' is a deeply personal one, inflected by one's past suffering, subsequent experiences, worldview and sense of the future. It is not a certain course and has many pathways.

One of the difficulties about transitional justice initiatives like the Khmer Rouge Tribunal is that they promise too much. Promises abound that the truth will be revealed as victims supposedly attain a sense of peace, justice, reconciliation, healing and closure. Such sweeping proclamations are bound to fail. Yet they appear again and again in trials and truth commissions and thereby set the mechanisms up for failure.

There are many reasons that transitional justice practitioners and personnel make such promises. For example, they play well to the donors who enable the mechanisms. But they are also the stuff of what I have called a 'transitional justice imaginary' (Hinton, 2014; on 'the imaginary,' see also Anderson, 2006; Castoriadis, 1987; Taylor, 2003), or a set of interrelated discourses, practices and institutional forms that help generate a sense of shared belonging among a group of people – in this case, members of the transitional justice community or larger international community.

This imaginary, while not monolithic, can nevertheless be found in a variety of transitional justice contexts. It has at least four key dimensions. The transitional justice imaginary is normative (linked to certain truth claims and moral assumptions), performative (an imagined community is constituted through enactment) and productive (it produces certain subject positions). It is also characterized by a temporality premised on linear time intervals (a pre- and a post-state), an orientation (war and peace) and a teleology (a straightforward movement between these two intervals or states). In particular, this transitional justice temporality (see Hinton, 2013) implicitly parses societies into a pre-state of conflict and a post-state of liberal democracy, along with a related set of binaries (violent/ peaceful, chaos/order, barbarism/civilization, primitive/sophisticated, irrational/rational, trauma/health, and so forth). To effect this transition, history is shrunk and erased, filtering out the grey zones that disrupt this teleological narrative of past and future.

The temporal jurisdiction of the Khmer Rouge Tribunal highlights this point, as complicated pasts are backgrounded the proceedings even as truth claims are made. This temporal foreshortening is paradoxical, for, according to its own logic, truth is required for closure, yet the temporal modality of transitional justice is one of shrinkage and thus renders a truncated history. In the end, such insights ask us to reflect critically upon the presuppositions of transitional justice and ask what sorts of truths are produced and for what reasons. From the vantage of this 'critical transitional justice studies' perspective (Hinton, 2010), one can see how time is manipulated to assert an imaginary that casts the post-conflict society into a subordinate position even as it asserts a teleology of movement toward a liberal democratic end.

One of the key dangers of this transitional justice imaginary is that it directs attention away from social practice and the ways in which the meaning and understanding of such transitional justice processes are negotiated on the ground. As opposed to attaining some sort of unilineal sense of closure or healing from the tribunal, people like Vann Nath grapple with the past in different ways through their life-course.

In his memoir, *A Cambodian Prison Portrait: One Year in the Khmer Rouge's S-21*, Vann Nath (1998) recalls meeting Him Huy, one of his former captors at S-21, in 1996. He experienced a range of emotions, including anger, before coming to pity Huy. During the Khmer Rouge period, this man was like:

> a savage bull, a lion. None of the prisoners, including myself, had dared to look him in the face then. Now, he was in a deadlock, with no more fangs or horns. Seeing him in this situation, somehow I felt pity for him.
>
> (Vann Nath, 1998, p. 113)

When Pol Pot, the leader of the Khmer Rouge, died two years later, Vann Nath was once again 'flooded with a jumble of confused thoughts and emotions' (1998, p. 116). On the one hand, he felt relieved because 'the bloodiest master criminal had disappeared forever from this world.' On the other hand, he felt sorrow that 'I would never fulfill my long-held desire to see Pol Pot standing in the dock, facing a court to answer for his crimes' (p. 117).

In the end, however, Vann Nath viewed the death of Pol Pot and other leaders who died without being tried through a Buddhist frame. His book concludes:

> I believe there will be justice. A person harvests what he has sown. According to the Buddhist religion, good actions produce good results, bad actions produce bad results. The peasant harvests the rice, the fisherman catches the fish. Pol Pot and his henchmen will harvest the actions they committed. They will reap what they have sown.
>
> (Vann Nath, 1998, p. 118)

Here we encounter yet another form of temporality, what we might call 'vernacular time.' Vernacular time refers to the specific local understandings and temporal practices operative in a given locality. In this case, Vann Nath notes a particular Buddhist vernacular conception of time that is frequently evoked, both through speech and through nonverbal and ritual acts, in Cambodia. From this Buddhist perspective, our being is constituted and reconstituted in a cyclical fashion. On a cosmic level, the universe is created and then degrades before being renewed. Ontologically, the doctrine of *samsara*, or the cosmological cycle of life, death and rebirth, holds that being is fleeting, a momentary coalescence of constitutive elements. Each moment of coalescence is conditioned by what preceded it, a notion that is reflected in the doctrine of karma (*kamma*) that Vann Nath invoked in the passage above. Those who do good will receive good; those who do bad deeds will suffer the consequences. A form of cosmic justice is at work here, as punishment for bad deeds is an inevitable part of being.

This Buddhist vernacular of time, of course, stands at odds with the linearity and progressive teleology of juridical time and related conceptions in the transitional justice imaginary, which asserts a binary of trauma/ill-health and health/closure that is overcome through the tribunal. For if there are other ways of achieving closure, such as through Buddhist ritual belief and practices centred around the notion of meritorious and demeritorious action, one of the key justifications of the ECCC would be undermined. A similar argument could be made about related notions of Buddhist forgiving and forgetting. A more modest, yet powerful way of approaching time and healing would embrace an openness to different ways of coping with and dealing with the past, ranging from religious understanding to juridical mechanisms.

We can glimpse some of the ways in which Vann Nath sought his path forward. Buddhism was one of the cornerstones of his understanding of the world, a set of beliefs and practices that had taken shape in his youth while studying at a pagoda (Rithy Panh, 2011). It provided him with a way to cope with his past suffering and to approach his future experiences, such as his encounter with Him Huy and his response to Pol Pot's death.

Art also seemed to provide Vann Nath with a way of grappling with the past, at first by painting images from S-21 and then later by participating in painting workshops with young students.[3] This engagement with the younger generation was very important to Vann Nath. He chose not to become a civil party, foregoing a form of participation centred on rights for one that was more humanistically oriented (though clearly civil parties have a variety of motives for their participation, including humanistic ones).[4] He did this in part because of health concerns but also because he did not want to assert a primacy over other survivors. He also did not want reparations, perhaps because he felt nothing could compensate for his suffering (Trial Chamber, 2009, p. 103; see also Rithy Panh, 2011).

When asked why he still wanted to testify, Vann Nath stated that ever since he was detained at S-21, he:

determined that if one day I survived ... I would compile the events to reflect on what happened so that the younger generation would know ... So I had to reveal, I had to write, I had to compile, and it can [serve] as a mirror to the younger generation of the lives of those who were accused with no reason, who committed no wrong ... I do not want anything more than that.

(Trial Chamber, 2009, pp. 54–5)

Here also we find an interesting conjunction of vernacular and transitional justice temporality, as the Buddhist emphasis on clear understanding dovetails with juridical notions of truth and evidence.

Did Vann Nath achieve this sense of justice after the Duch trial and upon seeing the surviving senior leaders of the Khmer Rouge stand trial on the first day of the initial hearing? It is impossible to know for certain, though, even if he felt some ambivalence, overall he seemed to have a positive attitude toward the court, as he indicated to me that day we attended the opening of Case 002. He also seemed pleased in some ways by the initial Duch verdict (he did not live long enough to see Duch's final sentence of life imprisonment), as illustrated by the fact that he participated in verdict distributions organized by the ECCC's Public Affairs office.

Figure 9.3 Vann Nath at Duch Verdict Distribution, August 12, 2010. Courtesy of the ECCC (www.eccc.gov.kh/en/gallery/photo/duch-verdict-distribution-8)

Figure 9.4 Duch verdict, painting by Vann Nath. Courtesy of the Documentation Center of Cambodia

But through his paintings, public statements about the past, Buddhist practices and beliefs, engagement with the younger generation, testimony during the Duch trial, participation in court outreach events and other activities, Vann Nath seems to have moved closer to something like healing and closure to the extent to which it can ever be attained by a survivor.

Before he died, Vann Nath completed one last painting. It depicts Duch sitting between two columns of skulls and bones that recede into the distance of a gloomy horizon. Vultures circle in the sky above, perhaps a Buddhist symbol of the attachment and craving that drive people to sin. Before Duch, who gazes mournfully into the distance, lies a copy of the verdict from his trial.

This new painting seems familiar. After gazing at it for a while, it appears that Vann Nath may have modelled the painting on his own S-21 self-portrait. Both figures assume the same posture with the same dejected expression. The two walls of the S-21 cell have been replaced with the two columns of skulls. Instead of the iron shackles in the S-21 portrait, in the new painting Duch is 'bound' by the verdict, which sentences him to imprisonment. But the new painting is also a Buddhist one, suggesting that, like a shadow, the deeds of Duch's past trail behind him, conditioning his future.

Justice, temporality and shame

I close with another image and moment, ones that bring the second key term in this volume, shame, into discussion. During his testimony, Vann Nath was asked to explain the art he had created after DK, ranging from the depiction of himself alone in a prison cell at S-21 to scenes of torture and execution. Much of this art hangs on the walls of the Tuol Sleng Genocide Museum, though some if it does not, including a series of 13 black-and-white sketches.

'Uncle, Uncle!' Judge Non Nil instructed as one of the sketches was displayed on the court monitor. 'Look at this drawing, Uncle Nath.' In this sketch there are two men, who appear to be guards. And a man sits by a water basin and is putting his left hand into the water. 'What does it mean, Uncle? Who does the sketch depict? Did you see this happen to another prisoner? Or is it a sketch of you, yourself?' (Trial Chamber, 2009, p. 40; also in Khmer version, p. 33).

'Your Honor, Mr. President,' Vann Nath began, his voice flat and eyes downcast, almost closed, 'This image is a sketch of me, myself, on the very first day I was allowed to come down from my cell. The sketch is a recollection that I drew as a souvenir of that time, a remembrance of when I began to have hope that I might live a little longer, perhaps even survive' (Trial Chamber, 2009, p. 40; also in Khmer version, p. 33).

The man in the water basin sketch, Vann Nath explained, was an image of himself shortly after his first meeting with Duch; he was given three days to clean up and rest before he would begin to paint. 'They brought me there to shave my beard and cut my hair,' Vann Nath told the court as the sketch remained frozen on the court monitor. 'And they let me bathe, as you can see there. More than a month had passed since the time I was first arrested until that moment when I was allowed to bathe by the water basin.'

'But what was most important about that moment,' Vann Nath continued, his voice flat and gaze cast down, 'was that by the basin there was a piece of mirror, a little bigger than the size of a toe. I found it right there by the water basin.' Vann Nath had picked up the piece of mirror with his

Figure 9.5 Vann Nath sketch, 'Self-portrait with a mirror' (1995), introduced as evidence at the ECCC in 2009. Image courtesy of the ECCC

right hand and 'raised it up to see the reflection of my face. When I looked at my reflection in the piece of mirror, I saw that my face was so exhausted and withered.' The two guards, Vann Nath noted, 'were sitting there watching me in case there was a problem. So I drew this sketch to depict myself at that time. That's what I'd like to tell Your Honor.'

There are rich literatures on the mirror and the gaze, ones that are beyond the scope of this essay. What many of them share, however, is the notion of a gaze, both by self and from others, through which subjectivity is constructed. It is, however, often one of lack. As Vann Nath gazes into the piece of mirror, for example, he sees a reflection, an idealized image, an impossibility. For, even if Vann Nath is able to reclaim some of his sense of self and humanity and thereby mitigate his shame as an abject 'traitor' in the new revolutionary society, there remains a necessary disjuncture between the ideal and the reality, a lack that may suddenly burst into view, revealed, what I have elsewhere called the redactic (Hinton, 2016). This lack contains the kernel of shame, one that may take root depending on the moment and the gaze.

Vann Nath's sketch vividly renders this moment of disjuncture, which he signals by linking it to memory (*souvenir*), a remembered image of self and the reality of how he now appears. 'My body was like that of an animal from hell,' Vann Nath had told the court. Indeed, S-21 was an institution that transformed human beings into enemy others that had to be marked, controlled, contained and diminished. This process was also bound up with time, ranging from the routines at the prison that structured the (barely) lived experience of the prisoners to the interrogations. Indeed, these interrogations were meant to produce a new rendering of time: a past rewritten to accord with their presumed guilt. This rewriting was also an ending, since the completion of a confession – which inscribed their revolutionary 'lack' and shame – was soon followed by execution.

This lack is also related to the notion of transition. Transitional justice temporality, as I noted earlier, involves a movement between two states, a regressive past and a progressive future with the transitional justice mechanisms serving as the vehicle of transformation. This notion of transition has a long genealogy. It is directly related to Enlightenment ideals, which assert the power of a reason capable of guiding (sometimes massive) social change and are often bound up with the idea of progressive time. A number of scholars, from Condorcet to Marx, have laid out stage theories suggesting a rise from a 'backward' state of being (as primitive or barbaric other) to the 'progressive' state of civilization at the top of the linear temporal scale.

Such stage theories assert a classificatory order, placing large groups of people into a temporally distanced and negatively marked place (Fabian, 1983). This act produces a lack. The 'backward other' is proclaimed to lack the qualities of civilization, to be 'uncultivated.' It is also a position of shame, one that, in the case of transitional justice, is extended to encompass entire societies. Transitional justice may render justice of a sort, but it also produces shame through its temporal framings of 'the backward other' – not just perpetrators but the society as a whole.

These temporal emplotments have a direct parallel to the violence at S-21. The DK regime, if inspired by Maoism and other socialist precedents, was at root Marxist-Leninism as the Party Statures clearly stated. Marxism was predicated on stage theory as societies were assumed to transition through different social forms linked to given material modalities. This linear process would culminate in revolution, a radical reorganization of society in which time began anew. The French Revolution provided a model of radical revolution guided by reason; it was a precedent the Khmer Rouge leadership, many of whom had studied in France, knew well. Revolution, in other words, is a model of transition, one that found further manifestation in the revolutions in Russia, China and Vietnam.

During DK, the notion of transition and change, and the potential lack thereof, also mediated the view of prisoners at S-21. Like society, which had to leap from a regressive state of capitalism (and communist 'lack') to one of revolutionary socialism, each person in DK had to continuously 'sharpen the consciousness' as they forged a pure mind that accorded with the Party line. The S-21 prisoners were those who had not done so, serving, more broadly, as symbolic containers for the larger 'lack' of a revolution that inevitably failed in its attempt to achieve impossible utopian goals (creating a utopian communist society filled with pure, uniform, revolutionary beings) that were always 'to come' (Derrida, 1990) – what I earlier referred as an aporia of genocide.

Their symbolic 'lack' both contaminated and threatened the revolution even as their abject, polluting, shameful state reflected and contained the larger 'lack' of the state and failures of its revolutionary leaders. The prisoners thereby also contained the leadership's shame and existential dread and terror, which may arise when a reality (in this case, the idealized revolutionary society) threatens to fragment. This projected lack and shame were 'revealed' through interrogation and torture leading to confession (which affirmed their subversion and justified their abjection), their degrading treatment, and prison conditions producing bodily deterioration and defoulment. It is this shame, embedded in a revolutionary and carceral temporality, which is manifest in Vann Nath's sketch, reflected by what he sees in the mirror as well as the gaze of his Khmer Rouge guards. The sketch also reflects a particular phenomenology of shame, including Cambodian conceptions of honour and 'face' (and the loss or lack thereof as in the case of S-21 prisoners; see Hinton, 2005).

This temporal lack also has parallels in the juridical process. On the one hand, transitional justice itself produces a lack as it asserts Cambodia's pre-existing position at a lower state (authoritarianism) and movement toward, but still at a distance from (as a 'transitional society') the end stage toward which it moves, a 'civilized' liberal democracy. Transitional justice is represented as serving as the mechanism of this movement. It is bestowed by the 'gift' of donors that masks, especially in the case of the US, the donors' own culpability while asserting their superiority as 'the givers' over the subordinate receivers (Maus, 2000).

On the other hand, there is a lack that is potentially addressed by justice, meted out by the verdict. Vann Nath's portrait of Duch, sitting before a copy of the verdict, highlights this shame even as it is also embedded in local Buddhist understandings and Cambodian conceptions of face and shame. The portrait illustrates how time and justice were interlinked for Vann Nath, a fusion of a phenomenology of shame (the 'lack') and revolutionary, juridical and Buddhist temporalities as Duch is now imprisoned for his bad deeds in the Khmer Rouge past, one from which Vann Nath had at last been released.

Notes

1 Since 2009, the author has been conducting research, ranging from on-site observations to participant-observation to semi-structured interviews, on the Khmer Rouge Tribunal. This research was supported by grants from the United States Institute of Peace (USIP) and Rutgers Research Council and a 2011–12 fellowship from the Institute for Advanced Study in Princeton. The views, ideas and conclusions expressed in the essay are, of course, my own and do not necessarily reflect the view of the USIP or any of these other institutions. I'd like to thank Rafiki Ubaldo and Nicole Cooley for their helpful suggestions on this essay. The book editors, Ladson Hinton and Hessel Willemsen, provided extensive feedback that helped clarify and strengthen the arguments at many points. My thanks go to them as well. I also owe thanks to Youk Chhang and the Documentation Center of Cambodia and to the ECCC Public Affairs Section for permission to use the images in this chapter. This paper is a substantially revised version of the following essay, "Justice and Time at the Khmer Rouge Tribunal: In Memory of Vann Nath, Painter and S-21 Survivor," *Genocide Studies and Prevention* 8(2): 7–17, 2014.
2 Author field notes, Press Conference, Extraordinary Chambers in the Courts of Cambodia, Phnom Penh: Cambodia, June 30, 2011. See also: http://vimeo.com/26064118, accessed December 20, 2011.
3 Vann Nath's paintings can be found at many sites on the Internet. See, for example, the webpage devoted to Vann Nath at 'Vann Nath – Paint Propaganda or Die – The Art History Archive' (www.arthistoryarchive.com/arthistory/asian/Vann-Nath.html, accessed July 5, 2012).
4 On this point, see also Youk Chhang (2011).

References

Anderson, B. (2006). *Imagined Communities: Reflections on the Origin and Spread of Nationalism*. New York: Verso.

Arendt, H. (1994). *Eichmann in Jerusalem: A Report on the Banality of Evil*. New York: Penguin.

Bauman, Z. (1991). *Modernity and the Holocaust*. Ithaca, NY: Cornell University Press.

Castoriadis, C. (1987). *The Imaginary Institution of Society*. Cambridge, MA: MIT Press.

Chandler, D.P. (1999). *Voices from S-21: Terror and History in Pol Pot's Secret Prison*. Berkeley, CA: University of California Press.

Chhang, Y. (2011). 'Vann Nath: A Witness to History (S-21 Survivor Passed Away),' Documentation Center of Cambodia, September 5 (www.d.dccam.org/Projects/Living_Doc/Photos/2011/S-21_Survivor_Passed_Away/index.html, accessed December 13, 2011).

Derrida, J. (1990). 'The Force of Law: The "Mystical Foundation of Authority."' *Cardozo Law Review* 11: 920–1045.

Di Certo, B. (2011). 'Health Woes Slow KRT,' *Phnom Penh Post*, December 8 (www.phnompenhpost.com/index.php/2011120853239/National-news/health-woes-slow-krt.html, accessed December 13, 2011).

Fabian, J. (1983). *Time and the Other: How Anthropology Makes it Object*. New York: Columbia University Press.

Fawthrop, T. & Jarvis, H. (2004). *Getting Away with Genocide: Elusive Justice and the Khmer Rouge Tribunal*. London: Pluto.

Geertz, C. (1977). *The Interpretation of Cultures*. New York: Basic Books Classics.

Geertz, C. (1983). *Local Knowledge: Further Essays in Interpretive Anthropology*. New York: Basic Books.

Hinton, A.L. (2005). *Why Did They Kill? Cambodia in the Shadow of Genocide*. Berkeley, CA: University of California Press.

Hinton, A.L. (ed.) (2010). Introduction: Toward an Anthropology of Transitional Justice. In A.L. Hinton (ed.), *Transitional Justice: Global Mechanisms and Local Realities after Genocide and Mass Violence*, 1–24, New Brunswick, NJ: Rutgers University Press.

Hinton, A.L. (2013). Transitional Justice Time: Uncle San, Aunty Yan, and the Khmer Rouge Tribunal. In Deborah Mayerson & Annie Pohlman (eds), *Genocide and Mass Atrocities in Asia: Legacies and Prevention*, 86–98, New York: Routledge.

Hinton, A.L. (2014). The Transitional Justice Imaginary: Uncle San, Aunty Yan and Victim Participation at the Khmer Rouge Tribunal. In Inge Vanfraechme,

Antony Pemberton, & Felix Mukwiza Ndahinda (eds), *Justice for Victims: Perspectives on Rights, Transition, and Reconciliation*, 247–261. New York: Routledge.

Hinton, A.L. (2016). *Man or Monster? The Trial of a Khmer Rouge Torturer*. Durham, NC: Duke University Press.

Hinton, A.L. (2017). Wonder Woman, the Gutter, and Critical Genocide Studies. In Fazil Moradi, Ralph Buchenhorst & Maria Six-Hohenbalken (eds), *Memory and Genocide: On What Remains and the Possibility of Representation*, 165–174. New York: Routledge.

Ieng Sary Defence Team (2011). 'Ieng Sary's Notice to the Trial Chamber that he will not testify during Trial' Phnom Penh: Extraordinary Chambers in the Courts of Cambodia, October 24 (www.eccc.gov.kh/sites/default/files/documents/courtdoc/E101_4_EN.PDF, accessed December 6, 2011).

Kiernan, B. (1996). *The Pol Pot Regime: Race, Power, and Genocide in Cambodia under the Khmer Rouge, 1975–79*. New Haven, CT: Yale University Press.

Kong Sothanarith (2011). 'Tribunal Parties Want Faster Prosecution at UN Court,' VOA Khmer, September 7 (www.voanews.com/khmer-english/news/Tribunal-Parties-Want-Faster-Prosecution-at-UN-Court-129378318.html, accessed December 13, 2011).

Letisinger, M. (2009). 'First ex-Khmer Rouge Member Faces Genocide Court,' CNN, February 16 (http://edition.cnn.com/2009/WORLD/asiapcf/02/16/cambodia.genocide/index.html, accessed December 13, 2011).

Maus, M. (2000). *The Gift: The Form and Reason for Exchange in Archaic Societies*. New York: W. W. Norton.

Rithy Panh (2011). 'Allocution de Rithy Panh,' September 14, 2011, e-mail from Association le Cercle des Amis de Vann Nath.

Scott, J.C. (1998). *Seeing Like a State: How Certain Schemes to Improve the Human Condition Have Failed*. New Haven, CT: Yale University Press.

Shapiro, T. Rees (2011). 'Vann Nath, whose artistry allowed him to survive Cambodian prison, dies.' *Washington Post*, September 6 (www.washingtonpost.com/local/obituaries/vann-nath-whose-artistry-allowed-him-to-survive-cambodian-prison-dies/2011/09/06/gIQARPhA8J_story.html, accessed December 6, 2011).

Taylor, C. (2003). *Modern Social Imaginaries*. Durham, NC: Duke University Press.

Trial Chamber (2009). Extraordinary Chambers in the Courts of Cambodia, 'Transcript of Trial Proceedings – Kaing Guek Eav "Duch" Public,' Trial Day 35, June 29, 2009.

Trial Chamber (2011a). 'Transcript of Initial Hearing – Nuon Chea, Ieng Sary, Ieng Thirith, Khieu Samphan Public,' Phnom Penh: Extraordinary Chambers in the Courts of Cambodia, June 27, 2011.

Trial Chamber (2011b). 'Transcript of Initial Hearing – Nuon Chea, Ieng Sary, Ieng Thirith, Khieu Samphan Public,' Phnom Penh: Extraordinary Chambers in the Courts of Cambodia, June 28, 2011.

Trial Chamber (2011c). Severance Order Pursuant to Internal Rule 89ter. Phnom Penh: Extraordinary Chambers in the Courts of Cambodia, September 22 (www.eccc.gov.kh/en/document/court/severance-order-pursuant-internal-rule-89ter, accessed December 6, 2011).

Trial Chamber (2011d). Trial Chamber Decision on Ieng Thirith's Fitness to Stand Trial. Phnom Penh: Extraordinary Chambers in the Courts of Cambodia, November 17 (www.eccc.gov.kh/en/articles/trial-chamber-decision-ieng-thirith's-fitness-stand-trial, accessed December 6, 2011).

United Nations (1999). 'Report of the Group of Experts for Cambodia established pursuant to General Assembly Resolution 52/135,' February 18, 1999 (http://unakrt-online.org/Docs/GA%20Documents/1999%20Experts%20Report.pdf, accessed December 20, 2011).

United Nations (2003). Agreement between the United Nations and the Royal Government of Cambodia concerning the Prosecution under Cambodian Law of Crimes Committed during the period of Democratic Kampuchea,' June 6, 2003 (www.eccc.gov.kh/sites/default/files/legal-documents/Agreement_between_UN_and_RGC.pdf, accessed December 20, 2011).

Vann Nath (1998). *A Cambodian Prison Portrait: One Year in the Khmer Rouge's S-21*. Bangkok: White Lotus.

Chapter 10

The four modalities of temporality and the problem of shame

Murray Stein

The psychological connection between temporality and shame is not a simple matter, to say the least, especially when one takes the unconscious into account. First of all, the topic of temporality is complex, and the link to shame is therefore also more than a simple registering and remembering of shameful things done present and past. Hinton cites Serres as speaking of temporality as a 'folded and crumpled handkerchief' (Hinton, 2015, p. 365). In this handkerchief, we inevitably find the stains of shame. How do they get there? And can they be ameliorated or even removed? If not, what is their purpose for individuation?

In this chapter, I would like to unfold and iron out this crumpled piece of fabric somewhat and try to look at the threads that go into its construction and see how and when shame enters into its weave and possibly how the problem of shame may be integrated into conscious life through an experience of the self.

Four modalities of temporality

What is time? Yiassemides begins her study of time and timelessness with the sentence, 'Time is an extremely obscure concept,' and she quotes the Mad Hatter from Lewis Carroll's *Alice's Adventures in Wonderland*: 'If you knew Time as well as I do . . . you wouldn't talk about . . . *it. It's him*' (Yiassemides, 2014, p. xiii, original emphasis). Already we have two metaphors for time: handkerchief and Father Time. Others could be added, such as the great archetypal images of river (or snake), procession (or train) and wheel (von Franz, 1992, p. 136). Each metaphor offers a perspective on the human experience of temporality.

My approach will be more analytical and abstract, however, and will not attempt to answer the question of what time is essentially but rather to suggest that four basic modalities of temporality play a role in human consciousness in various ways and at different stages of life: achronicity, chronicity, synchronicity and dyschronicity.[1] For purposes of this discussion, I will arrange them into two polarity pairs as shown in this diagram:

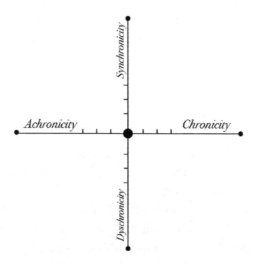

Figure 10.1 Four modes of temporality

The horizontal axis indicates temporality on a scale from absence to presence of the sense of chronological time. The vertical axis indicates parallel and divergent time lines that exist in real time,[2] and may fall together in consciousness. All share the term 'chronicity,' from the Greek word 'chronos,' meaning 'time.'

Definitions

The simplest and closest to everyday common sense of the four modes of psychological temporality is 'chronicity,' which indicates the normal sense of a past-present-future continuum in the waking state once a person has acquired a sense of real time and continuity of memory. Temporality as chronicity is the conscious state of awareness of the regular movement of objects like the sun and the hands of a clock in the world around us. Von Franz quotes Macrobius: 'Insofar as time is a fixed measure, it is derived from the revolutions of the sky. Time begins there, and from this is believed to have been born Kronos who is Chronos. This Kronos-Saturn is the creator of time' (Von Franz, 1978, p. 74). From time immemorial, humans have observed and recorded the changing seasons, the movement of the stars in the night sky, the moving slant of light that falls on a sundial, and the changes that occur in the body as the years pass by. Using this chronistic modality of temporality, it is possible to construct a personal narrative based on a time frame with specific dates and related contexts, which may resemble a piece of fabric into which are woven memories of the past and anticipations of possible futures. Memories of painful experiences of shame can leave dark and indelible marks in such a personal narrative.

A related but contrasting mode of psychological temporality is what I am calling 'achronicity.' This is a kind of negative mode of temporality, a zero in time, a beginning point in myth and psychological development. This is experienced as timelessness and outside of time frames. Before the number one, which might represent chronicity, there is the number zero, achronicity. Achronicity refers to the absence in consciousness of the sense of objective time ('real time'). All takes place in the present tense, and time, if registered at all in this modality, is gossamer-like, a thin veil draped lightly over consciousness but not leaving a deep impression. Here memory may or may not feature as a factor. While the clock continues ticking on the table, the psyche is unaware of its movement. This is experienced by infants, sleepers, daydreamers, deep readers, meditators and mystics, the aged and demented, creative people at work, in short by all of us. If shame registers here, it tends to be vague and generalized, perhaps not attached to specific objects, events or persons, but rather something more of a mood than a feeling linked to context, and if linked to a specific memory, then to a memory repressed.

Achronicity and chronicity lie on a spectrum with many gradations between the extremes, and they may flow smoothly or roughly into and out of one another. This is depicted by the horizontal axis in the drawing above.

The vertical axis is psychologically more complex. The two modes of temporality featured here are able to create some of the deeper wrinkles in the fabric of temporality and may account for shame felt in a strange and impersonal or transgenerational register. The two temporalities on this axis are made up of a complexity of simultaneous time-lines. To become fully aware of them requires observing and remembering one's dreams and fantasies, i.e., the themes and story-lines in the unconscious.

The upward extension of this axis rising above the horizontal line consists of a mode of psychological temporality that Jung named 'synchronicity.' He refers to this as *acausal correspondences*, which consist in a parallel arrangement of facts in time' (Adler, 1975, p. 46). Synchronicity consists in a surprising and unexpected but meaningful convergence of chronological sequences between either: a) the inner world of psyche and the outer world of material objects, or b) two causally unconnected parallel sequences in the material world (for detailed discussions see Atmanspacher, 2013; Cambray, 2009; Connolly, 2015; Jung, 1952/1969; Main, 2004; Von Franz, 1974; Yiassemides, 2014). Synchronicity creates a fold in the fabric of temporality that brings together two separate time-lines. Shame may or may not feature prominently in this mode of temporality. No blame can be derived specifically from this twist in time because there is no causal connection between the sequences. It is attributed purely to chance: perhaps not to random chance, as Pauli surmised (Pauli, 1954/2002, p. 127), but to chance nevertheless.

On the extension downward on the vertical axis is the psychological temporality that I am calling 'dyschronicity.' This is the contrary opposite of synchronicity, a kind of shadow temporality: two parallel sequences in time are experienced and lived simultaneously but not as convergent. Shame is often embedded here, but often it is not of a personal character in that it may be transgenerational.

The problem of shame in the achronicity-chronicity pair of temporality modalities

Achronicity

The universe begins from a state of objective achronicity. Time does not exist before the Big Bang, when the material universe exploded into being (Stein, 2016, p. 3). Prior to this, there is only a kind of God-alone-space, which in the Mazdean book of Genesis, for instance, is called 'the place and abode of Ōhrmazd. Some call it the infinite Light . . . The Time of the garment [of Ōhrmazd] is infinite' (Corbin, 1951/1957, p. 121). Creation myths tell of the moment when the world came into being as taking place *in illo tempore*, 'in that time' (Eliade, 1958/1968, p. 395). Achronicity is pre-temporal, infinite and boundless. It is a no-time temporality.

In fact, achronicity is myth's modality of temporality generally. Myth is not contained within chronological time, but rather it contains a time-like feature within it as a kind of internal coherence. Essentially, myth is achronistic in that it does not require historical consciousness or context for meaning. Rather, myth stands alone as 'iconic constancy,' as Blumenberg observes:

> Iconic constancy is the most characteristic element in the description of myths. The constancy of its core contents allows myth to appear, embedded as an 'erratic' element, even in traditional contexts of a different kind ... Its high level of durability ensures its diffusion in time and space, its independence of circumstances of place and epoch. The Greek *mython mytheisthai* [to tell a 'myth'] means to tell a story that is not dated and not datable, so that it cannot be localized in any chronicle, but a story that compensates for this lack by being 'significant' in itself.
>
> (Blumenberg, 1990, p. 149)

While myths exist essentially in achronistic temporality, they do enter into chronicity through being told, heard and remembered, and thus they take their place within personal and cultural historical narratives and as such can engender cultural or collective shame, as in the case of 'original sin.' On the other hand, rituals are able to transform chronological time into mythical achronicity *in illo tempore* because the ritual, a dance, say, 'is a repetition, and consequently a reactualization, of *illud tempus*, "those days"' (Eliade, 1959, pp. 28–9).

'In the beginning . . .' (Genesis 1:1), the opening phrase of the Bible, leaves no room for a description of reality 'before' the beginning. The Bible begins with the creation of time. Real time did not exist before there were objects in space. Time is a function – the regular rhythms of movements of objects in relation to one another in space. At the moment of creation, the continuous flow of real time can begin because objects now exist. Jung put it as follows: 'If there is no body moving in space, there can be no time either' (Adler, 1975, p. 45). Only the Divine exists outside of time and space, *in illo tempore*, in mythical or imaginal time and space. Divinity (singular and plural) resides within achronistic temporality. This is an eternal present. It also applies to the realm of pure psyche, as Jung writes in a letter: 'As in the psychic world there are no bodies moving in space, there is also no time. The archetypal world is "eternal," i.e., outside time' (Adler, 1975, p. 46).

In the biblical account of the beginning, the human sense of time as Adam and Eve experience it remains mythical, or achronistic, even after the six days of creation have been duly counted out and they have taken their place in the Garden of Eden. This indicates the essential difference between human psychic temporality and objective, or real, time. Adam and Eve do not exist within what we would recognize as psychological chronicity, that is, with a sense of time passing continuously from present to future and with a history accumulating in its wake, because they live in an eternal round of day and night without significant change and development. Moreover, they walk and talk easily and regularly directly with God, so there is no division between the human psychic world and the divine archetypal world. Chronistic temporality has not yet begun. While in the Garden of Eden, Adam and Eve live in psychological achronicity, and while this prevails they are without shame. History (i.e., chronicity), which is made of the passage of real time with the conscious linear accumulation of remembered incidents, developments and changes, begins only after the 'Fall' and the expulsion from Eden.

In the development of an individual's conscious sense of time, this type of temporality prevails in foetal consciousness and well into the period of infancy. In the modality of psychological achronicity, experiences are registered individually, but because memory is not yet in play they remain unconnected to each other or to contexts in which they took place. In neuroscience, this is called 'semantic consciousness' (Hinton, 2015, p. 363). These are moments registered but not tied together in a continuous narrative by memory.

Humans, if they live long enough and fall into certain pathological neurological conditions like dementia, may end up where they began, in the temporality modality of chronic 'achronicity.' I vividly recall a scene in an assisted care ward for the demented where two aged men were seated on a bench staring placidly straight ahead into the space in front of them. Across the hallway and in easy eyesight, a clock was ticking and showing the time. Slowly the hands moved on the time-face from number to number. It was early afternoon on a Sunday. The men did not stir from their places. They seemed to be profoundly unaware of time past, present or future. A sign next to the clock showed that lunch was served daily at 11:30 am. It was now 2:30 pm, so presumably the two men had eaten and were now taking a rest on the bench. Their eyes were wide open, but they did not move even to blink. In whatever state of consciousness they may have been at this moment, it seemed to have no relation to chronological time. They were living in the psychological temporality of perpetual achronicity with no clocks or calendars in mind. Memory no longer functioned to string experiences together. They lived in an eternal present. Their mode of temporality in consciousness was akin to myth and infancy, *in illo tempore*.

Throughout normal healthy life, however, we are also constantly moving between the achronistic mode and a registered sense of chronological time. But we are not stuck in achronicity by neurological deficiency. We can slide along the scale from one position on the horizontal axis to another. When we sleep, when we daydream or fall into reverie, when we meditate or do active imagination, when we gaze blankly into empty space or smell a rose, we are momentarily in achronistic temporality to one degree or another. In fact, most of our days are heavily dotted with achronistic periods, and a careful inventory of consciousness makes it evident that much of our lives is passed in this modality. When time seems to escape us, or the hours on the clock get dramatically compressed and we lose track of hour, day or year, we are in this mode or perhaps halfway in and halfway out of it. Generally, while awake we slide between achronicity and chronicity easily enough and can move along this axis by acts of will.

The experiences registered within the achronicity modality may include shame stains, but not usually so. An exception is with people strongly embedded in a system of strict rules, often religious laws and mandates that strictly forbid entertaining certain thoughts or feelings. If these surface in achronistic moments (fantasies, dreams, random associations) before they can be repressed and relegated to the basement of unconsciousness, shame will result. For these people, psychotherapy is not an option because they cannot tolerate their shadow affects and thoughts and therefore cannot integrate them. Fear of shame and guilt block the way. The net result is chronic neurotic conflict.

Chronicity

In the biblical tale, psychological chronicity begins when Adam and Eve are exiled from the Garden of Eden and the easy flow of conversation between creature and Creator is broken off. The experience of time changes from a round of eternal repetitions of easy-going need-satisfaction cycles to a linear sequence of moments in historical time that demand heavy effort and directed consciousness to proceed from need to fulfilment, with long gaps of frustration often in between. A continuous memory of past events and experiences now takes hold and shapes a narrative as the world begins to change and evolve in human consciousness. In neuroscience, this is called the onset of 'episodic memory,' and it begins for most people around the age of four (Hinton, 2015, p. 364). A sense of the future as well, including the awareness of death, takes its place in consciousness. Beginnings and endings take place in chronological time. To live with this sense of temporality is to live in the modality of chronicity.

Adam and Eve, having eaten the fruit of the tree of knowledge of good and evil, leave Eden in shame and, soon enough, conflict and power struggles enter the picture. Normal human life begins. Envy gathers like a cloud between their sons, Cain and Abel, and shadow enactments ensue. Crime and punishment become features of human history. The mark of shame becomes indelibly inscribed on the forehead of Cain, the criminal brother, and assumes centrality in his identity. Causal links between past and present and the consequences and responsibilities they entail become the law of life in the temporality modality of chronicity.

I clearly recall that I was four or five years old when my father taught me to tell time. It was an Easter Sunday morning, and before going to church my pastor father gave me a lesson in time. He took a clock about the size of his hand and showed me how the pointers moved, or could be moved, on the face. The small pointer showed the hour, he said, and the large pointer showed the minute. The numbers pointed to indicated the time. I knew enough about time to understand these words. So far, so good. He turned the dial on the back of the clock and made the hands move. Then he set the clock at a certain time and asked me to tell him what time it showed. We did this several times, and soon I got the hang of it. Proudly I announced to my Sunday School friends that I could tell time now! It was a breakthrough in learning for me, and it is a moment in time I have never forgotten. It is a permanent and constant part of my life's narrative. Ever since, I have felt that time is my friend, and I rarely lose track of time and am almost never late for meetings and appointments. If I slip up, I feel ashamed. I have a good sense of chronological time and live comfortably within this type of temporality. I am also interested in history that reaches back in time to the origins of human culture and even to the beginnings of the universe, and I place myself within a precise historical and cultural context. Perhaps by coincidence, my earliest memory of experiencing shame dates from about this same age.

At the point in psychological development when chronicity takes permanent hold in consciousness, a separation takes place in the psyche. The emerging ego parts company with the unconscious, and the ego becomes more and more a singular psychic unit unto itself as distinct from other parts of the inner world. The psyche differentiates, in short, and repression begins to occur. Ego defences form and identity begins to take shape. This birth into chronicity is a kind of second birth of human consciousness, and with this comes the stable awareness of opposites such as good and evil, innocence and shame, success and failure, and life and death. The ego's time sense now becomes one of chronicity, and the psyche's timeless achronicity becomes hidden in the unconscious and left to the world of dreams and fantasy. In childhood, achronicity is restored during play, and creativity throughout life continues to depend on making contact with the ability to play and therefore on temporary re-entry into the mode of achronicity.

In some cultures, notably in those of the East such as Japan, the separation of ego from unconscious is much less drastic and 'softer.' Myth and history are not as sharply distinguishable, and a normal reality sense may include fantasy importantly in a way that is not the case in the West. Chronicity and achronicity are closer to one another, indeed somewhat intertwined. Here I am following the lines of thought laid down by Hayao Kawai (1988) and Claude Levi-Strauss (2013).

It is worth noting that Japan is known as a 'shame-culture' in contrast to the 'guilt-cultures' of the West. The anthropologist Ruth Benedict made this observation initially in her classic work, *The Chrysanthemum and the Sword*. This feature of Japanese culture seems to follow from the closer proximity between achronistic and chronistic modalities of temporality in the population. Some people think that this indicates a lower or lesser level of ego development in this culture because shame is more associated with early ego development while guilt follows more advanced ego development. But in fact shame cannot be separated from guilt as though the latter were a product of greater ego development. As we see in the biblical account of the Fall, guilt actually precedes shame, and certainly they come wrapped together in a package. In fact, it is often the case that guilt, as inner self-judgement and condemnation for something done, produces a profound sense of shame.

It has often been argued, too, that guilt is more isolated to a single act in a specific context, whereas shame generalizes to the whole self, but in fact guilt often bleeds beyond the discrete confines of a guilty action and affects the whole psyche-body, including the unconscious. One sees this phenomenon in detail in Dostoyevsky's novel, *Crime and Punishment* (1866/1987). Raskolnikov judges himself guilty and thereafter begins to experience excruciating shame in every facet of his being. Paul Ricoeur notes this same development in Kafka's work: 'To be accursed without being cursed by anybody is the highest degree of accursedness' (Edelman, 1998, p. 19). Shame is this 'highest degree of accursedness,' and it often comes about as the consequence of guilt.

One could say perhaps that in shame-cultures the bleeding from guilt into shame happens more quickly, predictably, and profusely than it does in guilt-cultures. This may be because the ego, which takes responsibility for actions and therefore bears guilt, is not as completely isolated from the rest of the self. The boundary between the ego and the unconscious is more permeable, and so the experience of shame is more immediate and total. However, this by no means excludes the experience of guilt. Shame and guilt are simply more tightly woven together.

Both shame and guilt enter the psychic picture forcefully with the establishment of the modality of chronicity. In cultures where the chronicity modality is extremely recessive, shame may also be relatively light or even absent. This would be a subject for further research by psychological or cultural anthropology.

As 'semantic consciousness' turns into 'episodic memory' in a person, a continuous memory takes form and a narrative takes shape, made up of associated and linked memories. Of course, this woven-together narrative undergoes constant revision in life, and in a sense it must be recreated every day upon awakening from sleep. It is also subject to a process of radical redesign from time to time as a person's life passes through the phases of individuation from childhood to adolescence, adulthood, midlife, old age and the approach to death. It is not as solid and intact as it might seem at first glance. In fact, upon close inspection, it is full of holes and gaps that get filled in from time to time with what Jung called *zurückphantasieren* ('retro-fantasizing') (Laplanche & Pontalis, 1973, p. 112) where current feelings and fantasies are transposed and taken for ('remembered' as) past events.[3] In analysis, constant work is done on unweaving and reweaving the narrative based on new insights and emergent memories. A danger here is that this may become nothing more than a sophisticated form of 'retro-fantasizing,' as has been seen when therapists wilfully supported or even inserted vague fantasies in the present into patients' narratives as 'memories' of childhood trauma. Early and formative experiences of shame and guilt, of course, naturally take their place in this emerging and constantly transforming narrative of chronicity and assume an important feature there.

The sense of psychological temporality as chronicity is an orientation assumed by consciousness with reference to the material world surrounding us and to our place in it. This is a key function of the 'reality principle,' as housed with the ego. This modality is a representation in consciousness of temporality as real time ruling over inner or subjective temporalities, which include achronicity, synchronicity and dyschronicity. When we live with a keen awareness of the clock and calendar and think of ourselves in relation to history, personal and collective, and place ourselves essentially within these contexts, we live in a world where chronicity is king. The ego, oriented by chronicity, is the sun around which all other temporalities revolve. The development in this direction begins early in life and lasts throughout, as long as one remains sound of mind. Mental status tests look to this as a key feature of sanity. Psychosis is a break in the dominance of chronicity within consciousness, when other forms of temporality take over and the ego loses its central place. Then subjective factors like feelings, thoughts and fantasies assume dominance, and with them come other temporality modalities such as achronicity (dementia), synchronicity (paranoia) and dyschronicity (dissociation) to replace the ego's grasp on chronicity and real time.

The sense of the world and life as strictly determined by chronicity has great advantages for humankind; it includes a sense of human life as developmental and finite. One is aware of the inevitability of death, and one monitors one's age more carefully as the probabilities for the end of one's personal history increase. This psychological temporality mode introduces, and holds, shame and guilt into consciousness, and along with this come necessarily the appearance of ethics and the elaboration of moral rules. Ethics depends on an awareness of object relations and causality in time and space.

Human culture depends on psychological chronicity as a powerful and indeed dominant fact of consciousness. In a sense, an acute awareness of shame is a price we pay for culture.

The synchronicity-dyschronicity pair of temporality modalities

Synchronicity

The type of temporality modality that Adam and Eve live within while in the Garden of Eden is achronistic (mythical), but it is also synchronistic: in Eden, there is complete and smooth harmony between supply and demand, between inner need and outer fulfilment, between psyche and world. This is the archetypal template for temporality in the modality of synchronicity, when inner (psyche) and outer (objective world) are in a harmonious and syntonic relationship. In this state of consciousness, there is no sense of shame. Synchronicity in itself is shame-free, but if it is taken up into the chronicity of the ego's normal experience of life and considered in a different light, perhaps ethical, it may take on an aspect of shame.

Synchronicity refers to an acausal or chance falling together in time of the inner (image, thought, feeling) and the outer (material objects, creatures), and objective meaning is revealed in the event (Jung, 1952/1969). It is a coincidental and meaningful confluence of psyche and matter, inner and outer, subjective and objective temporalities. The timing of the psyche, conscious or unconscious, and the timing of events in the objective world simply happen by chance to coincide meaningfully. Two lines of temporality in this instance become intertwined as one within consciousness.

Erich Neumann writes of infancy in terms that imply this same type of syntony between inner and outer worlds. The foetus while contained in the mother's womb passes this stage of life in a state of achronicity. After birth, this gradually passes over into what later in her arms and at her breast becomes a prefiguration of the synchronistic state:

> This childhood experience ... is the ontogenetic embodiment of the primal unitary reality in which the partial worlds of outside and inside, objective world and psyche do not exist ... In this phase there is a primary unity of mother and child.
>
> (Neumann, 1973/2002, p. 11)

Nature facilitates the closely coordinated timing of need and satisfaction, as mother's acts of feeding and infant's need to be fed are more or less well timed to coincide. The inner is met by the outer in a timely fashion when infant cries and mother responds. This is a personal prototype of temporality as synchronicity: psyche and world are in a state of syntony. For development, this is a transitional state moving from achronicity to chronicity, and it is, like the Original Parents, without shame.

An early and preverbal experience of shame may occur in this phase of infant development, however, if the expressed need is not met or the mirroring of mother fails to meet the gaze of the infant. Edelman, referring to the work of Kaufman (1989), writes: 'Facial gazing is . . . the earliest form of communion. If the fundamental expectations are not met during this activity, shame is constellated' (Edelman, 1998, p. 29). Since this occurs within the psychological temporality of achronicity, however, it is not carried forward in time and woven into the narrative of memory. It will simply remain an experience of shame unassociated to time or place, and since the context is missing it will be akin to what Bion called beta elements, which do not get psychically metabolized. If repeated often enough, these early experiences of shame may become the foundation for a generalized sense of shame, or basic fault (Balint, 1969/1979), in the sense of self, a primal wound that does not heal and creates a free-floating and pervasive undertone of shame in a person's moods later in life. They may become what Jung calls a complex, a complex of shame. This would be attributable to the breakdown of synchronistic meetings of inner and outer, infant and mother, need and satisfaction, in the early developmental process.

The experience of syntony that comes out of the synchronistic match-ups between infant and mother is objectively meaningful in that it supports the healthy survival of the species. The beneficiaries of good-enough mothering are more fit than those who do not have this experience. This will lay the ground for later optimism and faith, qualities of mind that are good for thriving in later life. This foundational experience of syntony in infancy is a personal template for later experiences of synchronicity, which reflects the archetypal Edenic one. The later experiences of synchronicity, which take place and are recorded into memory after the ego has been formed and inner and outer worlds have been separated, show similar coincidences between need and satisfaction, inner and outer worlds, in a meaningful way.

The overlapping of chronicities, inner with outer, that takes place in synchronicity also brings the perception of transcendent meaning to a specific moment in time. The experience of temporality as synchronistic is therefore referred to sometimes as *kairos* (a kind of elevated or spiritually significant season or period of time) as opposed to *chronos* (ordinary sequential time).

Hinton references André Green as speaking of 'moments of breakthrough of temporality ... or exploded time ... in which 'the strictures of time are "exploded," and a more "open ensemble" of psychic life emerges' (Hinton, 2015, p. 358). This is a lovely poetic description of synchronicity temporality. Connolly describes several such synchronistic experiences in the clinical setting in similar terms (Connolly, 2015, p. 167ff.). On a more mythological note, Von Franz writes about this phenomenon that '*kairos* signifies the "right order" in time. The association of *kairos* with goddesses weaving time alludes ... to the idea of a "field" in which "meaningful connections" are interwoven like threads in a fabric' (Von Franz, 1974, p. 256).

Dyschronicity

Because conscious and unconscious are separated in the human psyche after a point in psychological development, there is a strong possibility that the timing between them becomes disconnected. This is the usual neurotic condition that we confront in analysis. Instead of experiencing a state of simple chronicity in consciousness or one of achronicity or synchronicity, a state of dyschronicity prevails either subtly or blatantly. Two different time programmes, instead of falling 'together, with' as in synchronicity, form a disconnected parallel sequence and create a mismatch of temporalities in the psyche. They remain apart and are often quite unconnected in consciousness. A contradiction between one aspect of psyche's time and another occurs, with the result that there is a type of dystonia, a more or less severe lack of coordination, in the temporality system as a whole. This creates a deep wrinkle in the fabric of temporality, which may be registered in consciousness or not. When it becomes conscious, a possibility exists for working with this conflict or dissociation in analysis.

For years I have been fascinated by a passage in Jung's late autobiographical work, *Memories, Dreams, Reflections*, where he recounts the experience of living in two different centuries, the seventeenth and the twentieth, at the same time:

> It was wartime. I was on the Italian front and driving back from the front line with a little man, a peasant, in his horse-drawn wagon ... We had to cross a bridge and then go through a tunnel ... Arriving at the end of the tunnel, we saw before us a sunny landscape, and I recognized the region around Verona ... The road led through

lovely springtime countryside ... Then, diagonally across the road, I caught sight of a large building, a manor house of grand proportions, rather like the palace of a North Italian duke ... The little coachman and myself drove in through a gate, and from here we could see, through a second gate at the far end, the sunlit landscape again ... Just as we reached the middle of the courtyard, in front of the main entrance, something unexpected happened: with a dull clang, both gates flew shut. The peasant leaped down from his seat and exclaimed, 'Now we are caught in the seventeenth century.' Resignedly I thought, 'Well, that's that! But what is there to do about it? Now we shall be caught for years.' Then the consoling thought came to me: 'Someday, years from now, I shall get out again.' ... Not until much later did I realize that it [i.e., the dream] referred to alchemy, for that science reached its height in the seventeenth century.

(Jung/Jaffé, 1961/1989, pp. 202–3)

This dream reflects a strange doubling in Jung's sense of temporality, even an acute disturbance, and it echoes his childhood feeling of living with two personalities, Number One located in the present time and Number Two in the eighteenth century (Jung/Jaffé, 1961/1989, pp. 23–83).[4] In his waking life at the time of this dream (1926), he was a highly successful middle-aged professional and family man of the twentieth century, but in his dream he retreats in time from World War I and is eventually locked into the seventeenth century. This signifies a large gap between the temporality lived in everyday conscious life by the steady beat of a reliable Swiss watch and the temporality of his unconscious as registered in this impressive dream, a discrepant doubling of Jung's sense of temporal identity into two seemingly disconnected time frames. Inner and outer temporalities are hugely discrepant. It is a dystonic state at first and totally uncoordinated. Later it will become extremely meaningful. This particular dream, which may well have had a long prehistory in his unconscious as indicated in his memories of a childhood with two personalities separated in time by centuries as well, made a deep impression on the mature Jung and drove him to a sense of mission that would take years to complete. He worked mightily to reconcile these two overlaid temporalities in his identity, even into his advanced years.[5] It was a dyschronicity that made a difference.

One can find many examples of dyschronicity in literature and in life. Nostalgia is a form of dyschronicity if taken to the extreme of living simultaneously in two time periods. William Faulkner was a master story-teller of this psychological condition. One found this condition floridly lived out in the American 'old South' where many people continued to live well into the twentieth century in the long bygone days of wine and roses of the pre-Civil War period. Cervantes' novel, *Don Quixote*, offers a humorous and touching example of a character living within two tempo-ralities simultaneously, his current and mundane time period and the romantic days of knights and ladies of centuries before. Like Jung, he lives in two disparate temporalities. Unlike Jung, he does not manage to bring them together in a meaningful way, although he does in the end break out of his delusion. An example from film is Woody Allen's marvel-lous comedy, *Midnight in Paris*. By day the protagonist lives in the twenty-first century, and by night he finds himself in the Paris of the 1920s where his adventures are far more colourful and concordant than his day-time life. The film brilliantly resolves the conflict that gathers as a result of this dyschronicity. An example of dyschronicity from the manuals of psychopathology is the paraphilia known as *autoneplophilia*, or adult baby syndrome. Here a person in the body of an adult simultaneously chooses to remain in an infant's psyche. Adult and baby co-inhabit the ego's sense of temporality.[6] Another form of this is the refusal to accept the body's ageing. Cosmetic surgeons thrive on this form of psychological dyschronicity. People live two lives: one in an ageing body, and another in the cosmetized body of a youthful psyche. This discrepancy can lead to spasmodic episodes of shame because fantasy images of self and the real-ity of one's body do not match. Thus shame gets woven into the fabric of temporality via dyschronicity.

Two cases of dyschronicity

In analytical practice, we may come upon the phenomenon of dyschronic-ity as we delve into the unconscious and discover autonomous complexes at work in the psyche. Viktor, a Swiss man in his mid-fifties, told me a dream early in his analysis. He said that he dreamed of being attacked by a group of wild natives, 'primitives,' in a far-away foreign country. This took place in what seemed like another century. He was travelling by horse-drawn wagon through a high desert area with a few other people when suddenly they noticed on the ridges above them and up ahead the figures of a large number of threatening half-clad men preparing to attack their party. He awoke in a panic, and he now described this to me as a nightmare similar to others of being attacked he had experienced in the past. He had no particular associations to the primitive attackers or to the setting of the dream, other than from the movies, and nothing in his recent past suggested an image like this one. There was no specific residue from the previous days. It was a strange and puzzling dream, obviously symbolic. I thought about the transference even though this did not fit with anything we had experienced up to this early point in the analysis, but I took it to be a signal of possible trouble ahead. At this point, it was as though this dream belonged to another person, in another time and place, and with no connection to the dreamer, a European man through and through who had never travelled in such areas of the world. There was a time disjunction between his waking consciousness and the dream scene, as though it had happened in an earlier century and to another self.

The dream shows a large discontinuity between the dreamer's conscious life in the present, where normal chronicity rules and where he was appropriately oriented to reality and generally competent in his various activities, and his inner life in the temporality of the unconscious operating in psychic time. Two distinct and discrepant temporalities are running their programmes, the one current in his present life and the other far in the past of previous generations. As further analysis revealed, this was a dissociation that formed as a result of many early childhood traumas. These traumas were largely split off from his ego-consciousness and were hidden behind his upper middle-class social identity as a husband, father and active businessman. In actuality, he was living in a psychic set-up that was severely uncoordinated between his ego's time and his unconscious time and its complexes. As a child, he had never felt safe for a variety of reasons, and so his defences then and now in adulthood were hypervigilant and ever at the ready to protect himself from abuse and attack. The unconscious scene of being under attack vividly portrayed the difficulties that had brought him into analysis: explosive and sudden defensive rage attacks, violent reactions at little or no provocation, disruptive anxieties of an irrational nature, and frequent breakdowns in relationships with intimate others. The dream image pictures a split-off feeling-toned complex with the usual polarities: a surprised and innocent victim, and abusive attackers. In an uncanny way, this scene would be repeated regularly in Viktor's life.

An activated complex means that past events can suddenly overshadow the present in the emotional life of a person and often generate highly overcharged and inappropriate reactions. In Victor's life, this would happen when a waiter accidentally spilled a cup of coffee or the housemaid failed to clean his bathroom properly. In these instances, the complex would discharge an amount of affect that would better be used in an extreme situation like the scene pictured in his dream. Suddenly, chronicity would give way to dyschronicity, and what was simply an accident or an oversight would be interpreted as a life-threatening attack.

In time, his dreams became more explicitly relevant to Viktor's present life and his emotional reactions to situations in the present better attuned to actual temporality in the present. The two temporality systems began to converge, and modulation of emotion could be better achieved. The childhood traumas became memories and could be largely integrated into his autobiographical narrative. Dyschronicity was reduced, a sense of routine chronicity in waking life was strengthened, and synchronicity could emerge in the appearances of meaningful coordination between psyche and world in everyday life.

An important side-effect of this gradual integration was that a sense of shame actually developed and grew stronger as present temporality replaced dyschronicity. The outbursts were no longer dissociated and so had to be acknowledged. As chronicity replaced dyschronicity, shame entered the psychic field and led to the possibility of apology and reparation. Thus we see again that shame is linked to temporality as chronicity. As Hinton has suggested, shame may become a teacher for culture and individuation (Hinton, 1999).

Another case of dyschronicity, similar to Viktor's in some respects, but considerably more severe and painful, was that of Gertrude, a highly sensitive German analysand in her sixties. The relevant part of her story is that she had previously decided to explore a form of intense regression therapy that had left her with a broken sense of self from which she could not recover. What she had 'remembered' and powerfully experienced in that therapy was the trauma of being a Jew in Nazi Germany and being sent with her young daughter to a death camp. There she had been separated from her and knew that she had been violently raped and brutally murdered. Even though she had survived the camp by some quirk of fate, she was left utterly bereft and did not know how to continue her life in the face of such evil and loss. When Gertrude came to see me, she was still mired in a deep depression. She felt that her life had been irrevocably changed by the experience of a 'past life.' She was living in two time frames. In the present, she was a fairly comfortably well-off professional woman with a healthy family; in the past, she was a devastated camp survivor. The sense of this tragic and horrifying past utterly overshadowed her present. She was depressed, anxious and without hope for anything of positive value in the future. She was suffering from a memory of a life that was not hers, at least not in the chronicity temporality modality of her life.

The telling fact behind this case of dyschronicity was that in the previous generations her parents and grandparents had been complicit in the Holocaust. Even though their participation in the events of those times was largely indirect, the collective guilt for what had happened infected them, but largely at unconscious levels. Therefore they could not speak about it even if they had wished to do so. Today, therapists recognize the effects of 'transgenerational transmission of trauma' (Schellinski, 2014), and this was such a case. The paradox was that the transmission of collective guilt, inherited by Gertrude as a cultural complex (Singer & Kaplinski, 2010), had been reversed so that she now experienced the suffering of the victims rather than the guilt of the perpetrators. Shame and guilt had been transformed into the opposite, into innocent suffering, not in order to escape the shame primarily, in my opinion, but to expiate the cultural guilt through vicarious suffering. This was the meaning of dyschronicity in this case. Gertrude had to bear the suffering inflicted on the victims of earlier generations of perpetrators. Dyschronicity had found a permanent home in Gertrude's consciousness, and no amount of reductive analysis could remove it. It had to be borne as though it were her suffering, added to which was the shadow of survivor guilt since she had escaped execution. Grasping the suffering in this way would make it possible for her to search out meaning in it, for herself and for her generation. Here, too, shame and guilt, as Hinton (1999) has suggested, could become enlisted in the project of individuation.

A further reflection on temporality and the problem of shame – the role of the transcendent function

The diagram below shows the four modalities of temporality feeding into a central psychic agency, ego-consciousness.

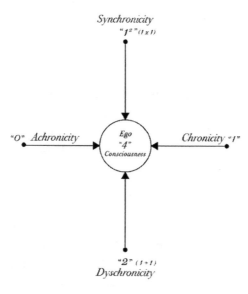

Figure 10.2 Times four

As the centre of consciousness, the ego may register the four modalities, and with maturity it is able to contain them and include them in a coherent narrative. Jung's autobiography, *Memories, Dreams, Reflections,* for instance, includes all four modalities in the narrative. For purposes of further analysis, I have assigned a numerical value to each of the temporalities as follows. Pure achronicity is given the value of Zero, indicating the emptiness of chronological consciousness in this modality. The chronicity modality is given the value of One, signifying full consciousness of chronological time as a single flowing stream of events from past to present to future. The modality of synchronicity is assigned the numerical value of One squared: again One, but with two parallel chronicities twisted into a single moment of chronological time. The dyschronicity modality is given the value of Two, which indicates two temporalities running in parallel but separated in the psyche. At the centre, within an ego-consciousness aware of all four modalities, these numerical values add up to the number Four. The ego is the container, too, of whatever stains of shame blemish the fabric of a personal narrative, provided they are conscious and not repressed or forgotten. These stains (both conscious and unconscious) may derive from pre-verbal early infancy or other periods of pure achronicity in life (the achronicity arm), from experiences within the chronological memory of the person (the chronicity arm), from transpersonal sources (the synchronicity arm), and from transgenerational transmissions (the dyschronicity arm). All of these stains of shame may be collected by the central agency of consciousness and combined into the total narrative of the person's history. This is a person who has faced the shadow, made it conscious, and is able to carry this as memory in consciousness. For such a person, shame will be a teacher of humility. This is an advanced stage of individuation, hence it attains to the number Four.

The problem of complete integration of the modalities themselves remains, however. The ego is able to count them and to reflect on them but not by its own efforts to integrate them. Integration means unification, or what Jung in his late writing on alchemy called 'conjunction' from the Latin phrase *mysterium coniunctionis* ('mystical conjunction'), the title of his last major work. For unification or conjunction to take place, a larger and more powerful agency is required, one that can embrace the opposites, i.e., the two pairs of temporality modality, and contain them as facets of a single unit of a superior psychological structure.

Our reflection on this high degree of integration of the four modalities and the contents they bring with them into the fabric of temporality will border on the ontological and the theological. This level of deep integration is symbolized by Pauli at the conclusion of his 'Piano Lesson' by the golden 'Ring *i*,' which is presented to him in the narrative by his female teacher.

It is a mandala with the mathematical symbol *i* at the centre. This symbol, *i*, is an imaginary unit that opens up new dimensions within

Figure 10.3 The Ring *i*

mathematical fields so that 'complex numbers' can be created, which combine real and imaginary numbers. The symbol i is a sort of magical unifier of opposites, in alchemical terms a Mercurius figure. The golden 'Ring i' transforms the centre of identity, previously occupied by the ego, and replaces the dominance of chronistic temporality with a synthetic union of all four modalities.

'It makes time into a static image,' Pauli exclaims to his teacher (Pauli, 1954/2002, p. 134). In the terms used in this essay, it transcends the four modalities of temporality and folds them into a single unit or monad. It is a symbol of the self, the central agency of the psyche as a whole and superordinate to the ego. The diagram (below) illustrates the constellation of the self and represents the installation of the ego-self axis (Neumann 1952/1989) at the centre of consciousness.

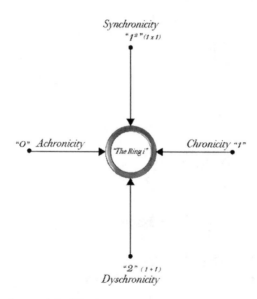

Figure 10.4 Times four and the Ring i

This constellation of the ego-self axis introduces the timeless into consciousness alongside the temporality modalities, not to replace them but to accompany them as an overtone. Von Franz concludes her book, *Time, Rhythm and Repose*, with the same perception: 'from the timeless God flows the "flow of grace" which creates an ever-present now – so that God is simultaneously stillness and everlasting flux' (1978, p. 32). The dialectical play between the ego and the self accounts for this simultaneity. Von Franz shows the levels of temporality and their arrangement in Figure 10.5, which also indicates the displacement of the ego from the centre to the periphery, while the self assumes the position of centre, or 'sun,' around which the ego revolves.

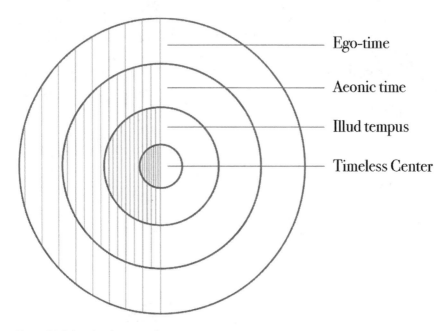

Figure 10.5 Levels of temporality

'Ego-time' in this diagram is chronicity in the personal sphere, while 'aeonic time' is chronicity extended to larger frameworks of chronological time such as the Platonic year consisting of 2,000 years, which are called Aeons. '*Illud Tempus*' is mythic time and therefore achronistic, the framework in which the archetypes reside and execute their wills by creating synchronicities and dyschronicities in real time. 'The timeless centre' is the self and equivalent to Pauli's 'Ring *i*,' where time becomes 'a static image.' As such, it is a transcendent agency beyond the temporalities but with a creative impact on time through initiating synchronistic phenomena ('acts of creation in time' [Jung]) via the various lesser archetypal agencies. The symbol, 'Ring *i*,' includes recognition of reciprocity between ego and self such that they interact with one another dynamically and drive an evolutionary process forward in human consciousness.

What is the effect of the constellation of the ego-self axis on the shame stains in the temporality handkerchief? So long as sheer temporality in its various modalities dominates consciousness exclusively, shame remains, although in a pure achronicity modality it may tend to fade into the vacuum left by the absence of memory. But assuming that the four modalities remain intact and are subsumed by the self constellation, by the 'Ring i,' what happens to shame?

Returning to the biblical narrative, running from the tale of Adam and Eve in the book of Genesis onward through the entire Bible the problem of shame and guilt ('sin') remains indelibly a feature of the human condition. Once chronistic temporality takes hold, shame becomes resident in consciousness and remains. This is human reality. The handkerchief is stained, and as time passes it gets more and more so and crumpled by the fluctuating temporality modalities. In the Old Testament view, the stain can be somewhat reduced by strict obedience to the Mosaic Law and by observance of its vast array of ethical implications, but it cannot be removed, and constantly it threatens to expand and deepen. In fact, the application of the Law increases the sense of sin because it raises consciousness of personal and individual as well as collective responsibility. The fall from grace into shame and the consequent expulsion from the Garden of Eden created a radical and permanent blemish on humanity, which had originally been created in the image of God (*imago Dei*), and this called for a radical solution.

Such a solution is offered in the New Testament. When Christ, as the New Adam, replaces the Old Adam, he restores the *imago Dei* in a singular human being to its original state of perfection. In Christ, there is no element of sin, no shame, despite his having entered into temporality as an ordinary flesh-and-blood human being. Mythic purity is restored because Christ is also Divine. The Christian solution to the problem of shame, then, takes form in the possibility of making an identification with the Christ figure. The stain is washed clean in the Christ symbol, and this can be transmitted to the believer through identification with Him. With relief, St Paul cries out: 'Wretch that I am, who will rescue me from this doomed body? Thanks be to God – [it is done] through Jesus Christ our Lord!' (Romans 7:24–5, Fitzmyer translation, 1993, p. 472). Following shortly upon the Ascension of Christ, the descent of the Holy Spirit on the Day of Pentecost and the reception of the spirit into human consciousness created a new spiritual centre in the psyche of the believers (Acts 2:4). In the mystical language of St. Paul: 'It is no longer I who live, but Christ who lives in me' (Galatians 2:20). The Christians, as they now were called, no longer lived out of a chronicity-dominated ego but out of a transcendent spiritual identity associated with Christ. The blemished, folded, crumpled handkerchief of temporality was washed clean and transformed into a spiritualized fabric. Temporality lost its power, in the view of the early Christians. Christ has conquered the power of temporality, as they would affirm.

In this religious narrative of release from all modalities of temporality and the shame that becomes resident in consciousness with them, the psyche is seen as having recovered a transcendent centre in consciousness, whence it originated as *imago Dei*, rather than maintaining its primary residence exclusively in the alienated ego that developed in history. Psychologically, this possibly represents an advanced stage of individuation and not a regression, provided that the ego-self axis is constellated in the centre of consciousness and the dialectic between ego and self is maintained. If the ego does not vanish into the void of unconsciousness but rather becomes subordinated to a larger agency through the 'transcendent function' (Jung, 1916/1969), then a reciprocal relationship between ego and self replaces the ego alone as the centre of consciousness. This creates a kind of dual identity with a binary structure. Here time and the timeless walk together, the secular person and the sacred. The problem of shame within the fabric of temporality is partially resolved, therefore by being taken up as a part of the larger self, which as a union of opposites is able to integrate, i.e., *unify*, the light and the dark, the innocent and the shameful, and the temporal and the eternal into a unique singularity. This translates into a state of self-acceptance. As Paul Tillich announced in his famous sermon, 'You Are Accepted': 'Accept that you are accepted . . . You are accepted. *You are accepted*, accepted by that which is greater than you, and the name of which you do not know' (Tillich, 1948, p. 162, original emphasis). Many mystical traditions, such as Cabbala, Hasidism (Magid, 2015), Sufism, Yoga, Zen Buddhism (Izutsu, 1977) and others, have made identical moves toward transcending temporality, even if only momentarily. This is a goal of individuation as conceived by Jung and those following him in depth psychology. All arrive at the position symbolized by Pauli's 'Ring i,' a place beyond sheer temporality and shame and characterized by compassion, grace and a sense of wholeness realized.

From a realistic and psychological point of view, it is wise, however, to think of this goal of individuation as something sought for and attained momentarily from time to time in experiences of ego-transcendence.

The return to temporality, and especially to the chronicity modality, is inevitable and often abrupt. Humans, as long as they live and breathe in a physical body, continue to live in temporality and therefore with the problem of shame. Within temporality, shame can become a guide and counsellor, as Hinton (1999) describes, functioning to keep the human ego aware of its finite condition and its limitations. Shame is endemic and built into human experience because we live in the temporalities. In that sense, shame is 'ontological,' that is to say, it is archetypal, and therefore built into the structure of human experience. Because the ego-self axis is constructed dialectically, there is a continual interaction between time and eternity. To think of a permanent escape from temporality and shame while in this life is a dangerous illusion and leads to utopian fantasies that inevitably collapse and produce only further experiences of ever-deeper shame.

Notes

1 I have created this neologism for the purposes of this chapter. To my knowledge, no one has discussed this phenomenon before, although it is well known among Jungian psychoanalysts. I chose the prefix dys- (from Gr. meaning 'bad,' 'hard,' 'unlucky') because it indicates a difficult, often abnormal and sometimes painful state.
2 I use the phrase 'real time' to indicate time as measured by clocks, i.e., objective time, which exists beyond human recognition of it. It is non-psychological temporality.
3 Hinton offers a useful discussion of *Nachträglichkeit*, the revision of memory in light of reflections back on earlier experiences such as early childhood traumas. See Hinton, 2015, p. 361ff.
4 This perception of having two very different temporal personalities organizes the entire chapter on childhood titled 'School Years.'
5 Jung's last great work, *Mysterium Coniunctionis* (*CW* 14), is the culmination of this project.
6 The only instance of a Jungian discussion of this paraphilia, to my knowledge, is a paper by the late Prof. Leland Roloff (1992) in his Chicago IAAP Congress lecture.

References

Adler, G. (ed.) (1975). *C.G. Jung Letters*, Vol. 2. Princeton, NJ: Princeton University Press.
Atmanspacher, H. (2013). A structural-phenomenological typology of the mind-matter correlations. *Journal of Analytical Psychology*, 58, 2, 219–245.

Balint, M. (1968/1979). *The Basic Fault*. New York: Brunner/Mazel.

Benedict, R. (1989). *The Chrysanthemum and the Sword: Patterns of Japanese Culture*. Boston, MA: Houghton Mifflin.

Blumenberg, H. (1990). *Work on Myth*. Cambridge, MA, and London: MIT Press.

Cambray, J. (2009). *Synchronicity: Nature and Psyche in an Interconnected Universe*. College Station, TX: Texas A & M University Press.

Connolly, A. (2015). Bridging the reductive and the synthetic: some reflections on the clinical implications of synchronicity. *Journal of Analytical Psychology*, 60, 2, 159–178.

Corbin, H. (1951/1957). Cyclical time in Mazdaism and Ismailism. In Joseph Campbell (ed.), *Man and Time*. Princeton, NJ: Princeton University Press, 115–172.

Dostoyevsky, F. (1866/1987). *Crime and Punishment*. London: Wordsworth Editions, 1987.

Edelman, S.P. (1998). *Turning the Gorgon: A Meditation on Shame*. Woodstock, CT: Spring Publications.

Eliade, M. (1958/1968). *Patterns in Comparative Religion*. Cleveland, OH: The World Publishing Company.

Eliade, M. (1959). *Cosmos and History: The Myth of the Eternal Return*. New York: Harper Torchbooks.

Fitzmyer, J. (1993). *Romans: The Anchor Yale Bible*. New Haven, CT, and London: Yale University Press.

Hinton, L. (1999). Shame as a teacher. In Mary Ann Mattoon (ed.), *Florence 1998 – Destruction and Creation*. Einsiedeln: Daimon Verlag, pp. 172–185.

Hinton, L. (2015). Temporality and the torments of time, *Journal of Analytical Psychology*, 60, 3, 353–370.

Izutsu, T. (1977). *Toward a Philosophy of Zen Buddhism*. Boulder, CO: Prajna Press.

Jung, C.G. (1916/1969). The transcendent function. In *The Collected Works of C.G. Jung*, Vol. 8. Princeton, NJ: Princeton University Press.

Jung, C.G. (1952/1969). Synchronicity: An acausal connecting principle. *The Collected Works of C.G. Jung* (Vol. 8.). Princeton, NJ: Princeton University Press.

Jung, C.G., with Jaffé, A. (1961/1989). *Memories, Dreams, Reflections*. New York: Random House.

Kaufman, G. (1989). *The Psychology of Shame*. New York: Springer Publishing Company.

Kawai, H. 1988. *The Japanese Psyche*. Dallas, TX: Spring Publications.

Laplanche, J. & Pontalis, J.-B. (1973). *The Language of Psycho-Analysis*. New York: Norton.

Levi-Strauss, C. (2013). *The Other Face of the Moon*. Cambridge, MA, and London: The Belknap Press of Harvard University Press.

Magid, S. (2015). *Hasidism Incarnate: Hasidism, Christianity, and the Construction of Modern Judaism*. Stanford, CA: Stanford University Press.

Main, R. (2004). *The Rupture of Time: Synchronicity and Jung's Critique of Modern Western Culture*. Hove and New York: Brunner-Routledge.

Neumann, E. (1952/1989). The psyche and the transformation of the reality planes. In *The Place of Creation*, Princeton, NJ: Princeton University Press, 3–62.

Neumann, E. (1973/2002). *The Child*. London: Karnac Books.

Pauli, W. (1954/2002). The piano lesson. *Harvest*, 49, 2, 122–134.

Roloff, L. (1992). Living, ignoring, and regressing. *Chicago 92*. Einsiedeln: Daimon Verlag, 195–211.

Schellinski, K. (2014). Horror inherited: Transgenerational transmission of collective trauma in dreams. In G. Gudaité and M. Stein (eds), *Confronting Cultural Trauma*. New Orleans, LA: Spring Journal Books, 11–30.

Singer, T. & Kaplinski, C. (2010). Cultural complexes in analysis. In M. Stein (ed.), *Jungian Psychoanalysis*. Chicago, IL: Open Court, 22–37.

Stein, M. (2016). On synchronizing time and eternity. *International Journal of Jungian Studies*, 8, 1, 1–14.

Tillich, P. (1948). *The Shaking of the Foundations*. New York: Charles Scribner's Sons.

Von Franz, M.-L. (1974). *Number and Time*. Evanston, IL: Northwestern University Press.

Von Franz, M.-L. (1978). *Time: Rhythm and Repose*. New York: Thames and Hudson.

Von Franz, M.-L. (1992). *Psyche and Matter*. Boston, MA, and London: Shambhala.

Yiassemides, A. (2014). *Time and Timelessness: Temporality in the Theory of Carl Jung*. London and New York: Routledge.

Chapter 11

Disavowal in Jungian psychology
A case study of disenchantment and the timing of shame

Michael Whan

Introduction

The Jung I write of is the narrative figure in the genetic tale of analytical psychology, the *psychologist* 'Jung' of *Memories, Dreams, Reflections*, the *Collected Works* and other texts. This is the Jung who said: 'I can only make direct statements, only "tell stories". Whether or not the stories are "true" is not the problem. The only question is whether what I tell is *my* fable, *my* truth' (Jung, 1963, p. 3).[1] Yet, Jung had written, 'In history there is never a way back' (1976, p. 346), asserting the historicity of historical time; hence of *historical truth*. Contrarily, he also held to a concept of temporality rooted in the psyche's 'mythic ground'. For Jung, myth spoke the soul's language. Essentially, myth represented a cyclic temporality, an 'eternal return' to an originary, primordial time; a 'once-upon-a-time' that underlay psychic experience. The idea of the *arche-type* means the ruling or commanding *typos* ('blow', 'strike') that creates the fundamental psychic patterns. Despite acknowledgement of the linear movement of historical time, for Jung, the psyche was more deeply rooted in *a*-temporality.

Yet, Jung underwent a number of critical experiences of disenchantment, which inherently negated this notion of atemporality and the mythic and religious underpinning of his thought. These experiences threatened the 're-enchantment' project of his psychology, a project continued today among some so-called 'post-Jungians'. In this account, I contend that Jung responded to these disenchantment experiences through disavowal. In turn, this necessitated taking certain defensive positions, in which an activated shame and its relation to temporality played a crucial role in how Jung reacted to where his own thinking led. My contention is that Jung disowned his own experiences and insight into the soul's self-disenchantment, resorting rather to a defensive psychology of re-enchantment – itself an inflated notion, as if we are ever able to '*re*-enchant' against the *real* of the historical present.

Essentially, the concept of psychology followed here is that psychology is the *logos* of the *soul* (psyche), and that the soul's dialectical movement into modernity consists of a series of historical *negations*, in which it has surpassed the logical life of its previous *forms of consciousness*. The soul has disenchanted, self-emptied (*kenósis*) itself of its former mythic, religious, and metaphysical modes of being. In modernity, the soul, *as psycho-logy*, now reflects itself back into itself. Psychology serves as the soul's self-reflection, its self-relation.

Initiating disenchantment

Recalling his childhood neurosis in his twelfth year, when he suffered fainting spells whenever he had to attend school or do homework, Jung writes that in the process of recovering and self-realization, he had felt 'ashamed of' himself: 'The neurosis . . . was a shameful secret, a defeat' (1963, pp. 30–2). In the same year, Jung had a critical episode, an experience in the Basel Cathedral square, in which he saw the 'radiant sunshine, the roof of the cathedral glittered, the sun sparkling from the new, brightly glazed tiles'. Jung felt 'overwhelmed by the beauty of the sight, and thought: "The world is beautiful and the church is beautiful, and God made all this and sits above it far away in the blue sky on a golden throne and . . .".' At this point, Jung's blissful experience abruptly ended and there 'came a great hole in my thoughts and a choking sensation'. He felt 'numbed' and told himself: 'Don't go on thinking now! Something terrible is coming, something I do not want to think, something I dare not even approach' (ibid., p. 36). For two days, Jung sought to avoid 'the forbidden thought, which I did not yet know' and which 'tried to break out'. On the third night however, the thought broke through Jung's resistance. Jung rationalized 'the forbidden thought' as deriving from God's will, in order 'to test [Jung's] obedience'. As Jung put it, he gathered up his courage and 'let the thought come':

> I saw before me the cathedral, the blue sky. God sits on his golden throne, high above the world – and from under the throne an enormous turd falls upon the sparkling new roof, shatters it, and breaks the walls of the cathedral asunder.
>
> (Ibid., p. 39)

Interestingly, both these incidents occurred in the vicinity of the Basel Cathedral square. For Jung's neurotic fainting fits occurred after being pushed by another boy in the square, and Jung hitting his head on a curb stone. Similarly, like the time of the cathedral experience, this happened at 12 noon. In his rigorous study of the cathedral experience, Giegerich alludes to Nietzsche's 'high noon': 'It was a midday that One turned to Two . . .' (Nietzsche, 2008, p. 180). In the episode of the fainting fits, Jung was eventually able to see through the fits to their neurotic purpose. He was able to step back reflectively from his fainting behaviour to observe himself. That is to say, 'One turned into Two'. In that same year, Jung came to a further self-conscious realization of his subjectivity: 'I was taking the long road to school . . . when suddenly for a single moment I had the overwhelming impression of having just emerged from a dense cloud. I knew at once: now I am *myself*' (Jung, 1963, p. 32). Nevertheless, as Giegerich points out, though Jung here had 'arrived at the threshold to adulthood', this was not Jung's initiatory crossing of that threshold. Rather, Jung's '*specific initiation*' into true adulthood was based on 'the sense of his being introduced into a new knowing and into a new basic redefinition of his position in and towards the world . . . an initiation into disenchantment' (Giegerich, 2013, pp. 72–3). Continuing with his analysis of the initiatory experience, Giegerich observes that in the puberty initiations in traditional societies, a fundamental factor was 'a moment of disillusionment . . . [the] real purpose was . . . to open the mind . . . for the first time to empirical reality and ground it in the earth' (ibid.). Such initiations were an opening into adulthood in both a personal sense and 'into the particular form of adulthood corresponding to the culture and spirit of the time' (ibid., p. 75). Given that initiations in the true sense are no longer a collective or cultural aspect of modernity (save as *simulated* initiations, mere *likenesses*, not authentic), then it happens only 'as a private spontaneous experience'. The *telos* of Jung's experience, notes Giegerich, was 'to ruthlessly undeceive the innocently believing boy Jung, initiating him through an absolute disenchantment into the cultural truth of the age' (ibid., p. 76). Jung's response to his fantasy was the opposite. Instead of opening his mind to the image of God shitting on the cathedral, with its attendant *disenchantment* of the blissful oneness and innocence of the earlier part of the experience, he resisted it fiercely. Instead of letting the *telos* of disenchantment fulfil itself, Jung headed it off, eventually saying to himself, '*I must think*. It must be thought out beforehand'. Hence, intervening 'beforehand' in the fantasy's progress towards its end, he interpreted the shameful, sacrilegious image of God defecating on his sacred church as God's work, thereby cancelling out any notion that God had committed such a shameful act as intentional desecration. The ideal, blissful, enchanted 'Oneness' of the experience was preserved: God as the 'Oneness' remained the Creator of it all. The 'fundamental rupture' within the experience was disavowed and a 'primary oneness' maintained (Giegerich, 2013, pp. 74–5). Jung also misappropriated the temporal quality of the moment, the rupture of the enchantment/disenchantment, which would otherwise have held as the inner dialectical complexity of *disenchantment*, the unity of identity and difference.

At an empirical level, Jung, as both boy and adult, could, of course, conceive of the opposites of enchantment and disenchantment. Or, as Giegerich describes it, Jung was able to stay 'with the manifold of possible concrete opposites in empirical-practical life . . . in the experiential sphere of the ego' (ibid.). Jung could conceive and hold such opposites as *contents* or semantics of consciousness. But the *form* of consciousness (the religious form) remained immune from disenchantment. Jung's refusal to give up the notion of enchantment at the level of the form or syntactic level of consciousness carried over later into his very conception of psychology. Psychology, argues Giegerich, is 'concerned with *the* One and *the* Two quite abstractly, with *the* "psychic opposites" as such, without any semantic concretization'.[2] Regarding the initiatory *moment* with its rupture *of* time *in* time:

> The question is: ... what we might call "the world", the whole, the *logic* of consciousness suffered a division or is there still the logic of a primary unbroken unity ... It is a syntactical question, not a question on the level of the contents of consciousness or the contents of experience.
>
> (Giegerich, 2013, pp. 74–5, footnote 8)

Against the threat which Jung felt to the integrity of his 'eternal soul' through the disenchantment experience, by this very notion of his 'soul's' eternality through its 'everlastingness', he was able to preserve a temporal continuity from the temporal disruption of disenchantment.

For in making the whole experience into a test by God, the enchantment of the world and temporality was underpinned by the 'eternal'. Time was sustained by *timelessness*, a sacred timeless moment. Disenchantment would have robbed time of its eternal dimension: but, the moment was a moment *in* but not *of* time. The '*in* but not *of* time' was Jung's fabrication of the 'timeless', figured by the image of God and atemporal notion of his 'eternal soul'. Just as later, Jung's differentiation of the archetype-as-such and the archetypal image allows for two modes of temporality: the timelessness of the soul and the cultural-*historical* locus of the archetypal image. Hence, Jung acknowledges the particular 'symbol' or 'archetypal image' drawn from cultural history, from the particular imaginal modalities of *the* time, such as alchemical, gnostic, religious, as well as myth and fairy tale symbology. Such imagery reflects the historical present in which they arise. But deeper than this historical level, which Jung rather called the 'spirit of the times', lies the 'spirit of the deep', which his psychology valorizes as psychologically that of 'ultimate concern'. That is to say, Jung describes a mode of 'mythic time' that breaks in upon us, a 'timelessness' that imparts a sense of the 'eternal values' and meaning against the 'vacuity' of modernity.

Contrary to Jung's own interpretation of protecting his 'eternal soul' by thinking through 'beforehand' the meaning of the 'turd' shattering the roof and walls of the cathedral as God's own work, his was an egoic resistance to the soul's work of negation. Because of the *shame* Jung felt towards the fantasy, he, as it were, missed the moment, that is, its qualitative meaning. He had the experience, but missed the meaning. For the 'Oneness' and enchantment are retrospective projections, presuppositions, fabricated out of an already disenchanted state of mind. Enchantment comes out of the disenchanted mind. Through the fantasy of the 'Oneness' and enchanted world, the disenchanted mind is able to consciously articulate itself, its meaning: 'Disenchantment is the unity of itself and its opposite.' Even Jung's valorization of 'the divine beauty of the world' derives from his disenchantment, because in the fantasy's 'self-unfolding of its inner telos and the coming to light of its inner truth . . . Because we are here in the world of Two or of the opposites, the enchanted world's own *inner truth* is the disenchantment' (Giegerich, 2013, pp. 78–9). Despite Jung's affirmation of the cathedral experience as God's work, the disenchantment did enter Jung's awareness – but at a highly personal level. As such, it did not disturb the temporal frame, the logic of Jung's consciousness. Rather, Jung felt it as a *personal* failure, a deficit in Jung's subjective being, at the *semantic* or content level. It did not disrupt the logic of Jung's being-in-the-world.

Shame as defence against the rupture of time

Jung defended himself against this initiation into the rupture at an ontological level, by turning the disenchanting event into a matter of personal *shame*. The logic of Jung's consciousness did not suffer a self-division. Instead, defensively, Jung took the self-division *into* himself: to be suffered as the inner rupture of the ego-personality's sense of unity. In other words, he suffered the disenchantment at the *personal* level of shame; a disenchantment with himself. Thus, Jung could preserve the enchanted condition of 'Oneness', of a consciousness knowing God's grace, rather than knowing the end of the mythical, religious, and metaphysical logics of consciousness. Writing of the 'effect', the aftermath, of the experience, Jung states: 'it was a shaming experience.' Indeed, one 'effect' was that of:

> increasing my sense of inferiority. I am a devil or a swine, I thought; I am infinitely depraved ... I often thought of myself as a corrupt and inferior person ... I had fallen into something bad, something evil and sinister, though at the same time it was a kind of distinction.
>
> (Jung, 1963, pp. 40–1)

Whilst Jung's feelings of shame led to a feeling of isolation, 'unendurable loneliness', of inferiority, of secrecy, it also was rescued as 'part of the great secret'. Here, Jung describes the experience of shame. He speaks of the global aspect of it; his whole being is involved, a global negative self-evaluation. Pertinent also is the felt experience of shame's self-consciousness, especially remembering that it was in the same year he came to a self-consciousness of himself. Shame brings a sense of a *personal* or subjective inner life. Jung's feeling of self-consciousness was amplified by the idea of *being seen* by God. Jung's deepest religious values and principles were challenged by the disenchantment experience, laying the ground for his need to employ shame as a defence.

Looking back at this life event, Jung made this important observation: 'The greater my inferiority feelings became, the more incomprehensible did God's grace appear to me' (Jung, 1963, pp. 40–1). By internalizing the *negation* of disenchantment as personal shame, a negation which truly belonged to initiation into a different, cultural-historical mode of being in the world, a different constitutional logic of consciousness, Jung kept that insight at bay. Hence, through the 'incomprehensibility' of God's grace coupled with Jung's increasing inferiority feelings, his shame, Jung could sustain the obsolescent metaphysical logic of consciousness by way of the notion of God's grace. Despite the obvious suffering that the feeling of shame inflicted upon Jung, it had the value of keeping alive the enchantment of God's world. It was the price worth paying. Actually, the shame and the grace were two sides of the same. Jung's shame could know itself through the incomprehensibility of grace; and the experience of grace could be known through the affliction of being ashamed. Jung used them both as a bulwark against disenchantment as *ontological* rupture. Likewise, the sense of grace lent the experience of temporality a quality of *kairos*, of a divine moment in time; but a crisis moment displaced from that of disenchantment.

The claustrophobic sense of time, the finitude, in feeling shame was mitigated by the timelessness, the infinity, the transcendence, of God's grace. To be ashamed, is to be caught in what is felt as an inescapable finite moment, yet because I am wholly in it – my being is completely flooded with shame, cannot get out of it – it contrarily feels unbounded, infinite. That is to say, an utterly abject limitation and sense of exposure, the exposure feeling limitless. The shame suffered cannot be evaded, even if no one else is present as witness. I am wholly interiorized into the negating and immediate gaze of the 'other', an inner 'other' whose gaze enwraps me completely, in the immediacy of abject self-consciousness. I am utterly caught in the finitude of my being-there – a 'being-there' I wish I could escape from, a present moment which captures me in its finitude, and which I feel wholly inside of, having no sense of an 'outside' I can hide in. The sense of failure here is one of a chronic, elusive feeling of existential shame: I feel my whole being in some way as a failure, that I am 'nothing, a nobody'. Yet, Jung found an escape from the absolute humiliation of shame: 'But then I began searching through the New Testament and read . . . that reprobates are the chosen ones' (Jung, 1963, p. 41). By turning the whole episode into a matter of God's Will, Jung was able to constellate a feeling of grace out of the depths of his shame, a sense of being one of the 'chosen ones'. Jung's use of shame brought him to feel an intimate bond with God. Further, by keeping the whole experience *secret* – a common defence, the impulse to hide to protect against shame's fear of exposure – the mix of shame and grace, as a 'complex of opposites', could incubate as experiential contents of Jung's consciousness. His shame and inferiority were valorized by knowing that God's gaze was upon him. As such, the experience of time was dignified by the *kairotic* moment. Instead of the 'emptying', disillusioning experience of historical rupture, the shame that he felt *in* the light of grace provided the moment of the 'fullness' of time. Whereas the disenchantment, the *kenósis*, would have fulfilled itself, *if* Jung had allowed the fantasy to reach its *telos*; seeing the experience in terms of God's work enabled Jung's ego-personality to save the metaphysical 'whole'.

Reflecting on this moment in Jung's boyhood and comparing it to Jung's recognition of his childhood neurosis as a 'shameful secret', Giegerich notes how Jung was 'quite willing to acknowledge the shamefully neurotic quality' of his fainting fits and accept the responsibility of personal adulthood. Yet, 'in the truly *psychological* sphere' where the concerns were religious and metaphysical, Jung failed to live up to the moment:

> it seemed to him more precious to hold on to the *child's* highest principle and his own subjective preferences than to be honest: true to his own truth, his own real thought experience (which came from the objective psyche and corresponded to the truth of modern adulthood).
> (Giegerich, 2013, p. 81, footnote 14)

In misappropriating the negation of disenchantment as a personally shameful moment, Jung obfuscated it, concealing its meaning. Jung transferred the shame of not living up to his own truth into the personal sphere, in which his shame served as an entrance for the experience of grace and intimacy with God as one of his 'chosen . . . reprobates'. Shame served as a neurotic self-defence, for, rather be disenchanted with oneself than suffer 'the disenchantment of the world', the loss of metaphysical innocence. Jung's shame helped conceal his experience of 'metaphysical nakedness' by affecting a personalized shameful 'Edenic nakedness'.

Stepping back from insight into the soul's self-negation

Fundamentally, the experience served paradigmatically for his later approach to psychological thought. No doubt, Jung as a great psychologist had formidable, original and incomparable insights into the nature of psychology – yet he also stepped back at various points from following through *thinkingly* to where they led. Jung's notion of psychology as 'psychology *with* soul', psychology as the *logos* of the soul, is a theoretical and practical recognition of the existing, living *concept* of psychology, and whether or not it *measures* up to itself. As Jung stated: 'We should never forget that in any psychological discussion we are not saying anything *about* the psyche, but that the psyche is always speaking about *itself*' (*CW* 9i, para. 483). This is the fundamental principle of Jung's psychology: no Archimedean position *outside* the psyche. Hence, psychology is the *methodological* principle of an *absolute interiority*. In Jung's conception of psychology, the psyche is both subject *and* object. Thinking psychologically requires an absolute adherence to whatever transpires, no matter our subjective preferences. Yet, Jung too, against his own stance as a great psychologist, did step back from what the soul was telling him: step back from thinking.

At times, Jung recognized that psychology, as the *logos* of the *soul*, was in actuality *the* locus of the soul in modernity, the only place in which to speak authentically and meaningfully (*logos*) of soul. Namely, it was where the soul – as Jung saw – could speak about and from itself. Thus, Jung states insightfully: 'I see in the fact that we have a psychology a symptom that proves the profound convulsions of the general soul . . . Only in this situation, in this *predicament*, do we discover the soul' (*CW* 10, paras 158–61). Psychology, as a creature of modernity, is the 'symptomatic' voice of the soul. What, then, is this '*predicament*'? In the essay, 'Archetypes of the Collective Unconscious', Jung cautioned against the flight from the nihilistic condition of modernity into 'spiritual' irreality:

> the growing impoverishment of symbols has meaning. It is a development that has an inner consistency ... It seems to me that it would be far better stoutly to avow our spiritual poverty, our symbollessness, instead of feigning a legacy to which we are not the legitimate heirs at all.
>
> (*CW* 9i, para. 28)

Continuing, Jung writes: 'Anyone who has lost the historical symbols . . . cannot be satisfied with substitutes'. It is better, he declares, to 'renounce the false riches of the spirit . . . in order, finally, to dwell . . . alone, where in the cold light of consciousness, the blank barrenness of the world reaches to the very stars' (*CW* 9i, paras 28–9). With these words, Jung truly avows the meaning and nature of the soul's *logos* in the historical *present*. Here, Jung the psychologist truly listens to and follows the *logos*, the soul's logical life. Giegerich has further elaborated on Jung's insights:

> In the alchemy of the (Western) soul's history, the soul has ... moved through a series of logical constitutions of consciousness, from a stage of shamanism (as a whole mode of being-in-the-world) to that of the mythological and ritualistic polytheism and further to Christian monotheism with its trinity of metaphysics, science, and technology, which is the sublation of the two previous stages. It now seems to be at a point where the traditional-Christian constitution of the soul negates itself without the resulting new definition of the soul's state already being clearly visible.
>
> (Giegerich, 1998, p. 76)

Jung, of course, never formulated things this way, yet is it not implicit in his notion of the 'inner consistency' of 'our symbollessness', the 'growing impoverishment of symbols'? Well, not quite, for the term 'impoverishment' implies a negative judgement, that there is something wrong with it, which contrasts with the idea of an 'inner consistency', which suggests a certain meaningfulness. Nevertheless, what matters is that here Jung recognizes the *kenósis*, the soul's self-negation, its self-emptying, of its former mythic, religious and metaphysical truths. Jung, of course, does not speak in terms of 'self-emptying' or 'self-negation', but rather of 'impoverishment', which is radically different; hence, the feeling-tone of his reaction as negative.

It is precisely here that Jung blocks his own insights. For again, he turns from the negation of disenchantment, thereby turning from the temporality of modernity. This turn reappears latterly as a *feigned legacy* in much contemporary Jungian psychology, which Giegerich has critiqued as 'shameless' (1998, p. 37). On the one side, there is 'a branch of psychology that is . . . matter-of-fact', scientistic/science-lite, and 'shallow'. On the other, 'we have a lot of psychology . . . inflated, emotional, full of sentimentalism and mystifications (but no less shallow)'. A lot of Jungian psychology does *not* heed Jung's call to better stay with 'the cold light of consciousness'. Instead, the patient's material gets reconfigured in terms of fairytale plots, mythic 'gods' and 'goddesses', shamanic 'initiations': 'one innocent, helpless fairytale after another is subjected to trivial inter- pretations in terms of personalistic psychology'. This is done 'to provide a higher aura for rather commonplace case histories'. A vast 'literary' project of case histories has developed with a professional readership party to the intimacies of (confidentially disguised) people's lives, a kind of sophisticated exposé, in which the various case histories serve up 'character-types' and 'plots', more like the *genre* of the 'psychological novel' – interestingly a *genre* Jung was deeply suspicious of as *truly* psychological, recognizing its contrivance.

In newspapers and on TV, there is a similar intrusion into private lives, and much psychological 'case history', though more articulate in the lan- guages of current-day psychologies, mirrors this breaking of the hermetic seal. Giegerich writes: 'this literal shamelessness can probably be inter- preted as the objective reflection of the *logical* shamelessness of our general psychological attitude' (ibid., p. 38). The irony of this intense focus on our subjective 'inner life' is that it is exactly the opposite. It is the work of the soul's externalization and self-display. Hence, psycho- therapy, which as a profession would argue for its defence of the 'inner life', of intimacy and privacy, is actually complicit in the undoing of this 'inner life'. The work of disenchantment that Jung turned from in his cathedral experience nevertheless found its way into the heart of the very profession Jung founded. Contrary, to much contemporary Jungian ana- lytic writing, Jung published few case histories. But this reservation has not been taken up among those who practise under the sign of 'Jungian'. Indeed, all the reference to fairytale and myth is part of this self-display. As Giegerich puts it:

> it is itself yet the soul's work, the objective psyche's turn against itself, the destruction of the "inner", of the sense of interiority on the subjective level, of the feeling of shame ... The ultimate aim is a world that is exclusively surface.
>
> (Giegerich, 2007, p. 302)

Jung's feeling of shame consequent on the cathedral experience is but the twin of the logical shamelessness which underlines our 'general psycho- logical attitude'. Indeed, has the vast publication of articles and books, full of 'case history' become a symptom of psychotherapy's shameless loss of the *feeling* for interiority, the inner life of patients being emptied out in the profession's self-display, imitating the medical model (where 'case history' has a valid empirical value)?

As already asserted, following Giegerich, the temporal image of 'high noon' in Jung's cathedral experience marks it out as a profound moment. From the disenchantment perspective, it signified a rupture, a break in historical time, a 'before' and 'after'. In terms of the experience itself as *initiatory* for the boy Jung, it is the end of the morning of childhood and entry into the afternoon of adulthood. By personalizing the negativity of the disenchantment, given in the unfolding of the fantasy of God defecating on the cathedral, breaking open its walls and by turning it into a subjective feeling of shame and inferiority, consoled through divine grace, Jung could bridge over this fracture in the fabric of time. Jung's defensive use of shame helped him to resist the full import of disenchantment, so he could truly let unfold into his concept of psychology. That is to say, it enabled him to disengage from the soul's self-emptying of its previous historical forms of consciousness. From Jung's account, the cathedral experience had been traumatic. For, given the experience as one of disenchantment, it was more than personal. Jung was plugged in by his soul to historical temporality. For history 'is itself that trauma from which it suffers. It suffers from the rupture' of secularization, Enlightenment, loss of tradition, values and meaning. It is further 'a counter-movement . . . to correct or mend the rupture through a meaning-producing understanding'. History itself creates the very rupture of 'the irrevocable pastness of the Past', which it 'wants to mend'. Indeed, says Giegerich, history is like psychology, which in its 'fight against neurosis is the neurosis itself'. And, he continues, 'Neurosis as well as history, in their deepest essence, are not reactions to a previous split; they are a ritual itself in which dissociation more and more and ever anew realizes itself' (Giegerich, 2008, pp. 367–8). Here, Jung's use of shame as evasion concealed and repressed the temporal aspect of the experience as the historical rupture of disenchantment. Indeed, as already noted, Jung's reaction – full of shame and inferiority – allowed him to retrospectively re-imagine the enchanted world of God's grace, even though such a notion was itself projected out of disenchantment. The suffering of shame by the ego-personality turned the negation of disillusionment against the self-image on the ontic level, hence avoiding the trauma of the historical rupture at the ontological level. Later, in his psychology, Jung drew on this defensive reaction, keeping the disenchantment experience at arm's length, half-recognized, yet not taken to heart, so not to *let be* the soul's absolute negative interiorization into itself, its *kenotic* self-reflection into itself as *psychology only*.

Immunizing the inner dialogue from itself

Such a dissociation, as Giegerich identifies in both history and psychology, shows up later in Jungian psychology. I have posited the idea that Jung's response to shame and inferiority acted to conceal the negativity of disenchantment logic. It helped Jung keep the rupture of history at bay. For in proposing the notion of the 'archetype', of the mythic mode of being-in-the-world as an alive and immediate experience in the depths of the psyche, he could underpin the temporality of modernity with an *a*-temporality, a supposed originary or primordial level of experience. In this way then, Jung's psychology served to annul 'the irrevocable pastness of the Past' by positing a return – the analytic method – to the primordial depths, to the 'two million year old man'. Jung was able to conceal the dissociation from himself by not experiencing 'the dissociation *as* a dissociation or split'. His use of shame combined two modes of defence: namely, to '*feelingly experience* reality (including our own body) [shame as a profound bodily sensation]; the other is *ethics*'. Jung invoked the latter by way of personalized negation; he describes himself in terms of 'sin', of moral inferiority, likening himself to a 'reprobate'. The defensive claim implicit in the shame and the 'incomprehensibility' of grace is that:

> an ontic (personal) cement is supposed to glue together an ontological rupture … [in which] … the subsequently attempted healing of the split carries the split within itself and only transports it in a new way into what has seemingly been healed.
>
> (Giegerich, 2008, p. 372)

Used in this way, shame provided Jung the necessary 'felt experience', the personalized negativity, to divert from the historical rupture and seemingly heal it, thereby repressing the dissociation *as* dissociation. Through the experiences of both shame and grace, Jung could maintain a *logical innocence*.

I turn now to a critical moment in Jung's conception of psychology, a moment, I suggest, which both echoes the language with which Jung records the cathedral experience, and also betrays a dissociative element. In *Memories, Dreams, Reflections*, he recounts a particular moment, when asking himself: 'But in what myth does man live nowadays?' In answer, Jung declares that he does not live in the 'Christian myth'. He continues: 'Then do we no longer have any myth? No, evidently we no longer have any myth . . . ' (1963, p. 171). With this sentence, Jung seemingly acknowledges the temporal, logical rupture from any mythical mode of being-in-the-world. Psychology belongs to a different age and form of consciousness. The philosopher Ernst Cassirer wrote in his *Philosophy of Symbolic Forms*: 'The world views of myth and theoretical knowledge cannot coexist in the same area of thought. They are mutually exclusive: the beginning of one is the equivalent to the end of the other' (Cassirer, 1957, pp. 78–91). As a theoretical, speculative discipline, psychology therefore cannot lay claim to a mythical foundation, a grounding in 'gods' and 'goddesses'. Indeed, as a 'discipline', that is, as a rigorous mode of thinking in the sense of psychology as the *logos* of the soul, it would have no place in a truly mythic mode of consciousness. Psychology carries within itself the logical and temporal rupture between *mythos* and *logos* – which had already happened in ancient Greece. As Jung uniquely pointed out: 'the psyche has attained its present complexity by a series of acts of introjection. Its complexity has increased in proportion to *the despiritualization of nature*' (*CW* 9i, para. 54, emphasis added). Psychology, then, is *the* discipline of *interiority* and has itself been a critical factor in the process of demythologization, thus, of *disenchantment*. It has pushed off from the *naturalistic* mode of consciousness, from a naïve, immediate notion of the soul. As the soul's *logos*, *its* notion of soul comprises a complex, sublated, logical life.

Earlier in the passage from *Memories, Dreams, Reflections*, Jung, having asked himself whether man still lives *in* myth, and having answered that modern man, including himself, 'no longer have any myth', Jung suddenly reverses his direction of thought. He puts the question, 'But then what is your myth – the myth in which you do live'? According to this question, modern man is back *inside* myth. Jung here regresses the logic of psychology – from *logos* to *mythos*. Then, he states: 'At this point the dialogue with myself became uncomfortable, and I stopped thinking. I had reached a dead end'. Yet, again contradicting this last question, Jung recalled that in this same 'dialogue' with himself, he had a moment of 'unusual clarity', asserting: 'Now you possess a key to mythology' (1963, p. 171). Such a claim could only be said from a stand-point that had long ago surpassed mythic being-in-the-world. Namely, it is a firm *theoretical* claim. To make such a claim, Jung situates himself irrevocably in psychology; his approach to understanding myth is ines-capably psychological. But he misses the implication of his claim. What then to make of Jung's *discomfort* and his stopping thinking? It sounds like a fractured inner dialogue, a thought disturbance, in which the dia-lectic has split apart dissociatively, neither part listening to the other. Each *immunized* against the other position. It is a non-dialectical self-contradiction, seemingly a dissociation, because it fails to recognize itself *as dissociative*. Having told himself that he had a key to mythology, Jung remembers: 'But then something whispered to me, "Why open all gates?"' Not to 'open all gates' means *stop thinking*. At this point, Jung abandons psychology as the *logos* of the soul. He *disavows* the contradic-tion. The question, '"Why open all gates?"' arises precisely from the *sacrificium intellectus*. The question is, why the 'sacrifice' of thinking? For, does this not echo with the Jung of the cathedral experience, who also tried to stop thinking – until the thought burst through his defences? What looms large is again disenchantment: '"No, evidently we no longer have any myth."' Jung here avoids the temporality of the historical pres-ent which ineluctably underpins and shapes our dialogue with the historical past. Having the psychological 'key to mythology' signifies an 'empathetic understanding . . . [which] for the duration of such under-standing we leave' the *reality* of our time. And 'when we return to our own reality, likewise again leave behind what we have just understood, so that the "right hand" does not know what the "left hand" has under-stood' (Giegerich, 2008, pp. 384–5). But we do so wholly within the temporality of history: our 'return to myth' remains utterly within an historical standpoint, whether we recognize it or not. Addressing this matter, Giegerich refers to the word 'Guilt', in the German word '*Schuld*'. It contains a reference to the Norns, one being called 'Skuld'. This means 'a entanglement in the course of events; in that particular world, [in which] being human means owing a debt (*Schuld*) to the real events, namely, having an obligation to cause their meaning to radiate forth' (ibid.). In this seminal moment in his dialogue with himself about myth, a founding moment in Jung's psychology, Jung is drawn into such a 'fate-ful entanglement in the course of events'. Yet, he appears not to realize the knot of this 'entanglement', rather, he escapes it by *stopping* thinking, rather than cutting through with his powerful intellect. Thereby, he escapes the 'obligation' for his *psychological* thinking *to measure up to the truth of its concept as the logos of the soul.* Not only that, he dissociates his psychology from the meaning of the *real* events. Jung's momentary recognition that no longer does man live *in* myth, broke *open* a questioning about the logical status of modern consciousness. Like the earlier cathedral experience, this was an *initiatory* moment, initiating Jung's psychological thought into the truth of the age, into its disenchantment. But again, he takes flight into emotion, into shame and guilt, the 'uncomfortable' feeling, rather than *go on thinking.* Where the discomfort might have beckoned him back to thinking, he rather used it to stop thinking. At the same time, the discomfort arose from his refusal to think further. What Jung here distracts himself from is the recognition of the moment as a *temporal rupture.* For, 'the *essential* course of events is at right angles to successive time. Instead of flowing from event to event, from cause to effect, it remains within a particular, qualitatively determined moment as the inner intensity of that moment' (ibid., p. 387). When Jung stopped thinking, he abandoned the soul's logical life underlying the qualitative 'intensity' of the moment, to go on and reflect the contradiction he had just given voice to into itself: 'At this point the dialogue with myself became uncomfortable, and I stopped thinking.'

Conclusion: disavowing what the objective psyche said

What was so 'uncomfortable'? Did not Jung *interrupt* the unfolding of his thought, just as he tried to block the unfolding of the cathedral fantasy? In both instances, it is the realization of disenchantment that is disavowed, the historical truth (*a-letheia*, 'unconcealment' at the ontological level). Jung here, I claim, suffers a feeling of *guilt* and *shame*, as he swerves away from where his thought has led. It is the discomfort of having uniquely articulated the meaning of psychology as the soul's *logos*, but then taken flight from its realization. The 'uncomfortable' feeling has a double edge: as defence, and *as* a defence contains a cognition of what it is a defence against. This feeling comes to determine his approach as *psycho-logist.* In this founding moment of analytical psychology, Jung eludes its qualitative determination, its dialectical *negation*, its 'inner intensity'. Jung's discomfort is the disclaimed consciousness, the shame

and guilt, the disavowed *initiation* into a different logical (*logos*) constitution of psychological consciousness. In his account, he has initially
allowed the question-and-answer movement of thought, given himself
over to its autonomy – but then reneged. Jung's second question – "'But
then what is your myth – the myth in which you do live?'" – dissociates
itself from the recognition of the *absence of myth*. Jung turned from the
alchemy of the historical moment, which is:

> the working on us of real events, the inscription of the 'text' of a given
> situation into our being: real life, the way it is in fact is, as the alchemical
> laboratory and man as the workpiece ... what is in the retort, being
> stewed and subjected to the alchemical *mortificatio* and *putrefactio*.
>
> (Giegerich, 2008, p. 387)

The shame and guilt (being 'uncomfortable') rose up in protest at Jung's
refusal at that time to live out and think through the nature of his question, a
truly psychological one, to live up to the obligation of his 'fateful entanglement': to let the meaning of disenchantment be fully *heeded*. His shame and
guilt sought to lead Jung back to the *essence* of the event, its eventfulness, to
the truth of its temporality. But he turned away and 'stopped thinking'.

What Jung did *not* allow in his thought was the loss of meaning. For
him, loss of meaning was the cause of modern neurosis:

> Only the symbolic life can express the soul ... When I live "the sym-
> bolic life": "I am something else, in which I am fulfilling my role, my
> role as one of the actors in the divine drama of life". Without this
> "symbolic life": "people ... can never step out of this mill – this
> awful, grinding, banal life in which they are 'nothing but'".
>
> (*CW* 18, para. 627)

Here, Jung rather conceives of the finitude of the all-too-human as itself
shameful, unless one can 'be' (fabricate oneself) as an 'actor' in the 'divine
drama' – just as with the cathedral experience, which he conceived of as
God's work, a 'divine drama'. What is neurotic though is not the loss of
meaning, but the *disavowal* or *denial* of loss of meaning. For Jung, as discussed earlier, only too well had insight into the soul's self-disenchantment,
when he perceived, that 'the growing impoverishment of symbols has
meaning ... an inner consistency'. Thus, it was better 'to renounce the false

riches of the spirit . . . in order, finally, to dwell . . . alone, where in the cold light of consciousness, the blank barrenness of the world reaches to the very stars.' With these words, Jung let the voice of the soul's *logos*, its self-emptying, self-negation, be heard, even if not truly heeded. But he did not tarry fully with the negative, let his consciousness undergo the historical mortification of disenchantment. Shame, in the guise of the 'uncomfortable' feeling, to which Jung responded by *not* thinking, was itself a portal into that disowned insight, when in that inner dialogue with himself, he answered: 'Then do we no longer have any myth? No, evidently we no longer have any myth.' The 'uncomfortable' feeling, the shame, issued forth from the soul at odds with itself, the objective psyche, seeking to keep Jung the psychologist held in the moment, to be inscribed and vulnerable, scarified with its 'text' *as* psychologist. The occasioning of shame in this broken-off inner dialogue instances the difference between a *syntactic* or *logical* shame from the *semantic*, defensive use of shame of the cathedral experience. For the semantic shame remained a content of consciousness which left consciousness in its innocent state, its form unchanged. The syntactic shame that erupted as an 'uncomfortable' feeling embodied a disruptive, transformative moment, initiating a different form of consciousness (Hinton, 2016). Shame was the 'advent' of disenchantment intending Jung's consciousness, seeking to penetrate and inscribe itself into it, to become the insight of his psychology. Shame sought to remind Jung of the dialectic that had been broken off: to go on thinking. In it was the 'gaze of the Other', meaning not God but the event itself addressing Jung, holding him in its 'gaze', so to speak *its objective* meaning, its temporality of 'no longer . . . any myth', deserting the 'uncomfortable' feeling objective psyche. Thereby, he escaped the *initiatory* moment, in which shame and guilt would have called him back to continue the dialogue with himself.

Notes

1 All emphases in quotations is from the original.
2 The terms *semantic* and *syntactic* (linguistic concepts), as employed here, express the difference between the *content* and the *form* of consciousness. When we speak a sentence, the concern is with its meaning, what it says. To the syntactic aspect belongs the abstract, formal, structural internal relations of the sentence, irrespective of its sense. Psychologically, the difference is between the contents of our subjective, personal inner life, its psychic level. To the psychological proper belongs the form of consciousness, the soul's logical life, the historical-cultural

mode of being-in-the-world, *as which* life is actually lived. Jungian psychology, for instance, speaks of 'living myth'. Of course, there is a great knowledge of myth, its figures, images, motifs; but these are only the content of consciousness. Modernity's form of consciousness – to which psychology ineluctably belongs – has long ago surpassed any authentic mythic mode of being-in-the-world. Take the *Star War* film series, which is plotted on mythological themes. These mythological themes are solely its content, its semantics. The form, the syntax, in which they are presented is wholly techno-logical, medial, cinematic. These are the powers that govern the historical logic in which life is actually lived. The mythic is but *simulated* content.

References

Cassirer, E. (1957). *Philosophy of Symbolic Forms*, Vol. III, R. Manheim (trans.), New Haven, CT: Yale University Press.

Giegerich, W. (1998). *The Soul's Logical Life: Towards a Rigorous Notion of Psychology*, Frankfurt am Main: Peter Lang.

Giegerich, W. (2005). *The Neurosis of Psychology*, New Orleans, LA: Spring Journal Books.

Giegerich, W. (2007). *Technology and the Soul: From the Nuclear Bomb to the World Wide Web*, *Collected English Papers*, Vol. II, New Orleans, LA: Spring Journal Books.

Giegerich, W. (2008). 'The Alchemy of History'. In *Soul Violence*, *Collected English Papers*, Vol. III, New Orleans, LA: Spring Journal Books.

Giegerich, W. (2013). 'The Disenchantment Complex. C.G. Jung and the Modern World'. In *The Flight into the Unconscious*: *An Analysis of C.G. Jung's Psychology Project*, *Collected English Papers*, Vol. V, New Orleans, LA: Spring Journal Books.

Jung, C.G. (1953–1977). Except where indicated references are by volume and paragraph number to the *Collected Works of C.G. Jung*, 20 volumes, Herbert Read, Michael Fordham & Gerhard Adler (eds), R.F.C. Hull (trans.). London and Princeton, NJ: Routledge and Princeton University Press.

Jung, C.G. (1963). *Memories, Dreams, Reflections.* Recorded and edited by Aniela Jaffé, Richard & Clara Winston (trans.). New York: Random House.

Jung, C.G. (1976). *Letters*, Vol. 2, 1951–61, selected and edited by Gerhard Adler in collaboration with Aniela Jaffé. Translation from the German by R.F.C. Hull, in two volumes. London: Routledge and Kegan Paul.

Hinton, L. (2016). Personal communication.

Nietzsche, F. (2008). *Beyond Good and Evil*. Marion Faber (trans.). Oxford: Oxford World Classics, Oxford University Press.

Index

Abel and Cain 221
abject bodies 9, 101–18
achronicity 11, 215, 216, 217–20, 233–6
act: Lacanian 82–7, 93–4; reflexive 166
Actaion and the hounds 18
Adam and Eve 1, 61–2, 219, 220–1, 225, 237
aeonic time 236
affects 103–4, 126, 136–7
Agamben, G. 112, 140–1
agoraphobia 29
agrarian work force 190
aidos 101
alchemy of the historical moment 258
aletheia 17
American Psychiatric Association (APA) 106
analyst's idealization 8, 33–56
analytic hollow 119, 122–3, 126, 129,
    133, 134
Anders, G. 161–9, 178
Ang Udom 198–9
Anima Mundi 14
animalistic dehumanization 111–12
annihilation 114
Antigone 175, 176–9, 181
Antigone (Sophocles) 176–9, 181
Antigone complex 10, 180–3
anxiety 29
Apollonian spirit 155
aporia of genocide 190–1, 209
archaic primacy 8, 33, 39–40, 42, 52–3
archetypal image 246
archetypal nature of shame 52
Arendt, H. 197–8
Aristotle 140
artefacts 158–65

Artemis 18
Ataria, Y. 112
atonement 152
Aufhebung (sublation) 54–5
Augustine, St 4, 101, 141
Auschwitz 112, 143
authority 174, 181; crisis of 181–2
autism spectrum disorder 25
automatisms (rhythms) 164–5
automatons 87–9, 97
autoneplophilia (adult baby syndrome) 229
autonoetic consciousness 141

Basel Cathedral square experience
    243–4, 253
being human 67–8, 71; shame of 171–6
belonging 21
Benedict, R. 222
better father, analyst as 42–7
Bible, the *see* Genesis
big Other 75, 93–4, 95
Bion, W. 22–3, 28, 153
Blake, H. 142
blame 49
Blumenberg, H. 218
body: abject bodies 9, 101–18; cultural
    112; as driver of temporality 10, 139–57
body image 110–11, 113
body ownership 110–11, 112–13
Bollas, C. 105
Borges, J.L. 6
brain damaged patients 141
brain development 27
Buddhism 187, 188, 202–3, 204, 205
bullying 45, 63

Cain and Abel 221
Cambodia 10–11, 186–213
capitalism 94, 171–2; consumerist 10, 15,
    172–3, 181; late-stage 17
carnival 152
case histories 252–3
Cassirer, E. 255
cathedral experience 243–4, 253
cause, fate as 87–9
Cervantes, M. 229
Chhang, Y. 193
child abuse: physical 42–7; sexual
    48–9, 106
China 197, 199
Christianity 141, 237–8
chronicity 11, 215–16, 220–4, 231,
    233–6, 237
chronological time 109
chronos 107–8
circular time 140–1
civility, loss of 3
cognition 38–9, 40
collective individuation 168–70, 176,
    179, 180
Colman, W. 135
conceptual metaphors 107
Connolly, A. 111, 152
consumerist capitalism 10, 15, 172–3, 181
content of consciousness 259–60
contingent, shock of the 161–3
Copernican revolution 15
cosmic justice 202
cosmological time 140
counter-shock 167–8, 180
crack in subjectivity 131–3, 135
Crime and Punishment (Dostoyevsky) 223
crisis of authority 181–2
Critchley, S. 65–6
cultural body 112
'Curious Case of Benjamin Button'
    (Fitzgerald) 148
'Curse of Canaan' 62–3

Darwinian revolution 15
Dasein 78–9, 96
data economy 178–9, 181
death 78–9, 143–4; inevitability of 10, 154
death camps, Nazi 102, 106, 110–14,
    231–2
death of God 21, 25, 181–2
death of time 102
decline of inner structure 25–6

default mode network 123–5
defence: shame as 247–9, 253–4; temporal
    defences 9, 119–38
dehumanization 102, 110–13, 165
deification of analyst 47–51
Deleuze, G. 158, 173
dementia 219–20
Demos, E.V. 150
Derrida, J. 4, 160, 189
Descartes, R. 66
desire 82; infinite 79, 81, 96–7
despair 92
destitution, subjective 89–92
determinism 87
diachronic shame 9, 58, 59, 64–71
diachronic unity of the self 108
diachronics 37–8, 53
diachronization 180–1
diachrony 8–9
*Diagnostic and Statistical Manual of
    Mental Disorders* 106
dialectic, the 39–40, 54–5
dialectical movement 21–2, 28
différance 160
digital data economy 178–9, 181
'Dimmesdal, Arthur' 71
Ding, das 96
Dionysian spirit 155
disavowal 11–12, 242–60
discipline of interiority 23–4
disembodiment 9, 102, 114–16;
    dehumanization and 110–13
disenchantment 11–12, 242–60
disgust 104–5, 112
disinhibition 170–1
disorientation 14–15
dissociation 115–16, 230–1; Jungian
    psychology 254–7
divided self 37
Don Quixote (Cervantes) 229
Dostoyevsky, F. 223
double continuity of time-consciousness
    53–4
doubt 86
dreams 105; dyschronicity 229–31; trauma
    and disembodiment 114–16
Duch, Comrade 186, 189, 195, 204; Vann
    Nath's painting of the verdict on 204–5,
    210
dynamics of shame 8–9, 57–73
dyschronicity 11, 215, 217, 227–9, 233–6;
    two cases of 229–32

eating disorders 120
Edelman, G. 6
Edelman, S.P. 226
ego: integration and the four modalities of temporality 232–9; separation from the unconscious 222
ego-self axis 235–9
ego-time 236
Eigen, M. 15, 27
Einstein, A. 142
election 67
embodiment 101–2, 110; and metaphor 106–7
emotion 126, 137
enchantment 245, 246; re-enchantment 243; see also disenchantment
Enlightenment 4
entropic time 140
entropy 140, 143, 154
Epimethean counter-shock 167–8
Epimetheus 27–8, 161–2
episodic memory 221, 223
epistemological shame 36
Erikson, E. 152
'essence precedes existence' view 4
ethical time 9, 74–100
ethics 173–4
evanescence 10, 139–57; temporality, shame and 151–4; time, identity and 141–3
Eve see Adam and Eve
Evil Eye 5
'existence precedes essence' view 4
existential emptiness 139, 151
existential function of shame 126–7
existential inertia 52
existential shame 9–10, 119–38, 152
experience 38
exposure 35, 36, 61–2, 68; genital 60, 61; soul 35
extimate Other 92–4
Extraordinary Chambers in the Courts of Cambodia (ECCC) 10–11, 186–213

failed perfection 37
fantasy 93; Jung's cathedral experience 243–4, 253; fundamental 89; retro-fantasizing 223–4
fate 74–5; as cause 87–9
faultiness 176
feeling 137
Ferrari, A.B. 145

Fitzgerald, F. Scott 148
flood, biblical 61
flow, states of 125, 134
Ford, H. 164
form of consciousness 259–60
four modalities of temporality 11, 214–41; definitions 215–17; role of the transcendent function 232–9; see also under individual modalities
freedom 163–4
French Revolution 209
Freud, S. 15, 68, 116, 160; evanescence 142; Hilflosigkeit 146; life and death 143–4; Nachträglichkeit 75, 77–8, 96, 147; seduction theory 154–6; shame 60, 61, 68, 105; shamelessness 63; trauma and incest 105; 'Wo es war, soll Ich wolden' 89–90
function of a trial 196–7
fundamental anthropological situation 146
fundamental fantasy 89
future, the: projective teleology 8, 33, 39–40, 41–2, 52–3; time, loss and 143–4
future anterior (future perfect) tense 81–2

Gallagher, S. 108–9, 110, 112
Garden of Eden 1, 61–2, 150, 219, 220–1, 225, 237
gaze 206–8; of the other 92–3
Genesis 61–3, 218; Adam and Eve and the Garden of Eden 1, 61–2, 150, 219, 220–1, 225, 237; Cain and Abel 221; Noah and the 'Curse of Canaan' 62–3
genital exposure 60, 61
genocide 15; aporia of 190–1, 209; Khmer Rouge Tribunal 10–11, 186–213; see also Nazi death camps
geopolitics 197, 199
Giegerich, W.: interiority 23–4; Jung 244, 245, 249, 251, 252, 253, 254, 256; soul 29; sublation 28; truth 18
'God is dead' 21, 25, 181–2
God's grace 248–9
guilt 17, 57, 58, 59, 106, 150; chronicity 222–3; Jung 256–8; survivor 106
Gyges 64

Ham 62
Hamlet (Shakespeare) 127–8
Hardt, J. 104–5
Hartman, G. 125

Hartmann, H. 142
Haslam, N. 111–12
haste 84
Haule, J. 121
Hawking, S. 140, 143, 154
Hawthorne, N. 57, 58–9
Hegel, G.W.F. 37, 46, 54–5, 69, 82
Heidegger, M. 4, 144, 154, 168–70, 176, 177–8
helplessness 9–10, 146
Herman, J. 113
Hesse, H. 152, 155
Hilflosigkeit (radical helplessness) 146
Him Huy 201–2
Hinton, L. 123, 127, 141, 151, 226–7
historical sedimentation 142
historicity 149, 155
hole in the paper sky of subjectivity 127–9, 131
Homo naledi 27
Homo sapiens 18, 27
Homo temporalis 141
honour, sense of 92
hope 21, 71
Hultberg, P. 126, 132
human time 109
humiliation 104
Husserl, E. 4, 53–4, 108–9
Hyldgaard, K. 2
hyper-diachronization 181–3
hyper-shame 183
hyper-synchronization 181

i 234–5
I 166, 168–70
iconic constancy 218
idealization of the analyst 8, 33–56
ideals, failure to live up to 35–7
identity: metaphor, time and personal identity 107–10; narrative 109; symbolic 90; time, evanescence and 141–3
Ieng Sary 187, 194, 198–9
Ieng Thirith 187, 194
illud tempus 236
Imaginary order 85, 95–6
immanence 54
immediacy of peace that is incumbent on me 69
immediational presence 8, 33, 39–40, 40–1, 42, 53
imposed shame 35

impoverishment of symbols 250–1, 258–9
incest 105
indifference 112
individuation 234, 238–9; collective 168–70, 176, 179, 180; psychic 168–70, 179, 180; technical 169–70, 179, 180
inevitability of death 10, 154
infants 145–7, 150–1, 225–6
inferiority 150, 247
infinite desire 79, 81, 96–7
infinity 66
instant of the glance 83
instrumental maieutics 160
instruments 164–5
integration of the four modalities of temporality 232–9
interiority 21–2, 22–3, 28; discipline of 23–4
interpretative method 153
intersubjectivity 82–7
intuiting psychic reality 153
inversion of intentionality 65–6
invisibility 64
it 166–7, 168–70

Jacoby, M. 149–50
Jacquard loom 171
Jacquin, M. 200
James, I. 141
Japan 222; Japanese students 25
Japheth 62
Jardine, A. 142
Jesus Christ 237–8; analyst revered as 47–51
Jews 112
Johnson, M. 107, 108
Jung, C.G. 126, 136–7, 217; cathedral square experience 243–4, 253; disavowal in Jungian psychology 11–12, 242–60; immunizing the inner dialogue from itself 254–7; initiation of disenchantment 243–7; living in two difference centuries at the same time 227–8; stepping back from insight into the soul's self–negation 249–54; trauma and dreaming 105; unconscious as inner otherness 121–2; youthful inflated ambition 7–8
juridical temporality 194–200
justice 4–5, 21, 61, 173–4, 176; Khmer Rouge Tribunal 10–11, 186–213; temporality, shame and 205–10

kairos 107, 109, 113
Kant, I. 4, 159
karate training 46–7
karma 202
Karnavas, M. 198–9
Kelly, J. 114
Kernberg, O.F. 149
Kertész, I. 74–5, 95, 111
Khieu Samphan 187, 194
Khmer Rouge Tribunal (KRT) 10–11,
    186–213
Kilborne, B. 119, 127–9, 131, 132
Kinston, W. 130
knowledge 164; proletarianization and loss
    of 171–3
Kohut, H. 35, 106
Kouider, S. 124
Kristeva, J. 112, 142

Lacan, J. 9, 46, 74–100; fate as cause
    87–9; *Nachträglichkeit* 75–6, 78–82,
    95; shame 92–4; subjectivization and
    subjective destitution 89–92; time, the
    Other and the act 82–7
lack 207–10; symbolic 209
lack-of-being 79
Lakoff, G. 107, 108
Laplanche, J. 29, 136, 154–5; infant and
    the Other 145–7; unconscious as inner
    otherness 119, 122–3
late-stage capitalism 17
law 173; *see also* Khmer Rouge Tribunal
    (KRT)
Levi, P. 9, 111, 112, 113, 114, 143, 158
Levinas, E. 8–9, 46, 65–71, 127, 150
Lewis, H.B. 103, 106
Lewis, M. 104, 106
Leys, R. 106
life, death and 143–4
Lindner, E.G. 104
'little other' 95
logical time 82–7
Lombardi, R. 140
loss: of meaning 258; time, loss and future
    143–4

M-13 195
Man in the Street 8, 19–22, 23, 24, 26
Marx, K. 171
Marxism 208–9
McCauley, C.R. 104–5
mechanistic dehumanization 111–12

medical vertex 22, 24
memory 6, 18–19; episodic 221, 223;
    technological 27
Mencken, H.L. 132
metaphor 9: embodiment and 106–7; loss
    of 102; time, personal identity and
    107–10
Metcalf, R. 60
Midnight in Paris 229
Miller, J.-A. 94
mirror 206–7
mirror stage 46
mnemotechnical individuation 179
mnemotechnologies 171, 176, 180
modesty 86–7, 93
moment of concluding 83, 84
moments of meeting 153
Montes Sánchez, A. 127, 129–30
mortality 10, 154
Mosaic Law 237
mother and infant 145–7, 150–1, 225–6
moving observer metaphor 108
moving time metaphor 108
Musselmann (walking corpse) 9, 112
myth 217–18; Jung 242, 255–7

Nachträglichkeit 9, 18, 75–82, 90, 91, 95,
    144, 147–8; temporality, the subject and
    Lacan's 78–82; trauma and Freud's
    77–8
narcissism 68
Narcissus and Goldmund (Hesse) 152, 155
narrative 223–4
narrative identity 109
Nazi death camps 102, 106, 110–14,
    231–2
negation 36, 139; of disenchantment 247–8,
    249; self-negation of the soul 249–54
Neill, C. 90, 97–8
Neumann, E. 225
neuroscience of perception 123–5
new experiences 139–40, 154
Nietzsche, F. 63, 155, 170, 181–2
Noah 62–3
Non Nil, Judge 206
nostalgia 228–9
nothingness 144
Nuon Chea 187, 193, 194, 195

objective self 150
Ogden, H.O. 153
orders of the Lacanian psyche 95–6

Orestes (Euripides) 127–8, 131
Other, the 144–7, 150–1; big Other 75,
   93–4, 95; diachronic shame 66–9;
   extimate 92–4; Lacan, time and the act
   82–7; little other 95; unconscious as
   inner otherness 119, 121–3

Paleolithic cave art 27
panic 29
Paradise *see* Garden of Eden
past, the: archaic primacy 8, 33, 39–40,
   42, 52–3; production of 147–8
Paul, St 237
Pauli, W. 234–5
People's Revolutionary Trial (PRT) 196, 198
perception: neuroscience of 123–5;
   of time 142
personal identity 107–10
personal shame 247–8
Pestman, M. 195–6
pharmacology of shame 10, 158–85
phenomenological time 109
phenomenotechnics of shame 165–8
physical abuse 42–7
Pines, M. 131
Pirandello, L. 127–8, 131
Plato 4, 14, 26–7, 60–1, 64, 140, 160
play 222; therapy as 47
Pol Pot 187, 202
politicians 158, 159
politics 175, 183; gift of political
   understanding 60–1; loss of confidence
   in 2–3
post-traumatic stress disorder (PTSD) 106
powerlessness 9–10
present, the (immediational presence) 33,
   39–40, 40–1, 42, 53
pride 58
primary metaphors 107
prisoner's dilemma 83–6, 90
private shame 130, 131
production of the past 147–8
projective teleology 8, 33, 39–40, 41–2,
   52–3
proletarianization 15, 165, 171–3, 179
Promethean shame 161, 163–5
Prometheus 10, 27–8, 60, 161–2, 175
Protagoras 60–1
protention 108
proton pseudos (original lie) 77
'Prynne, Hester' 57, 58–9, 63, 71
psychic individuation 168–70, 179, 180

psychoanalytic revolution 15
psychological time 140
psychotic communications 28
puberty 71
purges 190, 191

raw life 8, 14–32
Real order 88–9, 96
reality principle 224
recognition 46
redactic 208
re-enchantment 243
reflexive act 166
religious vertex 22, 24
Renaissance 4
responsibility 67–8, 69–70, 75
retention 108; selective 41
retro-fantasizing 223–4
retrospective judge 93–4
reverie 20, 21, 28
revolution 209
Ricoeur, P. 109
Ring *i* 234–5, 236–7
rituals 218
Roesler, C. 116
Rose, J. 105
Rozin, P. 104–5

S-21 11, 186, 189, 191–3; genocide
   museum 193, 206
samsara 202
Sartre, J.-P. 103, 104, 139, 148, 153
scapegoating 5
Scarfone, D. 123, 143, 146, 147–8
Scarlet Letter, The (Hawthorne) 57, 58–9
Seattle street encounter 8, 19–22, 23,
   24, 26
secrecy 248–9
seduction theory 154–5
Segre, L. 112
selective retention 41
self: diachronic unity of 108; divided 37;
   objective and subjective 150; sense of
   149–50; synchronic unity of 108
self-agency 110–11, 112–13
self-consciousness 35–6
self-division 25
self-esteem 132, 150
self-hatred 120–1, 123–5, 133–5
self-negation of the soul 249–54
semantic consciousness 219, 223
semantic shame 259

semantics 245, 259–60
Semprun, J. 114
sense of time 142
sexual abuse 48–9, 106
sexual shame 166
sexuality 77
sexually charged messages 146
Shameless 63–4
shamelessness 63, 183; contemporary
    pervasiveness of 10, 158–61; of the
    general psychological attitude 252–3
Shem 62
shock 167; of the contingent 161–3; and
    counter-shock 167–8, 180
shyness 150
signifiers 80, 90–1, 96
skin shame 17
Sloterdijk, P. 170–1
slowing down 123–5, 135
social shame 130, 131
'socks with holes' phobia 22
Socrates 159
Son Sen 187
sophism 82–7, 97
Sophocles 176–9, 181
soul 23, 29; exposure 35; self-negation of
    249–54
Sovannary, M. 198
spatial metaphors 108
spatio-temporal configuration 140, 154
spectacle 6
spectators 65
speech 79–80
speed 6, 163–4
spirit 37
Stack, A. 122
stage theories 208
starvation 192
Stiegler, B. 21, 27, 169–70, 178–9;
    Antigone complex 10, 180–3; *Disbelief
    and Discredit* series 171–6; raw life 15;
    symbolic misery 2, 17; technics 27–8,
    160, 162; truth 18
stranger fear 5
street encounter 8, 19–22, 23, 24, 26
strict rules 220
Studinsky, S. 199
stupidity 173–4
subject, Lacan's *Nachträglichkeit* and
    75–6, 78–82
subjective destitution 89–92
subjective experience 53–4

subjective self 150
subjectivity: crack in 131–3, 135; hole in
    the paper sky of 127–9, 131
subjectivization 89–92
sublation 54–5
sublimation 174–5
suicide 178
superego 149
survivor guilt 106
symbolic identity 90
symbolic misery 2, 17
Symbolic order 88, 95–6
symbolic realization 24
synchronic shame 9, 57–8, 58–9, 63, 70
synchronic unity of the self 108
synchronicity 11, 215, 217, 225–7, 233–6
synchronization 180–1
syntactic shame 259
syntax 245, 259–60
syntony 226
Szpunar, K.K. 141

Ta Mok 187
Talero, M. 144
Tanaka, Y. 24–6
technical individuation 169–70, 179, 180
technics 20, 27–8; pharmacology of shame
    10, 158–85
technological memory 27
technologically induced shame 10
temporal defences 9, 119–38
temporal jurisdiction 195–7
temporal mediacy 33, 39–42, 52–3
temporal rupture 245, 247–9, 257
temporal tension 85
Terr, L.C. 142
Tillich, P. 238
time for comprehending 83–4, 86
timeless centre 236
timelessness 246
Tomkins, S. 103, 106, 150
tool-making 5
torture 191, 192, 193
transcendence 54
transcendent function 232–9
transference cure 51
transgenerational transmission of trauma
    231–2
transgression 101, 174–5
transition 208–9
transitional justice 208, 209–10; *see also*
    Khmer Rouge Tribunal

transitional justice imaginary 200–5
translation 155
trauma 2, 9, 101–18, 139–40, 154; and
    Freud's *Nachträglichkeit* 77–8; and
    shame 105–6; and temporality 113–14;
    transgenerational transmission of 231–2
truth 7, 16–19
tuché 87–9, 91, 97
Tulving, E. 5, 141
Tuol Sleng Genocide Museum 193, 206

unborn-ness 24–6
unconscious, as inner otherness 119,
    121–3
United Nations 197; 'Group of Experts'
    for Cambodia 197
United States 197, 199
Unpast, the 143
Unus Mundus 14

values 35–6, 94
Vann Nath 11, 186–7, 201–8, 210; death
    of 193–4; at the Khmer Rouge Tribunal
    189–93; paintings 192, 193, 204–5,
    206, 207, 209, 210
Vanheule, S. 102
Vatel the servant 92

Verhaeghe, P. 102
vernacular temporalities 200–5
Virilio, P. 15
Von Franz, M.-L. 215–16, 227, 235–6
vulnerability 60, 61

'want-to-be' 80–1
we 168–70
Wharton, B. 150
Wiesel, E. 102
Willemsen, H. 115
Williams, B. 93
Winnicott, D.W. 47, 144–5
'*Wo es war, soll Ich wolden*' (where is war,
    I shall be) 89–92
women 142–3
Woolf, V. 132
work 2
world soul (Anima Mundi) 14
writing 159–60, 176

Yiassemides, A. 214
youth 182

Zahavi, D. 109
Zeus 60–1
Žižek, S. 91